Magic

Recent Titles in
American Popular Culture
Series Editor: M. Thomas Inge

Film: A Reference Guide
Robert A. Armour

Women's Gothic and Romantic Fiction: A Reference Guide
Kay Mussell

Animation: A Reference Guide
Thomas W. Hoffer

Variety Entertainment and Outdoor Amusements: A Reference Guide
Don B. Wilmeth

Women in Popular Culture: A Reference Guide
Katherine Fishburn

Sports: A Reference Guide
Robert J. Higgs

Play and Playthings: A Reference Guide
Bernard Mergen

American Popular Music: A Reference Guide
Mark W. Booth

American Popular Illustration: A Reference Guide
James J. Best

Recreational Vehicles and Travel: A Resource Guide
Bernard Mergen

MAGIC

A REFERENCE GUIDE

Earle J. Coleman

AMERICAN POPULAR CULTURE

Greenwood Press
New York • Westport, Connecticut • London

Library of Congress Cataloging-in-Publication Data

Coleman, Earle Jerome.
Magic : a reference guide.

(American popular culture, ISSN 0193-6859)
Includes bibliographies and indexes.
1. Conjuring. 2. Conjuring—Bibliography.
I. Title. II. Series.
GV1547.C595 1987 016.7938 86-29611
ISBN 0-313-23397-7 (lib. bdg. : alk. paper)

Library of Congress Catalog Card Number: 86-29611
ISBN: 0-313-23397-7
ISSN: 0193-6859

First published in 1987

Greenwood Press, Inc.
88 Post Road West, Westport, Connecticut 06881

Printed in the United States of America

The paper used in this book complies with the Permanent Paper Standard issued by the National Information Standards Organization (Z39.48-1984).

10 9 8 7 6 5 4 3 2 1

TO "STOSH"
and all the other unsung magicians

CONTENTS

Preface ix

Introduction xi

1. Histories of Magic 1

2. Appreciation: On the Principles of Psychology and Showmanship that Underlie the Performance of Magic 11

3. The Creation of Illusion: Manuals on the Execution of Magic 31

4. Magic in Relation to Other Arts 145

5. Biographies and Autobiographies 163

APPENDIX: Selected Dates in the History of Conjuring 175

Magic Periodicals 181

Directories 182

Research Collections 182

Dealers 184

Author Index 187

Subject Index 193

PREFACE

This is perhaps the first study to focus upon the history, psychology, techniques, and aesthetics of magic. There have been scholarly works on each of these subjects, but I am not aware of any compendium that embraces all of these emphases. The text is essentially a bibliographic essay in which the discussion of key texts sometimes leads to theoretical remarks. Through these passages, I seek to express my personal philosophy of conjuring. Such comments will have served their purpose if they stimulate the reader to reflect upon the theory of magic. Each chapter consists of a topical and bibliographical essay followed by a listing of all works that have been discussed or noted.

Chapter 1 emphasizes outstanding histories of magic but also treats multifaceted texts that make a distinct historical contribution. Chapter 2 analyzes some of the major bibliographic sources on the principles of psychology and showmanship that separate the master magician from the average performer. Chapter 3 evaluates manuals on the execution of magic in the categories of general studies, card magic, close-up magic, coin magic, stage magic, miscellaneous magic and related skills, and spiritualism and mental magic. There is some overlap among the categories in Chapter 3. For example, writings on cards and coins do appear in the stage magic section when the particular routines presuppose a significant distance between the performer and his audience. Hence, the reader who is interested in a particular prop may wish to consult the subject index for all cases in which it is mentioned. Chapter 4 presents bibliographic material that defends the artistic status of magic, explores its relation to other arts, and identifies some of its most distinctive aesthetic features. Chapter 5 reviews selected biographies and autobiographies that treat luminaries from the nineteenth century to the present.

The Appendix comprises a chronology recognizing important dates in the history of magic and information on magic periodicals, magic directories, research collections, and dealers. Author and subject indexes follow the appendixes. Omissions, even serious ones, are inevitable in a single book of manageable size, but the writings cited are representative of the vast literature of conjuring.

One theme that recurs throughout the book, especially in chapter 4, is that there are ample rational grounds for regarding magic as an art. Being a professor of philosophy of art and a magician, I hope that my observations fortify the thesis that magic should be accorded the status of an art form.

For whatever merit my study may have, I am indebted to my late parents, Helen and Edward Coleman, who were never too weary to "take another card"; to my wife, Karen, who, as usual, helped me to see the forest as well as the trees; to my late brother, Jimmy, who sometimes needed to be bribed into watching me practice a new move "just one more time"; to my brother Edward and James "Zimmy" Zimmerman, who were my first co-conspirators in conjuring; to Okito (pseudonym for Theodore Bamberg), from whom I received my first personal instructions on sleight of hand; to Edward Marlo, the supreme "cardician" of all times, who was willing to teach a thirteen-year-old some of the finer points of finesse with playing cards; to Neil Foster, whose elegant manipulative magic and floating ball routine first enabled me to see the grace and beauty of stage magic; to Robert Lund, proprietor of the American Museum of Magic in Marshall, Michigan, whose kind remarks on the first portion of this book encouraged me to continue the project; to Don Alan, whose weekly television program inspired me and any number of other neophytes in the Chicago area; to Richard Weibel, the author of myriad articles on conjuring psychology, who has been gracious enough to correspond with me on the psychology of magic; to "Senator" Clarke Crandall and Jay and Frances Marshall, whose magic shops I haunted on so many Saturdays of my teenage years; to Roger "Woody" Landers, an impeccably smooth sleight-of-hand artist, whose library on close-up magic was of great assistance to me; to Don Theobald, a demonstrator at the old "Magic Center" in Chicago's "Loop," who saved me a small fortune by offering advice on what magic effects were and were not suitable for a youngster; and finally, I wish to thank the late "Stosh"—I never did learn his full name—another demonstrator at the Magic Center, whose flawless performance of the "throw change" (in which one card is mysteriously transformed into another) cast a magic spell over me, one from which—I am delighted to say—I have never escaped.

The final manuscript for this book was produced by the Information Processing Center, Dean's Office, College of Humanities and Sciences, Virginia Commonwealth University, Gene Dunaway, Systems Coordinator. The latter's thoughtful suggestions and kind assistance are greatly appreciated. I also wish to thank Joan F. Kalyan for her assistance with the preparation of the indexes and proofreading.

INTRODUCTION

Nevil Maskelyne and David Devant (*Maskelyne on the Performance of Magic* [New York: Dover, 1976; reprint of Part 1, *Our Magic*, 1911], p. 5) have noted that the nineteenth-century French prestidigitator Jean Eugene Robert-Houdin defined the theatrical magician as an actor who is playing the role of a conjurer, that is, a being whose supernatural powers enable him to accomplish what is naturally impossible. Magic, like the closely related performing art of pantomime, is basically grounded upon the production of illusions. In fact, every feat of magic depends upon presenting the spectator with a forgery or counterfeit of some object, action, or state of affairs. But while the pantomimist presents an intelligible illusion, the magician exhibits an unintelligible illusion; in the case of the former, one understands how it is effected (through skillful body control developed from a host of balletlike exercises); in the latter, attributing skill to the performer hardly qualifies as an explanation of how the effect is produced.

Magic and magicians are as at home in American popular culture as the long-running comic strip *Mandrake the Magician* by Lee Falk and Phil Davis. Indeed, magic or magical themes have figured prominently in American versions of such diverse forms of entertainment as the impromptu street performance, stage show, circus, dime museum, carnival, nightclub, novel, drama, short story, film, radio, and television. Occasionally, a term used by magicians has found its way into wider circulation in American society. The word *gimmick*, for instance, by which magicians describe a concealed device needed as the means for some magical effect, was eventually adopted by the advertising industry to designate anything that attracts attention by injecting an element of novelty. By definition, popular arts are widely enjoyed, but magic is more than popular; it is actually universal in its appeal. A native of China and a citizen of Italy may have real difficulty in grasping, much less appreciating, the dance, music, literature, painting, or architecture of each other's culture, but both individuals are readily entertained by the magician, for in causing a coin to vanish or levitating a woman, the conjurer violates the laws of nature under which all human beings live and with which their experience vividly familiarizes them.

One problem may be unique to the student of magic as a performing art. Because the effectiveness of magic is utterly dependent upon the concealment of its secrets, a good deal of the best magic literature is circulated on a very limited basis. Hence, specialized research collections, which include some of the more closely guarded writings of small trade publishers, are crucial to the serious student. Such essential collections will be discussed in the Appendix. European magicians and magic books will be cited when they have significantly shaped the development of magic in America. The following historical overview will set the stage for the specialized chapters that follow.

Turning to the beginnings of American magic and magicians, one discovers that the colonial climate was decidedly inhospitable to conjurers, actors, and other entertainers; in fact, all such performers were banned from Jamestown in 1612. Perhaps frivolous entertainment was simply deemed incompatible with the sternness that the struggle for survival demanded of the early colonists. While Virginia still outlawed public magic performances in 1740, a member of the state council, William Byrd II, is reported to have enjoyed a private magic show in June of that year; and, by June 1769, Virginia no longer forbade magicians, for George Washington wrote in his diary of September 19, 1769, "went to see slight [*sic*] of hand performed"; this presentation took place in Alexandria. Washington was also present when Peter Gardiner, a magician/puppeteer, presented his act on November 17, 1772, in Williamsburg. In the same year, Jacob Meyer, the first American magician to appear in Europe, was entertaining Catherine II in Focsani, Romania. Meyer favored the stage name "Philadelphia," which he borrowed from his native city and found had a sufficiently exotic ring to European ears. Just over a decade later, in 1783, the famous Philadelphian Benjamin Franklin was solidly defeated in chess by a chess-playing automaton, the brainchild of a Baron Wolfgang von Kempelen. The match took place in Versailles while Franklin was serving as the ambassador to France. As we shall see, it remained for another celebrated American to argue that the automaton was actually a magic stunt operated by a concealed, chess-playing assistant in the body of the mannequin figure. Seventeen eighty-three is also significant because it marks the birth of Richard Potter, the first American to succeed as a magician in his own country. Featuring effects such as the standard cups and balls (which will be discussed under the subject of close-up magic), Potter attracted appreciative crowds in Canada as well as the United States. As the dark-skinned son of a British tax collector and his black slave, he has the dubious distinction of being the first American magician to experience racial prejudice during a twelve-day engagement in Mobile, Alabama. In 1861, John Henry Anderson, a European who advertised himself as "The Great Wizard of the North," was vividly confronted with the fermenting slavery issue in the United

States. Irate citizens of Richmond, Virginia, destroyed the advance publicity posters of this charlatan from the North who dared to trespass upon Southern soil. Explaining that Anderson was from northern Scotland was to no avail.

On seeing the automaton chess player in Richmond, Virginia, the still largely unknown American writer and poet Edgar Allan Poe offered his theory of the phenomenon in the *Southern Literary Messenger* of April 1836. Later history revealed that Poe had been partially correct in his analysis of the talented machine. As he suspected, there actually was a concealed chess player, but this person was not located in the body of the automaton itself as Poe believed; rather, the unseen player was hidden in the desk upon which the mannequin rested.

In 1861, the outstanding German conjurer, Carl Herrmann, brought his magic to the White House, where he performed for President Lincoln. A contemporary, but native American magician, John Wyman, went further by performing for Presidents Van Buren and Fillmore, as well as entertaining Lincoln four times. It was Wyman who pioneered in exposing fraudulent spirit mediums who bilked the public, a crusade that obsessed Harry Houdini in his final years. But it was undoubtedly Signor Blitz of London who performed the most memorable magic for Lincoln. In July 1863, at an outdoor gathering, Blitz produced a pigeon from Lincoln's hat. Attached to the bird's wing was a slip of paper with the message, "Victory, General Grant." The reference, of course, was to the intense battle then being waged at Gettysburg.

By 1884, Harry Kellar, the first native American magician to achieve international fame, had begun his longest run, 267 performances at the Egyptian Hall in Philadelphia. During this engagement, members of the audience included two of his friends, the noted actor Edwin Booth and the equally prominent writer Mark Twain. Born in Erie, Pennsylvania, on July 11, 1849, Kellar performed on five continents before being recognized as a monarch of American magic. His stylishly mounted levitation of a woman illusion was justifiably the centerpiece of his full-evening show.

Although an often neglected topic, American Indian conjuring is the subject of an entire chapter in Milbourne Christopher's excellent *The Illustrated History of Magic*. In fact, much of the present historical sketch is derived from Christopher's landmark book. Chapter 1 of the present study presents additional material on Christopher's study. Perhaps it should not be surprising that Indian magicians favored producing snakes from bags over extracting rabbits from hats. At the Louisiana Exposition of 1904, Shungopavi, an Indian who billed himself as a medicine man, employed an eagle feather for flourishes in place of the traditional magic wand.

Harry Kellar passed his mantle to Howard Thurston, an American born in Columbus, Ohio, on July 20, 1869. Thurston, who specialized in large-scale illusions, presented his own version of the famous Indian rope trick in which a rope tossed upward remains in mid-air, a boy climbs the rope, and he eventually vanishes. It is worth mentioning parenthetically that the original Indian version of the effect, in which the mystery was presented outside in broad daylight, appears to be purely mythical. Thurston and other magicians offered substantial sums of money to buy a single performance of the trick, and in 1934 the *Times* of India offered 10,000 rupees for one performance; there were no takers. During the same year, Thurston brought an elaborate magic show to the White House of President Roosevelt. One year later, while on what he planned as his farewell tour, Thurston died in Charleston, West Virginia. Having held his title as the United States' leading illusionist for nearly three decades, he had surpassed even the expectations of his predecessor, Kellar.

At about the time that Thurston took over the Kellar show, Thomas Nelson Downs was establishing himself as the greatest coin manipulator in the history of magic. Born in Montour, Iowa, on March 26, 1867, Downs' masterful production of an apparently inexhaustible supply of coins from thin air ensured bookings at first-rate theaters in the United States and on the Continent. One of the most tragic episodes in the history of American magic took place in 1918, when a contemporary of Downs, William E. Robinson, was accidentally shot to death during the performance of his sensational bullet-catching effect. Robinson, who used the stage name Chung Ling Soo, through make-up and costuming convinced his audiences that he actually was an Oriental. A somewhat later figure, Theodore Bamberg (1875–1963), also masqueraded as an Oriental and actually managed to fool even his Oriental audiences.

If the first quarter of this century belonged uniquely to any magician, it belonged to the master escape artist Harry Houdini (1874–1926). Born in Budapest, the son of a rabbi, Houdini, whose real name was Ehrich Weiss, insisted in later years that he was American born. He undoubtedly felt like an American, given that he was brought to the United States while still a child. Several of the biographies on Houdini give credence to the cliché that truth can be stranger and more exciting than fiction. Among his effects were walking through a brick wall, causing an elephant to vanish on the stage of the New York Hippodrome Theatre, and escaping from an endless series of restraining devices—including handcuffs from Scotland Yard. Eventually, Houdini's exploits won him a motion picture contract; his first of several films, *The Grim Game*, was shot in 1919. At the height of his success he received $3,700 a week, the largest salary ever paid to a single performer at the Palladium in London. On each anniversary of Houdini's death, members of the Society of American Magicians demonstrate their regard for him by making a pilgrimage to his Long Island tomb.

During the first three decades of this century, American theater was truly enriched by the phenomenon that came to be known as the full-evening magic show. These productions were extravaganzas that sometimes actually lived up to the superlatives in their advertisements. Elephants, lions, tigers, bears, horses, doves, rabbits, ducks, eagles, camels, dozens of assistants, elaborate backdrops and scenes that changed frequently, and the use of over a hundred costumes for one performance were the kind of ingredients that contributed to these pageants. But the depression that hit in 1929 delivered a death blow to most of these elaborately framed presentations. In such an economic climate, the production costs of full-evening shows were prohibitive. The advent of "talkies" in motion pictures and the great popularity of radio also increased the economic risks of large-scale magic shows. Therefore, a majority of American magicians shifted to performing smaller nightclub acts. One magical genius of this era was Cardini (1899–1939). Born Richard Valentine Pitchford, in Wales, Cardini achieved international acclaim for his suave nightclub act, which featured unexcelled playing card and cigarette manipulations. For many aspiring American magicians, Cardini's routines became the paradigm of perfection. A few figures such as Harry Blackstone, who was born Henri Bouton in Chicago, and Dante, whose real name was Harry Jansen, carried the full-evening show into the 1940s. Fortunately for contemporary lovers of magic, Harry Blackstone, Jr., is now performing some of his father's magical masterpieces in the baroque environment of Las Vegas hotels. Any chronicle of contemporary American magicians would surely include Joseph Dunninger, whose mental magic gained him popularity from the 1930s through to the 1960s. Dunninger's predictions and demonstrations of telepathy made him extremely successful on stage, radio, and television. In fact, he is one of very few performers who has ever had a series on all three national television networks.

Magic today is happily enjoying a rebirth as magicians adapt their art of unreality to the realities of the final quarter of this century. Witness, for example, the popular Broadway play *The Magic Show*, which fused the color, flash, and mystery of the old full-evening show with rock music. Doug Henning, who starred in this Broadway play in the late 1970s, and David Copperfield have both made repeated appearances with their own one-hour magic specials on network television in the 1980s. In February 1983, Henning premiered his new magic play, *Merlin*, for New York drama critics. In April of the same year, on network television, Copperfield performed possibly the most ambitious illusion ever undertaken. With a live audience present, as well as the television cameras, he seemingly caused the Statue of Liberty to momentarily disappear. One of the oldest forms of magic, street conjuring, has been revitalized by artists like Jeff Sheridan, who perform in New York's Central Park. The intimacy of the television camera has enormously increased the audience for close-up magic, which would normally be visible to only one or two dozen spectators. A million dollar contract with a major Las Vegas hotel has recently been signed by the magic team of Sigfried and Roy, making them the most handsomely paid magicians in history. Causing tigers and other big cats to appear, vanish, or become transformed into human beings, Sigfried Fischbacker and Roy Horn have also appeared in their own program on network television. Senior magicians who lecture to magic societies are finding a growing number of members in these organizations. Bars and restaurants that feature magicians are proliferating throughout the country. In numerous schools, from the elementary level to the university, a number of magicians specialize in entertaining students. A further expanding market for magic acts has been created by the phenomenon of the theme park. Many of these amusement parks feature half-hour, condensed versions of the full-evening show. In fact, there has been a magic franchise. Mark Wilson, once the star of his own television series, has trained and choreographed performers for magic shows at the Busch Gardens theme parks. Even the Houdini escape act has been resurrected by magicians such as the "Amazing" Randi. Kreskin, drawing perhaps too heavily from the mentalist Dunninger, has made his mental magic pay through numerous television appearances. It is sobering to realize that the magician who makes one network television presentation has a greater audience than Houdini had in a lifetime. Shimada, the Japanese magician, has reintroduced the exquisite beauty of Oriental magic and is in demand at magic conventions throughout the world. A number of contemporary magicians are being lucratively rewarded for their "commercial magic," that is, magic that is employed to sell a product or service at trade shows and conventions. In our post-Watergate era, the magician can be seen as refreshingly honest; he is the one person who openly announces that he will deceive you and then lives up to his word.

Magic

1

HISTORIES OF MAGIC

While the present chapter is devoted to works on the history of conjuring, distinguishing between the history of magic and the lives of particular magicians can be difficult if not arbitrary; thus, our final chapter on the biographies and autobiographies of famous magicians will supplement the present one by enabling the reader to follow the course of magic through the careers of some of its most celebrated exponents. Before turning to books, one representative periodical should be noted. *The Linking Ring*, the official publication of the International Brotherhood of Magicians, is one of the most widely read journals that regularly publish material on the history of magic. A turn to three recent contributions reveals the scope and depth of the articles featured in this leading monthly.

Since April 1963, John Booth has written a monthly column (''Memoirs of a Magician's Ghost: The Autobiography of John Booth'') for *The Linking Ring*; and in the March 1983 issue, he reflects upon his twenty years and 240 installments: ''This series actually constitutes an unfinished book. . . . Like a living organism, it grows, changes and reflects the evolution of magic. In many respects it is a history of magic and the practitioners of it during the twentieth century as seen and interpreted through the eyes of a single, one-time professional magician, who has lived through all but the first twelve years of this century'' (41).

Booth divides his columns of two decades into four five-year intervals. From 1963 to 1968, his writing was autobiographical, focusing on his performances in Japan, China, India (the internationally known Indian magician Sorcar is treated here), and Tibet. From 1968 to 1973, he wrote of his travels in South America, the Middle East, Africa, the South Seas, and Australia. The magic indigenous to each of these areas, including an account of witch doctors, was thematic during this period. From 1973 to 1978, Booth eclectically explored the art of so-called animal psychics (supposedly telepathic animals and the like will be discussed under the heading of ''Spiritualism and Mental Magic'' in chapter 3), trade show magicians (performers who use magic to promote a company or corporation at conventions or conferences), and an account of Canadian magicians. From 1978 to 1983, he ''emphasized inside accounts of top professional magicians, their life stories, philosophy, methodology, and anecdotes.''

Booth expresses the hope that someone will prepare a general index for *The Linking Ring* in order that one could locate alphabetically the specific subjects of his monthly segments. He further expresses his intent to abstract material from his columns for publication in the form of books: ''These may be specific, important biographies, or essays on the various aspects of the magic art, its history, development, collectors, inventions, technology, psychology, and philosophy''(42). Until either a general index is available or Booth's material takes the form of specialized books, the historian of magic can bring little systematization to his study of Booth's writings. Booth further remarks: ''We like to think these memoirs are a contribution to the cultural side of magic, a record of its history, its followers, and involvement in the wider affairs of humanity during this fantastic century of invention and transformation'' (42).

Fellow magicians have already agreed with this assessment, for on September 13, 1981, at the Magic Castle (a combination of private club, restaurant, performing center, museum, and library) in Hollywood, California, Booth was honored with an Academy of Magic Arts' champagne party and presented with an honorary life membership in the form of a gold card.

The reader should be advised that myriad other columns in *The Linking Ring* itself and other magic periodicals (see the Appendix) have also made valuable contributions to the history of magic. At present, no reference work indexes the copious material that has been dispensed but, of necessity, also dispersed by such periodicals. The following two citations are presented merely as further examples.

In the December 1982 edition of *The Linking Ring*, one finds that Eugene E. Gloye's column (''Our Magical Heritage'') discusses early explanations of the standard magician's gimmick that is known as the thumb tip—a flesh-colored, thimblelike device that is worn on one's thumb and used in numerous effects. Gloye relates the fact that at the turn of the century it was used to conceal an extra slip of paper for the popular ''torn and restored'' paper effect. Also in this issue, Benjamin Robinson seeks to refute the thesis that the Oriental magician's publicity was far greater than his skill. Robinson's article, ''Indian Magic,'' provides good grounds for questioning the accuracy of statements about the Indian magician (Jadoo-wallah) made by his rivals in America and Europe. Robinson's essay was written as part of the requirements for a degree in Asian Studies from Connecticut College.

There is one specialized periodical that is highly deserving of mention. Those who wish to read recent research on the history of conjuring will profit greatly from *The Journal of Magic History*, which features a wide range of scholarly articles on various aspects of magic history. For instance, in the July 1979 issue, Steve Tigner, who edits the periodical, describes the magic performed by one of Britain's most illustrious novelists ("Charles Dickens in and about Magic: A Preliminary Sketch"). Here we learn that Dickens' magic was so impressive that one commentator suggested that it "would enable him to make a handsome subsistence. Let the bookseller trade go as it pleased!" (98)

BOOKS

To date, the definitive history of magic in English is Milbourne Christopher's *The Illustrated History of Magic*, a work of loving scholarship by a dean of American magicians. Christopher is one of the best-known magicians of this century and has served as the president of the Society of American Magicians, an institution whose past members include Harry Houdini. Christopher's close friendship with other famous magicians and his avid collecting of magic memorabilia give considerable weight to his interpretation of the history of conjuring and make him a highly qualified historian of twentieth-century magicians. He has the added distinction of having authored numerous texts on magic, as well as the "Magic" entry for the 1982 edition of the *Funk and Wagnall's New Encyclopedia*. Illustrations, color plates, photographs, and a fine bibliography complement Christopher's invaluable text.

For his earlier reflections on the history of magic, one may consult Christopher's *Panorama of Magic*, which deservedly endures as a standard work. Here again the author has turned to his private collection of engravings, prints, and publicity material. Dover Publications, which is responsible for this book, is an important source for reprints and first editions of high quality magic books. All of their magic texts are quite reasonably priced, and their reprints make available material that is so rare as to be otherwise prohibitively expensive for the average magician to obtain in the original form. Their free catalog is available by writing to Dover Publications Inc., 31 East 2d Street, Mineola, NY 11501.

Quite recently David Price has added a monumental volume to the literature, *Magic: A Pictorial History of Conjurers in the Theatre*. Packed with hundreds of illustrations, this tome is fully one hundred pages longer than Christopher's history text and is surely an indispensable companion volume. In fine, Price has made the first substantial and comprehensive contribution on the history of magic since Christopher's outstanding works.

Readers seeking a more speculative, provocative orientation will appreciate the observations of I. G. Edmonds. His *The Magic Makers: Magic and the Men Who Made It* thoughtfully traces magic from its roots in such ancient religious practices as fire-walking to its present-day theatrical expressions. Edmonds suggests that magic was present in all early religions and cites the magic "duel" between Moses and Aaron (see chapter 7 of "Exodus") in order to support his thesis. After a necessarily conjectural discussion of magic in antiquity, he examines medieval entertainers who practiced juggling, sword-swallowing, and sleight of hand, reminding us that, during the Middle Ages, the word "juggler" embraced what we mean today by the term "magician," as well as one skilled in tossing, catching, and balancing objects. We are also reminded that magic and religion did not always mesh—as illustrated by the friar who was imprisoned by his fellow Franciscans simply because he performed magic.

Edmonds speculates that the eighteenth-century magician Jacob Meyer was able to conjure up ghosts on stage by virtue of his prototype of the magic lantern. (In chapter 4 of the present study, we will observe some of the relationships between magic and the motion picture.) Edmonds defends the nineteenth-century French conjurer Jean Eugenè Robert-Houdin against the charge of unoriginality that was made by his namesake Harry Houdini. This issue brings Edmonds' study into the twentieth century and to such magic virtuosos as Harry Blackstone. In fine, Edmonds' book is rewarding reading, because he not only describes great magicians and their effects, but usually exposes their secrets. A word on the term "effect" is in order; magicians generally prefer to speak of magic "effects" instead of "tricks," for the latter carries nuances of that which is underhanded, puerile, or trivial.

Another well-known treatment is Sidney W. Clarke's *The Annals of Conjuring, from the Earliest Times to the Present Day*, which traces magic up to 1929. This treatise contains valuable material that first appeared serially in a British magazine called *The Magic Wand*. Commenting on *Annals*, Robert Gill, in *Magic As a Performing Art*, notes that it is particularly helpful as a major source of information on magicians during the Maskelyne era (38). The Maskelynes formed Britain's most illustrious dynasty of illusionists, three generations of conjurers who profoundly influenced British stage magic since the turn of this century. For a more compact account, Harlan Tarbell's monumental *The Tarbell Course in Magic* contains the author's worthwhile observations on the beginnings and early history of magic. The magician who seeks to grasp the genesis of his art will not neglect this classic statement.

For those who seek other brief treatments, two works are especially apt. Albert A. Hopkins' nineteenth-century masterpiece, *Magic: Stage Illusions and Scientific Diversions, Including Trick Photography,* is important to the historian of magic, since the introduction by Henry Ridgely Evans is a brisk survey of magic from antiquity to the nineteenth century. Again, *Pegasus Book of Magic and Magicians*, by Geoffrey Frederick Lamb, is a terse history of conjuring that begins in antiquity and covers an enormous sweep.

John Mulholland's Story of Magic, written during the first half of this century, is an enjoyable history of conjuring that treats not only classic figures, but such recent artists as Jack Gwynne, a prominent illusionist and inventor of magic effects, and the legendary Nate Leipzig. The history of magic has been further enriched through Mulholland's *Quicker than the Eye*, an anecdotal presentation that surveys magic and magicians throughout the world. Magic as performed by American Indians is just one of the intriguing topics to which the author turns his attention.

Henry Ridgely Evans' *History of Conjuring and Magic: From the Earliest Times to the End of the Eighteenth Century* is a monograph that testifies to its author's ability to be refreshingly succinct. Herein he provides a bird's-eye view of magic from its murky beginnings to the conclusion of the Age of Enlightenment. The author's contributions are not limited to monographs. Having over five hundred pages, *The Old and the New Magic* is Evans' longest study; it is also one of his earliest. An illuminating introduction by Dr. Paul Carus explores the roots of magic and sets the stage for Evans' elaborations. Magicians, their pet effects, and their methodologies are all thematic.

In *This is Magic: Secrets of the Conjurer's Craft,* Will Dexter, a prolific British author of magic texts, is primarily concerned with sketching the historical development of magic rather than with exposing magic effects. Thus, those seeking information about the secrets of magic may be disappointed, but those interested in the development of magic will find this work to be a dependable introduction to the history of conjuring.

Among the myriad books that focus on technique as well as history, the following are representative. *The Art of Magic*, coauthored by Douglas and Kari Hunt, with a foreword by magician-inventor Robert Harbin (pseudonym for Ned Williams), includes material on the history of magic as well as instruction in the fundamentals of conjuring. The authors complement their explanation of sleights (sleight-of-hand operations) and effects with thoughtful advice on routining, creating, and presenting magic. *Magician's Magic*, by Paul Curry, offers a pleasantly written historical sketch of magic that begins with the stirrings of the art in antiquity. A number of effects are also explained, including Curry's reputation-making "Out of This World" card mystery, in which the performer presents a convincing simulation of extrasensory perception. In *The Great Book of Magic*, Wendy Rydell and George Gilbert have presented a pictorially oriented combination of magic history and instruction in the performance of 150 time-tested effects. Produced by a publisher of high quality art books, this volume offers an unusually well-illustrated, selective history of conjuring. Bill Severn's *Magic and Magicians* is another chronicle of conjuring and a textbook of elementary magic. Severn, a talented and prolific author of magic books, engagingly describes great magicians of today and yesterday. *History of Magic*, by P. C. Sorcar, is a succinct survey of magic, as well as a primer on elementary magic effects. In *Magic as a Performing Art: A Bibliography of Conjuring,* Robert Gill describes *History of Magic* as "essentially a publicity piece for Sorcar." Of Sorcar, it can safely be said that he never let virtues like modesty or humility interfere with promoting his own excellence.

A number of books treat magic as practiced in the seventeenth, eighteenth, or nineteenth century. *Magic and Its Professors* is a standard reference work in which H. R. Evans offers a book-length supplement to his *History of Conjuring and Magic*. In *Magic and Its Professors*, Evans concentrates upon the magic effects and magicians that prevailed during the nineteenth century. For a late-nineteenth-century treatment of magic history, one can read H. J. Burlingame's

History of Magic and Magicians. Burlingame is well known for his comprehensive biographical portraits of Carl and Alexander Herrmann. Appearing in 1876, Thomas Frost's *The Lives of the Conjurors* was the first book-length history of magic and is understandably required reading for the would-be historian of magic. In *Magic as a Performing Art: A Bibliography of Conjuring,* Robert Gill comments as follows: "It provides an enthralling and authoritative history of magic and magicians, with anecdotes of their lives and effects. It is important to note that this work remained unchallenged for some fifty years"(68). His previous study did not restrict itself to magic themes. In *The Old Showmen and the Old London Fairs,* Frost expounds upon the magicians and other fascinating variety artists who performed at English fairs during the seventeenth, eighteenth, and nineteenth centuries. In *The Early Magic Shows*, John Mulholland, a distinguished historian and collector of magic, concentrates upon itinerant magicians who performed out-of-doors at fairs and wherever else a crowd could be gathered. This fine but all-too-brief booklet might be read in tandem with Geoffrey Frederick Lamb's *Victorian Magic* for a study in contrasts, since the wandering magician was apt to be considered a mountebank and the Victorian magician, performing before royalty, was gravitating toward the status of an artist.

For more on the out-of-doors entertainer, an illustrated history of the oldest and perhaps the purest form of magic, street magic, or the magic of the marketplace, is set forth by Edward Claflin in *Street Magic*, which was written in collaboration with Jeff Sheridan, an outstanding contemporary street magician who favors New York's Central Park as his "theater." Working without the benefit of stage lighting or elaborate apparatus, using household objects and often surrounded by spectators who are in close proximity, the street performer engages in a most demanding expression of magical entertainment. Claflin's apt choice of graphics and his succinct, articulate text make this study a charming, informal history of a little-known variety of magic. *Edgar Allan Poe and Baron von Kempelen's Chess-Playing Automaton,* one of H. R. Evans' specialized studies, was published by the International Brotherhood of Magicians and is, therefore, not in wide circulation. Those unfamiliar with the chess-playing "machine" may consult the introduction to the present work for a brief description of this nineteenth century novelty. Edwin Dawes' *The Great Illusionists* is a welcome addition to the history of conjuring that concentrates upon magic from the eighteenth century to the present. His first chapter, however, explores ancient magic and locates one magical mechanism in the era of Hero of Alexandria who lived in the first century before Christ. Subsequent chapters treat Jacob Meyer, Alexander Herrmann, John Nevil Maskelyne, John Henry Anderson, Ching Ling Soo, and, of course, Harry Houdini. With the latter's death in 1926, Dawes concludes his chronicle at the end of the first quarter of the twentieth century. This scholarly and engaging treatise is richly packed with sketches, engravings, photographs, and other pieces of magic memorabilia. Since the author is a professor of biochemistry, he often illuminates the recurring overlap between science and magic that marks the history of conjuring. Milbourne Christopher judges W. H. Cremer's *The Secret Out, or One Thousand Tricks* to be the best among various Victorian magic texts. Thus, while it is not a historical work as such, historians of magic, who wish to know the details of the Victorian magician's repertoire, will find Cremer's manual enlightening. *The Victorian Book of Magic: Or Professor Hoffmann's Curious and Innocent Diversions for Parlour and Refined Gatherings*, by Arthur Good, is largely of antiquarian interest and will nicely complement W. H. Cremer's book. Of related interest is Geoffrey Frederick Lamb's previously mentioned *Victorian Magic*. This is a lively examination of the magicians who excelled during that era. Lamb's engaging history is punctuated by remarkable episodes, as in the case of the magician's dove, which flew off with a spectator's expensive ring and never returned. The author's opening comments best express his well-realized intention: ''The Victorian period saw the rise of the magician as a respected figure in society. Conjuring developed from a fairground frolic to an acknowledged art. The present story tells of its development'' (1).

Beginning with John Henry Anderson, born in 1814 and the self-proclaimed ''Great Wizard of the North'' (this ''North'' being northern Scotland), Lamb surveys contributions to the evolution of contemporary theatrical magic by such practitioners as Jean Eugene Robert-Houdin, Buatier De Kolta (whose vanishing bird cage effect was popularized in the twentieth century by the American magician Harry Blackstone), and Bartolemeo Bosco, who had the distinction of performing for the king of Prussia and the emperor of France. Robert-Houdin's performance before the queen and Prince Albert epitomizes Lamb's contention that conjuring had attained the status of an art. Here one might wish to add a qualification, for although Lamb is correct in asserting that magic was accorded greater regard during the Victorian period, it is far from evident that magic has, even now, achieved the status of a full-fledged art. This issue will resurface in our chapter on magic in relation to other arts. Lamb's book concludes with an excellent bibliography.

D. W. Findlay has translated Marcel Laureau's *The Robert-Houdin Theatre, 1879–1914*. This transcript of a lecture given in 1948 provides a selective overview of the magic that was practiced during the period of Robert-Houdin. Due to the rarity of this booklet (only one hundred copies were printed), the would-be reader will, most likely, need to turn to a specialized research collection (see the Appendix).

Students of twentieth-century magic will be delighted by the varied contributions of the following works. *Adventures in Magic* is but one of Henry Ridgely Evans' superb contributions to the historical, biographical and bibliographical literature of magic. This monograph will please those interested in the first half of the present century; Okito (pseudonym for Theodore Bamberg), who exemplified the artistry of Oriental magic, is among those treated. The present writer had the good fortune to study magic under this internationally acclaimed magician and was awestruck by his explanation for why he looked like an Oriental even when not in his stage make-up—the metal clamps that had been used for so many years to pull down his eye lids had permanently constricted them. Desfor's *Great Magicians in Great Moments: A Photo Album by Irving Desfor* constitutes an artistic enrichment of the literature on magic history. For over four decades, Desfor's camera has recorded the greatest magicians both in action and with their guard dropped. Compiled by him and Lee Jacobs, this work stands as a milestone book. Lee Jacobs himself has reverently preserved the most colorful type of magic memorabilia by reproducing magic posters of such distinguished magicians as Harry Blackstone, Howard Thurston, and Harry Houdini. The text features anecdotes and episodes from Desfor's personal reflections and introductory comments by Charles Reynolds (magician, author of magic books, and a creative consultant for Doug Henning's magic play *Merlin*) and Robert Lund, who is the curator of The American Museum of Magic in Marshall, Michigan (Lund's museum will be discussed in the Appendix).

A visual feast for historians of magic has been delivered in the form of *100 Years of Magic Posters* edited by Charles and Regina Reynolds. Their brief introduction to this collection of reproductions of posters asserts that "magic is the oldest of the theatrical arts," for it can be traced to the shamans and priests of ancient religions. While such a claim is surely controversial (perhaps mime, dance, music, or drama itself were earlier expressions), the Reynolds' assertion does underline the great antiquity of magic. For as soon as there were human beings capable of being deceived and other humans capable of deceiving them, magic arose. Put more categorically, to deceive and to be deceived are necessary conditions for being human. But this is not to say that the practice of magic antedates, say, the ability to make and be moved by music.

The editors provide two headings under which the posters may be classified, the suggestive and the explicit. Among the latter, one finds a good many grisly presentations: a female assistant being consumed by flames (male-chauvinism is at least as old as magic), a demon trying to drown Houdini, a woman being crushed, another woman being sawed in half, and still another woman being stretched. These gruesome posters lead the Reynolds to conclude that the contemporary illusionist plays upon the death and resurrection themes of the earliest religions.

My First Fifty Years, by Frances Ireland Marshall, is an engaging capsule history of magic by a woman who has been a magician, author, magic shop proprietor, wife of two outstanding magicians (Laurie L. Ireland and Jay Marshall), and a warm friend to magicians of all stations throughout the world. This monograph commemorates the author's fifty-year involvement in the magic profession. A genuine authority on magic in general and Chicago magicians in particular, Marshall enlivens her wonder-filled account with numerous photographs, anecdotes, bits of gossip, and a fine sense of humor.

BIBLIOGRAPHY

Booth, John N. "Memoirs of a Magician's Ghost: The Autobiography of John Booth" *The Linking Ring* 63, no. 3 (1983): 41–44.

Burlingame, H. J. *History of Magic and Magicians*. Chicago: Chas. L. Burlingame, 1895.

Christopher, Milbourne. *The Illustrated History of Magic*. New York: Crowell, 1973.

———. *Panorama of Magic*. New York: Dover, 1962.

Claflin, Edward, and Jeff Sheridan. *Street Magic*. New York: Doubleday, 1977.

Clarke, Sidney W. *The Annals of Conjuring, from the Earliest Times to the Present Day*. London: Magic Wand, 1929.

Cremer, W. H., ed. *The Secret Out, or One Thousand Tricks*. London: John Camden Hotten, 1871.

Curry, Paul (introd. by Martin Gardner). *Magician's Magic*. New York: Whiting & Wheaton, 1965.

Dawes, Edwin A. *The Great Illusionists*. Secaucus, N.J.: Chartwell Books, 1979.

Desfor, Irving, and Lee Jacobs. *Great Magicians in Great Moments: A Photo Album by Irving Desfor*. Pomeroy, Ohio: Lee Jacobs Productions, 1983.

Dexter, Will. *This is Magic: Secrets of the Conjurer's Craft*. London: Arco, 1958.

Edmonds, I. G. *The Magic Makers: Magic and the Men Who Made It*. Nashville: Thomas Nelson, 1976.

Evans, Henry Ridgely. *Adventures in Magic*. New York: Leo Rullman, 1927.

———. *Edgar Allan Poe and Baron von Kempelen's Chess-Playing Automaton*. Kenton, Ohio: International Brotherhood of Magicians, 1939.

———. *History of Conjuring and Magic: From the Earliest Times to the End of the Eighteenth Century*. Kenton, Ohio: William W. Durbin, 1930.

———. *Magic and Its Professors*. New York: G. Routledge, 1902.

———. *The Old and the New Magic*. Chicago: Open Court Pub., 1906.

Frost, Thomas. *The Lives of the Conjurors*. London: Tinsley Bros., 1876.

———. *The Old Showmen and the Old London Fairs*. London: Tinsley Bros., 1874.

Gill, Robert. *Magic as a Performing Art: A Bibliography of Conjuring*. London: Bowker, 1976.

Gloye, Eugene E. "Our Magical Heritage." *The Linking Ring* 62, no. 12 (1982): 51–53.

Good, Arthur (introd. by C. Raymond Reynolds). *The Victorian Book of Magic: Or Professor Hoffmann's Curious and Innocent Diversions for Parlour and Refined Gatherings*. Japan: Stephen Greene, 1969. A translation of *La Science Amusante*. Paris: Larousse, 1889.

Hopkins, Albert A. *Magic: Stage Illusions and Scientific Diversions, Including Trick Photography*. New York: Benjamin Blom, 1897.

Hunt, Douglas, and Kari Hunt (foreword by Robert Harbin). *The Art of Magic*. New York: Atheneum, 1967.

Lamb, Geoffrey Frederick. *Pegasus Book of Magic and Magicians*. London: Dobson, 1967.

———. *Victorian Magic*. London: Routledge, 1976.

Laureau, Marcel. *The Robert-Houdin Theatre, 1879–1914*. Translated by D. W. Findlay. Shanklin, Isle of Wight: J. B. Findlay, 1968.

Marshall, Frances Ireland. *My First Fifty Years*. Chicago: Magic Inc., 1981.

Mulholland, John. *The Early Magic Shows*. New York: Author, 1945.

———. *John Mulholland's Story of Magic*. New York: Loring & Mussey, 1935.

———. *Quicker than the Eye*. Indianapolis: Bobbs-Merrill, 1932.

Price, David. *Magic: A Pictorial History of Conjurers in the Theatre*. London: Cornwall Books, 1985.

Reynolds, Charles, and Regina Reynolds. *100 Years of Magic Posters*. New York: A Darien House Book, 1976.

Robinson, Benjamin. ''Indian Magic.'' *The Linking Ring* 62, no. 12 (1982): 41–44.

Rydell, Wendy, and George Gilbert. *The Great Book of Magic*. New York: Abrams, 1976.

Severn, Bill. *Magic and Magicians*. New York: David McKay Company, 1958.

Sorcar, P. C. *History of Magic*. Calcutta: Indrajal Pub., 1960.

Tarbell, Harlan, ed. *The Tarbell Course in Magic*. 7 vols. New York: Louis Tannen Inc., 1941–1972.

Tigner, Steven S. ''Charles Dickens in and about Magic: A Preliminary Sketch.'' *The Journal of Magic History* 1, no. 2 (1979): 88–110.

2

APPRECIATION: ON THE PRINCIPLES OF PSYCHOLOGY AND SHOWMANSHIP THAT UNDERLIE THE PERFORMANCE OF MAGIC

This chapter surveys writings that discuss the principles of psychology and presentation, which, in turn, furnish important criteria for the criticism of magic performances. While the values of sound psychology and effective presentation have routinely been championed by outstanding magicians, sustained contributions to the literature of magic on these topics have, nonetheless, been sparse. For this reason, we will dwell at considerable length upon some of the relatively few publications that are available.

Given that magic periodicals are so numerous (see the Appendix) and that they are often over a half century old, it would require a separate and, indeed, lengthy volume to reflect their diverse contributions on the subjects of psychology and showmanship. Instead, our concentration will be upon the more manageable category of books and monographs. The following brief sampling of articles is presented simply to suggest the multitudinous and manifold writings dealing with psychology and presentation that are to be found in magic periodicals.

PERIODICALS

Undoubtedly, one of the most valuable single essays on magic psychology is Richard Weibel's "An Annotated Bibliography of Conjuring Psychology." Researchers can thank Steve Tigner, editor of *The Journal of Magic History* in which the article was published, and Milbourne Christopher for encouraging Weibel to compile and comment upon a list of sources. One year later, in 1980, Weibel supplied an addendum to his bibliography that was printed in the same periodical. Before moving from articles to books that discuss conjuring psychology, Weibel's enormous contribution to magic periodicals must be acknowledged. Since June 1950, when he published his first article, "Psychology of

Misdirection,'' in *The Sphinx* magazine, Weibel has developed his psychological perspective in over one hundred articles. Simply put, he is the most prolific writer on magic psychology with which we are familiar.

A majority of his articles have appeared in *The Linking Ring*, beginning with ''Parapsychology'' in 1952 and continuing to the present. But as noted previously, he has also contributed to *The Journal of Magic History*. In addition, he has written for *Invocation*, a periodical specializing in spiritualism and mental magic, and *M-U-M*, the official publication of The Society of American Magicians.

For a welcome statement on the psychology of magic in relation to the aged, one may read Trent E. Bessent's ''Senior Sorcery . . . Entertaining the Elderly.'' Herein one finds observations on the psychological and therapeutic aspects of entertaining senior citizens with magic. The present writer has discovered that some senior citizens, who have been classified as senile and therefore institutionalized, are capable of responding to magic effects. In fine, they are rational enough to respond with surprise when a magician appears to violate laws of logic or science. Writings that speak to the psychology of entertaining children with magic appear to be far more abundant than those that address the psychology of performing for senior citizens. Would it follow that if Robertson Davies, who authored the novel *World of Wonders*, is correct in asserting that children are too immature to appreciate magic, the elderly would be the best possible sort of audience? To our knowledge, the treatise that would address such questions is yet to be written.

Another minority, women, is also becoming thematic in magic today. In ''Why Are There Not More Women Magicians?'' Dorfay (pseudonym for Dorothy Wagg), a female magician and columnist for *Genii* magazine, reviews psychological considerations that have been proposed in response to her thematic question. Dorfay reports that when a distinguished panel of male magicians was asked to explain the paucity of female magicians, they replied as follows:

1. Girls are not made up, psychologically, to be magicians;
2. Girls would not be as graceful in their production movements;
3. In the early teenage years, when boys become interested in magic, girls cannot concentrate on anything to the extent that magic demands;
4. Girls are not strong enough to do most of the carrying and heavy work that magic demands;
5. Girls will not practice to the extent that is necessary to become a magician (258).

The balance of Dorfay's article is given over to rebuttals, by both male and female magicians, of the panel's conclusions. Indeed, one wonders what sort of argumentation or justification the panel could possibly offer for its sweeping and dubious assertions. As respondents to the panelists have demonstrated, each of the five claims is vulnerable to a forceful attack. Claim one would require considerable elaboration to be clarified, much less justified. Claim two seems patently false. Claim three strikes one as cruelly chauvinistic. Claim four, apart from its other defects, would hardly speak to the cases in which a magician uses "feather-weight" props such as silks. Claim five is nothing more than an unwarranted attribution of sloth to females.

For further controversial remarks on magic psychology, one can turn to "Why Are There . . . Sorceresses, Witches, and Wondrous Women?" by Joel A. Moskowitz, M.D. His lively comments include the following:

> Deep primitive mental processes drive the male to grasp the phallic symbol of the wand. Gender and psychology determine play choice of objects, e.g., boys will build a tower of blocks, girls a circle. The traditional objects of the conjurer's craft seem more fitting for the male in our society. Psychoanalytic interpretations of the need to palpate and manipulate coins and cards, to be bound and sealed in a womb-like device and to master and escape are beyond this essay. Pop psychological interpretations may seem obvious and trite yet not wholly untrue(259).

See the "Books" section of the present chapter for a longer psychological disquisition by Moskowitz. Obviously it is beyond debate that his views are debatable. Is the male magician who uses silks and flowers as props being effeminate? Surely some would contest an affirmative answer. But certainly Moskowitz is correct in pointing out that females have traditionally served as magicians' assistants and, as such, were necessarily in a position of subservience. Thus, the chauvinist of today has just one more thing to abhor when a contemporary female magician relegates males to the role of her assistants.

Another writer emphasizes manipulating the spectator's thought rather than "the need to palpate and manipulate coins and cards." This youthful magician's psychology of magic is expressed in "Behold . . . the Mind Is in the Hand of the Magician." For his essay, Timothy E. Samp received an award of excellence from the International Brotherhood of Magicians. Samp advances the thesis that the magician, like the scientist, is able to predict and control that with which he works. In the case of the magician, it is his audience that is so manipulated. Samp emphasizes influencing the spectator's attention by playing upon his everyday assumptions and by using appropriate "body language."

Just as the views of magicians, such as Samp, are essential for understanding the psychology of magic, the observations of the trained psychologist are equally indispensable. At the turn of the century, Norman Triplett wrote "The Psychology of Conjuring Deceptions," which appeared in *The American Journal of Psychology* in 1900. Richard Weibel, himself a prominent authority on conjuring psychology, in *The Journal of Magic History*, has described Triplett's article as follows: "This lengthy study draws upon a wide range of literary, practical, and experimental sources to construct a synoptic view of conjuring psychology; the origin of conjuring, trick classification, conjurer training, matters of attention, perception, suggestion, association, etc., and sociological and pedagogical implications"(161).

BOOKS

Richard Weibel's *Conjuring Psychology* is a monograph that consists of a collection of short essays and concludes with an annotated bibliography. The latter alone makes this study required reading for those who wish to explore the psychological principles upon which magic effects depend. Weibel has the distinction of having lectured on the psychology of magic before the faculty, graduate students, and senior undergraduate students in the Department of Psychology at Lehigh University, where he majored in psychology. Weibel's knowledge of psychology is complemented by his comprehensive grasp of magic, which began with an apprenticeship at the age of eleven. Thus, he is especially well qualified to elucidate the elements of conjuring psychology.

There is some repetition in his study, because it is largely an unedited set of statements with certain recurring themes. Here, however, repetition may be desirable, since he takes us through normally unchartered territory. Weibel's insights begin in his preface when he observes:

> Being fooled by a magician can be a blow to a person's ego; it can be basically frustrating—he can't come up with a successful explanation for what happened. It threatens his ego, it is demeaning, a put down, outsmarting and thus very aggressive arousing as psychiatrist Bill Nagler, M.D., points out. People quite basically hate to be fooled. But the psychic man can make use of the same conjuring trick, apply a different dress and gain acceptance, in fact belief, because there is that desire to believe in the existence of extra mental abilities. People actually want to be fooled by a psychic. They do not have that blow to their ego, they are not frustrated, threatened or demeaned, since the feat is "real": they have not been tricked or deceived(1).

Perhaps one psychological admonition should be made for the would-be magician who wishes to be perceived as an entertainer rather than as a smart aleck. Keep in mind the just-quoted opening statement from Weibel's *Conjuring Psychology*, in which he warns that people do not like to be deceived, for it is a blow to their ego. The prudent magician will prevent any such assaults on the spectator's ego by one psychological subterfuge or another. For example, the magician can appear just as amused and puzzled by the results of his efforts as the spectator. In doing so, the magician converts his magic from the status of an intellectual challenge to that of enjoyment for all—himself included. In short, the magician who uses comedy or does not take himself seriously will avoid the "wise-guy" syndrome of many neophytes who are so adept at losing friends and alienating people. Even the magician who performs a silent act can convey a good-natured, nonchallenging disposition through facial expressions and body language.

Since Weibel is not a professional psychologist, his writing is free of the specialist's jargon, which can obfuscate communication with nonpsychologists. In straightforward terms, he reviews and categorizes the factors that influence the spectator's attention (these naturally include desires and expectations) and identifies, for example, magic apparatus that capitalizes on psychological principles. A metal tube, narrower at one end so as to accommodate a secret compartment between its walls, is cited in order to illustrate the use of depth perception in fooling the eye.

Weibel illuminatingly likens the magician to the writer of mystery stories, because ''both exploit the closure process by constructing a story or appearance in such a way that the subject forms false figures while important clues are turned out''(4). Indeed, the aesthetic experience of seeing a magic effect and that of reading a mystery story are similar, for neither can be exactly repeated, because the element of surprise no longer exists. Here magic and mystery tales share a property with comedy in all its genres.

Weibel's observation that being well educated does not diminish one's susceptibility to being fooled may profit from expansion. The more educated one is, the easier it is to fool him or her. A highly educated spectator perceives and interprets through a rich complex of entrenched theories and concepts. As Weibel himself puts the matter, the highly educated are trapped by their training ''to think down certain paths.'' Weibel enriches our grasp of conjuring psychology by drawing from famous psychologists at the turn of the century. He quotes, for instance, from Joseph Jastrow's ''Psychology of Deception'': ''Expectation is a useful principle of conjuring illusions. First actually do that which you afterward wish the audience to believe that you continue to do. Coins caught in mid-air and thrown into a hat, a few really thrown in''(7).

Weibel further reports that when Jastrow tested two great magicians of his day, Alexander Herrmann and Harry Kellar, for tactile, aural, and visual acuity, motor skills, and memory, the results were so slight as to be insignificant. On the face of it, one might suspect that magicians would be keener in their perceptions, quicker in their reflexes, and more able with respect to memorizing. But, in fact, Kellar tested about average and Herrmann was actually below average. Apparently, these two magicians succeeded in fooling the public because their principles were greater than their physiological and psychological faculties.

Weibel also quotes from Alfred Binet's ''The Psychology of Prestidigitation,'' which appeared in *The Review des Deux Mondes* in 1894: ''Animals are subject to the same tricks. I juggle sugar-plums away before dogs, just as children react to the ball tossing trick''(8). The present writer has informally tested Binet's claim by performing sleight of hand for a gorilla at the National Zoo in Washington, D.C. The performance was rewarded with the gorilla's apparent expressions of amusement and puzzlement. If gorillas cannot be entertained and fooled by magic, they are, at least, adept at simulating such a state of bafflement.

While Binet established himself in psychology, for better or worse, by developing the first successful intelligence test, he was not a professional magician. Therefore, it is not surprising that his article was attacked by some magicians. Weibel relates that no less a magical luminary than Harry Houdini was severely critical of Binet. Weibel adds that Houdini's critique of some genuine blunders in Binet's essay contained errors that were at least as bad if not worse than those made by Binet. Weibel again quotes Binet, this time on the topic of expectation: ''When one of two actions or perceptions, which as a rule follow one another, presents itself to our eyes, our mind is so constructed that the presence of the one act or perception irresistibly suggests that other''(11). This remark is apt to call to mind the psychology of David Hume, the British philosopher of empiricism, who identified ''cause and effect'' as one of the means by which we associate ideas. Hume further argues that our faith that ''A'' is the cause of ''B'' depends, in part anyway, upon the fact that the two have always been conjoined in our past experience. Hume's conclusion is crucially relevant to the point at hand. He concluded that from the fact that ''A'' has always preceded ''B'' in the past, it does not logically follow that the next instance of ''A'' will be succeeded by ''B.''

Weibel's philosophy of child psychology is decidedly optimistic: ''No one enjoys a magician's tricks like young children.'' Consider the antithetical statement of the Canadian novelist Robertson Davies' *World of Wonders*: ''Children are a miserable audience for magic; everybody thinks they are fond of marvels, but they are generally literal-minded little toughs who want to know how everything is done; they have not yet attained to the sophistication that takes pleasure in being deceived''(303).

The truth about children and their response to magic seems to oscillate between the two extremes expressed by Weibel and Davies. Both parties would probably agree that magicians face a greater challenge in attempting to fool children than they encounter when trying to fool adults. This is merely a corollary of the fact that increased education lends one more vulnerable to the deceptions of the magician. Relative to adults, children have fewer concepts; hence, they are more like creatures of ''raw perception'' and more resistant to being misdirected by the magician's monologue or dialogue. According to Davies' position, adults who refuse to simply suspend their critical faculties and enjoy magic are in effect behaving childishly. To be childlike, by contrast, would be to drop one's guard, to be receptive, to voluntarily disengage one's intellect and simply appreciate the magician's performance as an aesthetic experience that is an end in itself.

Not only does Weibel draw from noted psychologists, but he also turns to prominent magicians like Ted Annemann. According to the latter's psychology of magic, anything goes in the way of method as long as one manages to fool and entertain the spectator. In other words, when it comes to magic, the end justifies the means. The American philosopher John Dewey and the Hindu thinker Gandhi both emphasized that when it comes to morality, the means and the ends cannot be abstracted from each other. Thus, ethically speaking, a good end is undermined if it is achieved by bad means. With magic, however, Annemann argues that whether an effect is accomplished through great dexterity or by some mechanical contrivance is irrelevant, for the magician should only be concerned with the impact of his effect upon spectators. So the magician who disarms and fools his audience by using marked or especially prepared playing cards rather than a recourse to pure sleight of hand, should not have a guilty conscience.

However, other magicians argue that the best magic employs only sleight of hand and the principles of psychology instead of concealed gimmicks or specially prepared apparatus. The dispute is reminiscent of one in the field of architecture. Some architects decry buildings that appear to solve an architectural problem using, say, wooden beams alone, but in actuality use concealed metal rods. Of course, the complaint is that the end result, the finished building, does not reflect or is not true to the means employed. In short, the architect has deceived us. But one can hardly apply this critique to the magician, for it is his or her role to deceive us. Perhaps it is only for the benefit of fellow magicians, who can detect the means used, that a magician need pause over what technique to employ. An audience of magicians is apt to prefer sleight of hand over special equipment.

Another reason to favor the methodology of sleight of hand over that of mechanical apparatus is that one long-standing conception of "art" is "skillfulness in execution." Thus, for the magician who aspires to the status of an artist, the means behind a magic effect are not immaterial. He or she will favor manipulative skill rather than mechanical gadgets or contrivances. One qualification is in order; suppose that a magician elects to perform an effect that relies upon a virtually self-working apparatus. This performer may still be an artist in the sense of a skilled individual, for he may excel in the skills of showmanship and presentation. From which it follows that the worst magician is one who uses self-working props, lacks the skills of presentation, and makes a mistake with nearly fool-proof equipment. A final argument in support of sleight of hand might relate such dexterity to the performer's presentation as follows: Premise one: Mastering sleight of hand gives one a sense of pride and self-confidence. Premise two: Self-confidence is a necessary ingredient for effective showmanship and presentation. Therefore, even one's presentational skills will be enhanced by the cultivation of sleight of hand.

Possibly the most interesting and impressive skill that Weibel discusses is the art of "muscle reading." By this technique, a blind-folded magician, holding the hand or wrist of a spectator, can locate a hidden object in a vast auditorium. If the spectator knows the location of the object, his imperceptible-to-him, unintentional, small muscle movements will serve as clues that direct the magician to the object. Weibel's study concludes with a slightly extended version of his article, "An Annotated Bibliography of Conjuring Psychology," which appeared in *The Journal of Magic History*. As noted earlier, Weibel continues to write a column, "Conjuring Psychology," for *The Linking Ring* magazine.

As we observed at the outset of the present chapter, literature on the psychology of magic is, indeed, scant. To date, psychologists, magicians, and those magicians who hold advanced degrees in psychology have made only modest contributions to the topic. That most remains to be said is evidenced by the fact that a superb magician, some would say the premier magician of our century—

Dai Vernon, has incorrectly characterized the phenomenology of the spectator's consciousness. Quoted in a souvenir program from the 1983 Broadway play *Merlin*, which starred Doug Henning, Vernon observes, "The magician leads the audiences' mind on ingenuously, step by step, to defeat its own logic." But surely the members of an audience are not deceived because they are victims of some perverted sort of logic. Rather, they employ the same inductive and deductive inferences that mark all logical thinking. Spectators are deceived not because their thinking violates the laws of logic, but because they begin their reasoning process with false premises. If one proceeds from a mistaken premise, then even the most impeccable logical reasoning cannot protect him from arriving at a false conclusion. Consider the well-known effect in which the magician shows two coins, a dime and a penny, and then causes one of the coins to disappear. A typical spectator might conclude that some invisibly quick sleight-of-hand maneuver was responsible for the disappearance of the coin. In fact, gimmicked coins are used. The dime has a penny tail side and fits into the penny, which is actually a shell with the head side of a penny on top. The spectator is not defeated by his own logic; he simply starts with the wrong premise: the coins are ordinary or unprepared. Given this assumption, even a flawless exercise in logical reasoning will culminate in a false hypothesis. In short, the magician is able to deceive spectators precisely because their thinking adheres to the dictates of logic.

In concluding on Weibel, one early work that he recommends should be cited. This nineteenth-century piece on the psychology of magic, written as an introductory essay by Max Dessoir, appears in H. J. Burlingame's *Magician's Handbook*. The book itself is a biographical account of the celebrated magicians Carl and Alexander Herrmann. Weibel has described Dessoir's thirty-five page essay as "the pioneering study, full of examples and historical comments."

Two prominent writers who share Weibel's interest in psychology of magic are Henning Nelms and Jason Randal. Nelms's *Magic and Showmanship: A Handbook for Conjurors* is a superb text on conjuring psychology as well as showmanship. "Misdirection" (distracting the spectator's attention from one's methodology) is just one of the valuable chapters in this outstanding study. Because showmanship is what separates the entertainer from the mere deceiver, it would be difficult to overestimate the worth of Nelms's work. Among very recent writings on conjuring psychology, Jason Randal's *The Psychology of Deception* is especially deserving of attention. Randal is a professional magician who holds a Ph.D. in social psychology; thus, it is not surprising that reviewers have turned to adjectives like "academic" and "intellectual" in describing Randal's study. It is germane to add that he has also been praised for his ability to clarify his admittedly complex subject. Perhaps most interesting to the scholar is the fact that the author's theses are supported by research and documentation, rather than mere "armchair psychologizing." Questions addressed include: Why will certain magicians always be award winners? What do all audiences really want to see? Why will some effects automatically succeed? Why may a seemingly great effect be all wrong for one's own act? Why may a slight change in approach make a big difference in success? How and why does the process of deception really work?

Michael Ammar's *A Manual of Magic Psychology: A Search for Pure Magic* is less theoretical than, say, the writings of Randal or Weibel. Certainly the professional psychologist would hold that Ammar's title reflects a popular use of the term "psychology," since what Ammar offers are practical suggestions for the presentation of magic. Rather than present an academic analysis of concepts and principles, he provides tips for enhancing the effectiveness of one's performance. His recommendations, such as scheduling regular training periods for self-improvement, clearly merit the attention of the fledgling magician. Moreover, Ammar has made an important contribution to the aesthetics of magic, which will be acknowledged in our chapter on magic in relation to art. In this regard, Ammar's thinking will repay the scrutiny of the more advanced performer.

For the insights of a thinker one generation before Ammar, one may study *Milbourne Christopher's Magic Book*, a volume that combines sound advice on the performance of magic with instructions for a wide variety of effects. One representative tip on presentation is that the magician should place the props he will use first at the front of his table, those he will use next at the middle, and those he will use last at the back edge of the table. This simple but easily overlooked procedure will facilitate moving smoothly from one effect to another. Also often ignored is Christopher's sage suggestion that the magician who aspires to excellence should repeat and hone his act rather than frequently change effects or routines just for the sake of novelty. In his chapter, "Direction and Misdirection," Christopher uses specific effects to effectively illustrate some varieties of misdirection. In one intriguing case, he says that if a spectator is asked to note and count the spots on a die, she can be misdirected from noticing variations in the colors on the sides of the die. For a more flagrant example of misdirection, Christopher reveals that Harry Blackstone capitalized on a "stumbling assistant accident" in order to execute his "live duck" vanish. It seems that Blackstone's assistant invariably "stumbled" just when Blackstone needed to divert attention from his about-to-disappear duck. Of additional interest for the psychology of magic are Christopher's remarks on how magicians "get out of it," or extricate themselves from embarrassment when an effect fails. One magician, who dropped a supposedly real egg that hit the floor with a thud, regained composure and command by a turn to humor, exclaiming that the egg must have been laid by the sort of chicken called a Plymouth Rock.

One might wish to compare the findings of a veteran like Christopher with those of a newcomer such as James Hope. His *The Holistic Approach to Magic: Seven Possible Ways to Perform the Impossible* is noteworthy for its emphasis upon the psychological underpinnings in the seven routines that are explained. Hope encourages the reader to bring into question the logic of his actions by inviting him to adopt the perspective of the spectator. David R. Goodsell, editor of *M-U-M* magazine, has complimented Hope: "The Holistic idea is interesting and pertinent to the philosophy of performing magic. I very much respect the effort Mr. Hope has put into the book, and I hope he writes again, because I honestly believe he has talent."

Miscellaneous additions to the literature include the next two studies. Henry Ridgely Evans, an exemplary historian and biographer of magic, has a chapter on conjuring psychology in his *History of Conjuring and Magic: From the Earliest Times to the End of the Eighteenth Century*. The author discusses Norman Triplett (a well-known psychologist at the turn of the century), Robert-Houdin, and optical illusions. This last topic becomes a central motif in the war-time efforts of a great British magician, Jasper Maskelyne (see chapter 5). For a "life and death" application of conjuring psychology, one can read his *Magic—Top Secret*. This fascinating narrative reveals that Maskelyne turned to the principles of optical illusion in order to deceive the Germans through camouflage during World War II. Not surprisingly, his name eventually appeared on the Gestapo blacklist of undesirables. The Maskelyne dynasty of magicians—covering three generations—represents one of Britain's greatest contributions to the world of magic.

In moving to the topic of showmanship, it should be noted that magicians make no sharp distinction between the principles of psychology and the elements of presentation. *Showmanship for Magicians*, by Dariel Fitzkee, is one of those all-too-rare books that deal with ways of presenting magic so as to enhance its entertainment value. Here the would-be magician is shown how to increase audience response irrespective of the performing conditions that prevail. Topics discussed include patter, routining, music reinforcement, audience analysis, drawing applause, costuming and make-up, grooming, timing, new approaches to standard effects, entrances, exits, bows, and encores. Mastery of such matters is, of course, the hallmark of the polished performer. It has been said of Harry Houdini, for instance, that part of his powerful performance was due to his method of walking out to meet his audience. Just before the curtains were pulled, he stood behind them and began walking toward them. Thus, as the curtains parted, he was already moving toward his spectators and ready to take command of the stage. Contrast this with the performer who stands immobile until the curtains part and then steps forward, perhaps stumbling in the process.

As in the case of Houdini, a bold personality figured importantly in Burling Hull's approach to presentation. *Gold Medal Showmanship for Magicians and Mentalists*, by Hull, distills the philosophy of showmanship of an author who received the prestigious Gold Medal Award from *The Linking Ring* magazine for his insightful articles on the topic. Obituaries of Hull, who died in 1983, invariably concentrated on his prolific writings (over fifty textbooks on magic), his inventions, or his curmudgeonly character. Hull's book is a superb treatise on showmanship in relation to stage presence, routining an act, stage illusions, escape artists, mentalists, and selling one's act. Other subjects discussed include techniques for presenting comedy magic and methods for obtaining dynamic publicity. It is probably the semiprofessional, who wishes to increase his bookings, that will profit most from Hull's informative manual.

Representing the many books that give some attention to presentation is *Magic With Faucett Ross*, by Lewis Ganson, which features a short introductory section that enunciates commonsense rules and guidelines for the performance of magic, the business side of magic, and showmanship. These brief remarks deserve serious attention, since Ganson is both an expert magician and the editor or author of numerous classics in the literature of magic.

The Magician's Assistant, by Jan Jones and friends, is a unique work from a usually overlooked perspective on magic. Ms. Jones, the wife and assistant of illusionist Chuck Jones, augments her own view of the announced topic by drawing from conversations with those who assisted such illustrious magicians as Harry Blackstone, Howard Thurston, and the "Great" Virgil. Part one of Jones' book comments upon make-up, costumes (including remarks on specific fabrics), poise, handling props, and appearing on television. Part two is punctuated with illuminating anecdotes. The third and final section intersperses pictorial history with engaging reminiscences of various assistants. Remarks on the deportment and attitude of the assistant may be of particular interest to the psychologist.

In *Showmanship Out of the Hat*, The Great Masoni (pseudonym for Eric Mason) surveys the fundamentals of presentation from the standpoint of an accomplished professional magician. This monograph will repay the attention of newcomers to magic. In *Magic As A Performing Art: A Bibliography of Conjuring*, Robert Gill notes that Masoni's suggestions on publicity will be of value to the more seasoned magician.

Of similar merit, Edward Maurice's *Showmanship and Presentation* is a justifiably well-regarded monograph, for the author contributes richly to his announced topics. Robert Gill describes it as "a standard text on the subject of showmanship, presentation, stagecraft and personality projection. No performer can fail to benefit from a study of this excellent book" (143). Richard Weibel agrees with Gill's high assessment, but feels that the work is, unfortunately, little known. Perhaps it should be noted that both "showmanship" and "presentation" pertain to modalities (manners of acting or doing); thus, some magicians use the two interchangeably in referring to the way magic is performed.

On a somewhat more introductory level, *John Mulholland's Book of Magic* offers fine advice on the presentation of magic in the form of tips on routining and some suggested routines; most of the book is given over to an explanation of close-up and stage effects. Its psychological value has been noted by Robert Gill: "It is an excellent book for the beginner, particularly with regard to the author's introduction on the theory and psychology of conjuring. . . . The final chapter reappraises each effect, and suggests how the principles might be adapted for other effects"(149).

For an interesting statement on the conjurer's mentality one may consult *The Magical Mind*, which was coauthored by John Mulholland and George M. Gordon. *The Professional Technique for Magicians,* by James Reneaux, presents worthwhile advice on showmanship by an active professional who has had the benefit of receiving tips on magic by no less a great than Harry Blackstone. In a representative passage, Reneaux relates that the latter once urged him to change his white collar more often, since it showed traces of stage make-up. When Reneaux objected that his audience would be too far away to notice it, Blackstone aptly replied by pointing out that Reneaux himself, however, would be aware of it.

Drawing from his own performances in New York, London, Paris, Rome, Tokyo, and elsewhere, Reneaux investigates the distinction between amateur and professional, the performer's task, routining, stage waits, staging, entrances and exits, confidence, make-up and dress, ethics (an often overlooked matter), tempo, pacing, rehearsing, music, lighting, and other staging techniques. Frances Ireland Marshall's preface to Reneaux's book is marked by her usual warmth and intelligence.

The following four works illustrate the attempt to apply the principles of psychology and showmanship to card magic in particular. Volume two of *Card Control*, by Jerry Andrus, may interest the psychologist, since the introduction is written by Ray Haman, who is a professor of psychology at the University of Oregon, as well as a devotee of magic. Andrew Galloway's *Diverting Card Magic* is a two-part monograph that applies the principles of misdirection to standard maneuvers with cards such as the pass (secretly cutting a deck of cards), the palm (concealing a card or cards in the palm of the hand), and the glide (appearing to remove the bottom card, but really removing the card that is second from the bottom of the deck). After his excellent advice in part one, the author devotes part two to effective mysteries with cards. One reviewer has aptly noted: "In part one the reader is shown how to keep the eyes of the spectator away from his hands at the moment the vital sleight is made. This information is worth many times the price of the book."

"Outs," Precautions, and Challenges, by Charles H. Hopkins, is the card magician's bible for extricating himself from embarrassing situations—whether due to a mistake on the performer's part or the seemingly impossible "test" conditions posed by the occasionally testy spectator. This is especially valuable material for the beginner, since it distills what has been learned by a seasoned magician. In his introduction, Hopkins states: "We know of no case where all the sleights, artifices, etc. have been gathered between the same covers and coupled with vital psychological principles for the specific purpose of getting card workers out of difficulties."

While Hopkins ostensibly treats card magic, many of his psychological observations apply not just to card magic but to other varieties as well. For instance, he advises that caution is in order if a spectator asks a magician to repeat an effect for a third party who has not seen it. This third person may feel as if she or he is being "set up" as a victim or butt of a practical joke. After all, the other two know what is going to happen, but the third party may wonder, "What is the 'gimmick' or 'catch'?" Hopkins suggests that the prudent magician will "defuse" the situation by saying that instead of doing an old effect, he'd like to try something brand new. This approach puts both spectators on the same footing; neither has any privileged information that the other lacks. Thus, the third person is allowed to relax.

This thoughtful book will add to the psychological resourcefulness of the neophyte magician and is also apt to benefit all but the most experienced of magical veterans. As a bonus, Hopkins' monograph includes an explanation of the "throw change," which some would say is quite simply the most stunning maneuver possible with playing cards. In this effect, a card that is shown and thrown onto a table is transformed into a different card. Card specialists may wish to consult Lynn Searles' *The Card Expert*, in which the author's introductory remarks are focused upon psychology.

Misdirection is the key weapon in the arsenal of the prestidigitator; *Anatomy of Misdirection*, by Joe Bruno, has been advertised in magic periodicals as "an award-winning article now in book length." At sixty-seven pages, the work is more of a monograph than a book, but measured against other writings on the topic, which tend to be meager, Bruno's work qualifies as a virtual tome. Bruno analyzes misdirection into fifteen principles, gives fifty examples, and includes fifteen routines. Basically, he classifies misdirection under the three headings of distraction, diversion, and relaxation.

Bruno's statement is one of the more recent efforts and is very deserving of study. Misdirection can be defined as the artful transference of a spectator's attention from what is crucial in the execution of an effect to what is irrelevant. This may take the form of a gesture, as when the magician points in the direction toward which he wishes his spectators to look. Simulation or pretense is another form of misdirection; suppose the magician wishes to make a coin vanish. He may simulate the action of transferring the coin from his right hand to his left hand. A moment later, when the left hand is shown empty, the coin will seem to have disappeared. Additional misdirection, in the form of surprise, may also enter in, for while the spectator's attention has been deflected from his coin-concealing right hand and is focused upon the opening of the left hand, the magician may take this opportunity to dispose of the coin in his right hand, perhaps by pocketing it or, if seated at a table, by secretly dropping it into his lap. For an example of verbal misdirection, imagine that the magician wishes to create the illusion that a pocket knife can change colors. Suppose further that one side of the knife is white and one side is black. Through manipulation, the magician appears to show both sides of the knife as being, say, white, but, in fact, by using his thumb and fingers to turn the knife over at the same time that he rotates his wrist, the magician can really show the same side of the knife twice.

Verbal misdirection can insure that even the most perceptive spectator will not detect the slightly irregular action. If the magician begins his effect by announcing, "I will now cause this pocket knife to disappear," the most astute spectator will now concentrate upon keeping track of the knife's location and will be far less likely to observe the somewhat unusual handling of the knife "turn." That this piece of misdirection was discovered independently by the present writer, as well as by a specialist in knife manipulation, testifies to the fundamental nature of the principles of misdirection.

A related rule of misdirection is that one should not state in advance what he plans to accomplish. To do so would be to eliminate the element of surprise and to risk being detected in one's methodology. For a cruder expression of misdirection, consider the running line of "patter" (traceable to a word meaning a rapid, mumbling recitation of prayers in liturgy) that can so befuddle the spectator that he does not see whatever secret operations are at work.

Dariel Fitzkee's *Magic by Misdirection* attends to the psychology of deception in a truly book-length addition to the literature of conjuring psychology. Psychological principles are illustrated through the use of well-chosen magic effects. Subjects treated include disguise and attention control, simulation, dissimulation, interpretation, maneuver, pretense, ruse, anticipation, diversion, monotony, premature consumation, confusion, and suggestion. This trail-blazing classic is a development of the author's *Misdirection for Magicians*, a sixty-seven page, mimeographed work. Because misdirection is an indispensable ingredient of effective magic, Fitzkee's book has become a standard work.

As the following will demonstrate, numerous contributions on misdirection take the form of short statements. In *Don't Look Now*, with just over two dozen pages, Al Leech sets forth what some regard as the best available exposition on the all-important topic of misdirection. Having been a professional journalist, Leech writes with enviable clarity and economy. Leech's psychological study addresses not only how best to fool the spectator, but how to make him like you. *Our Magic*, coauthored by John Nevil Maskelyne and David Devant, features a first-rate chapter on misdirection. The book as a whole, which is a singular masterpiece in the literature of conjuring, will be discussed in our chapter on magic in relation to art, for the authors approach magic as such, even subjecting it to an Aristotelian analysis.

The final chapter of Charles J. Pecor's *The Craft of Magic: Easy-to-Learn Illustrations for Spectacular Performances* is devoted to the effective presentation of magic. Here the author, a professor of speech and drama, comments on the distinction between practice and rehearsal, as well as how to develop confidence. Misdirection is divided into four categories: Use of the eye (the performer looks in the direction that he wants his spectators to look), body language, natural actions, and repetition. Pecor advises the magician to read a book on body language in order to learn the details of this nonverbal means of communication; only then can one perceive how it can be applied for purposes of misdirection. Natural actions are essential; for if only ordinary actions seem to precede the magician's climax, the latter will be apprehended as genuinely extraordinary. Repetition diminishes the spectator's perceptual acuity by inculcating in him a pattern of expectation that obfuscates what actually takes place. Just as repetition often precedes the surprising punch line of a joke, it can be employed by the magician to disarm his audience prior to his denouement. Pecor's helpful discussion also treats finding a unique style, routining magic, and dealing with anxiety.

Alan Z. Kronzek's *The Secrets of Alkazar* features whimsical illustrations and sage advice on misdirection for beginners. The author integrates his comments on attention-control with explanations for simple but effective magic effects such as the salt shaker through the table mystery. Repetition, as a variety of misdirection, is illustrated through the well-known "homing stones" effect in which one of three small objects placed in a pocket returns to join the other two in the hand. For more basic material, Arthur Sherwood spends five pages analyzing misdirection in David Devant's *Secrets of My Magic*.

In Lewis Ganson's *The Magic of Slydini*, a short chapter on misdirection demonstrates that there is more to "pure magic" (magic without special apparatus or gimmicks) than sleight of hand, for it is shown that even the most exquisite sleight of hand can be fortified by the addition of misdirection. In *Slydini Encores*, by Leon Nathanson, the reader is given a postgraduate course in sleight of hand and a flawless elucidation of misdirection. Through the latter, Slydini has raised the ruse of lapping (secretly using the lap in order to produce and vanish objects) to a consummate art form.

Creativity, a factor in every art, is related to magic in the following three works. Chapter 1 of Arthur Buckley's *Principles and Deceptions* is occupied with magic theory and may enlighten one on the topic of inventing magic effects. Little has been written on the creative process as it applies to magic; thus the interested reader must glean what he can from scattered remarks. When we asked polished magicians like Horace Bennett why so little has been said about creativity in the literature of magic, one answer prevailed: Creativity does not lend itself to articulation; in short, it is ineffable. Interestingly enough, if this is the case, it has not inhibited writers from discussing, at length, the creative process in relation to the more established arts of painting, sculpture, music, and poetry.

The Trick Brain, a companion volume to Fitzkee's *Magic by Misdirection* and *Showmanship for Magicians*, completes what has come to be known as the "Fitzkee Trilogy." In *The Trick Brain*, Fitzkee subsumes all magic effects under nineteen basic categories. Various methods for executing the nineteen fundamental effects are then analyzed in an attempt to exhaust all possibilities. Such analysis is conducted in order to illustrate the evolution of new effects and methods that emerge from this very investigation. It is Fitzkee's thesis that following a systematic procedure will culminate in the invention and refinement of magic effects. In fact, advertisements for his book promise that it delivers "an automatic trick inventor." It is not surprising that readers have been disappointed with this book, for it purports to do that which is impossible (reduce the creative act to an automatic response), and it necessarily fails. The very magicians who praise the other two components of his trilogy are the ones who, at best, are disenchanted with and, at worst, vitriolically critical of *The Trick*

Brain. This is not to say that the book is devoid of merit; it has been and will continue to be important in the literature of magic. But Fitzkee's contribution does not lie in any recipe for creativity; it is not what he says in general, but what he causes magicians to think about in particular that is of enduring value. Fitzkee's book succeeds whenever it stimulates the reader to reflect upon the relations between specific effects and specific methods, their combinations and permutations, for such reflections are often a necessary, if not a sufficient, condition for individual creativity.

Eric C. Lewis' *Magical Mentality: Creative Thought for Magicians* is a theoretical work that seeks to assist magicians in the creation of magic effects and themes. Its author is a fertile inventor and a prolific writer of magic texts. The reader may wish to compare Lewis' findings with those of Fitzkee in *The Trick Brain*.

Varying perspectives on magic in relation to child psychology are expressed in the following three studies. In "Educational Showmanship," which was submitted in 1973 as a master's thesis in the Department of Education at the University of Toledo, James Dyko deals with the academic application of magic for teaching special children. As Richard Weibel has pointed out to this author in correspondence, it is difficult to say where the boundaries of conjuring psychology lie. Some would hesitate to include magic as a means for therapy within this field. But if magic is therapeutically employed to modify a patient's psychological states, broadly speaking, such activity falls at least within the province of magic psychology.

Further additions to the literature on magic as a form of therapy are apt to be forthcoming, since David Copperfield, who has starred in his own magic specials on the Columbia Broadcasting System Television Network, is currently coordinating a nationwide effort through which magicians will instruct rehabilitation workers in the performance of elementary magic effects. These rehabilitation professionals will, in turn, teach magic to their patients. Three basic purposes underlie this instructional program. First, it is hoped that learning magic will motivate patients to use muscles that are usually inactive. Second, it is believed that if patients master even rudimentary feats of magic, they will be able to do something that the ordinary nonpatient cannot; thus, the patient will be able to bolster his own sense of self-esteem. Finally, magicians who are supportive of the project predict that it will enlarge the category of those who appreciate magic.

In *Theatrical Magic*, Eugene E. Gloye, a life-long magician who holds a Ph.D. in psychology, combines psychological analyses with instruction in a variety of stage magic effects. For those interested in the psychology of theatrical magic in general and the psychology of children's magic in particular, this is a one-of-a-kind book. Psychological topics include the psychology of the physical arrangements in magic, children's reactions to magic, and an analysis of interest in magic. Presentation-related subjects include styles, themes, stage arrangements, timing, design, and stage furniture.

The Sorcerer's Apprentice, Or the Uses of Magic in the Psychotherapy of

Children, by Joel A. Moskowitz, is a booklet of some two dozen pages that will interest those who wish to consider the therapeutic possibilities of magic. Moskowitz also reflects upon the psychological factors that influence one's becoming a magician. Those with a Freudian turn of mind will be especially taken by Moskowitz' speculations.

A long-standing psychological principle of magic is challenged in I. G. Edmonds' *The Magic Makers: Magic and the Men Who Made It*. Magicians have traditionally opposed exposing the secrets of magic on the grounds that to do so would be to disappoint, disenchant, or diminish the spectator's enjoyment of magic. It does seem psychologically unassailable that magic is dependent upon the element of surprise and that once the secret of an effect has been divulged, this feature cannot arise. But Edmonds argues that revealing the secrets of magic can be justified, because such revelations will make for more appreciative, sophisticated spectators of magic as an art.

Edmonds appeals to two prestigious magic authorities in support of his conviction, Nevil Maskelyne and David Devant. On their side is the fact that fellow magicians, who are in the know, are apt to be the most sympathetic audience for other magicians. Conjurers, at their best, are members of a brotherhood, each member of which is in a position to empathize with the agonies and ecstasies of another magician's performance. Only a magician is likely to detect the sleight-of-hand dexterity that is responsible for a given effect. Only a magician has struggled to master such esoteric feats of manipulation. Only someone who is magically informed is able to appreciate the subtleties of methodology or presentation. From all this, it would seem to follow that were laymen to learn the secrets of magic, they would then be somewhat in awe of the magician's proficiency, which can rival that of the concert pianist. In short, laymen would hold magicians in higher regard.

Although the preceding argument is valid, there is such a thing as paying too high a price to achieve one's goal, for in doing so, one may prevent the accomplishment of a more important goal. Exposing the secrets of magic would reduce it to the category of skill or dexterity; moreover, such exposure would undermine the magician's ability to instill a sense of wonder in his audience. In James Barrie's *Peter Pan* we are reminded of the sad fact that, as adults, we cannot return to our childhood. But a competent magician and an adult spectator, who temporarily suspends his critical faculties, can combine to falsify Barrie's proposition. What is most aesthetic and magical about magic is its ability to rekindle in adults a childlike sense of the mysterious or the miraculous. The perspective of Virginia Woolf, novelist, essayist, and critic, on Lewis Carroll's *Alice's Adventures in Wonderland* is germane at this point. For her, the point of the book was not so much to entertain children as it was to make adults children again. It is ironic that many relegate magic to the level of an entertainment form for children, since it is adults who need it most of all.

A further complication arises for those who espouse revealing the secrets of magic. Certain excellent effects are based on self-working apparatus. Would the average layman still want to see a woman "floating in air" once he knew the exact mechanics? Would the layman be satisfied, as magicians are, to simply appreciate the showmanship of the magician who presides over the levitation? An affirmative answer seems dubious. It must be remembered that laymen who learn how an effect is done will still not know how to do it themselves. The deepest appreciation of magic calls for knowledge of both kinds and is present, to one degree or another, in magicians alone. Preserving the secrets of magic elevates it from a mere exercise in skill to an art form that is emotionally expressive and capable specifically of eliciting in the spectator the childlike sense of the numinous that, although sometimes suppressed, is always a part of what it means to be fully human. Philosophers as ancient as Plato and Aristotle and scientists as recent as Albert Einstein have identified man's sense of wonder as the primordial source of philosophy, science, and art. Indeed, it is a necessary condition for the development of religion as well. Magic, at its most dramatic moments, speaks directly and admirably to this sense of wonder.

There exists a psychological point that is commonplace in writings on magic and, therefore, deserving of mention. Generally, the simpler an effect the greater its impact upon an audience. Suppose that a magician causes a silk to disappear by first putting it into a container and later showing that the container is empty. Surely the effect can be heightened by eliminating the extraneous. With skill, instead of a specially prepared container, the magician can cause the silk to disappear using only his bare hands. Or, even more directly, he could cause the silk to vanish in a flash from the single hand that holds it. The epistemological principle known as "Occam's razor" or the "principle of parsimony" dictates that when there are two equally plausible explanations for a phenomenon, one should choose the more economical. This principle has been converted into a psychological dictum by magicians: When an effect can be accomplished by either of two methods, choose the simpler, for to do so will be to enhance the effect.

BIBLIOGRAPHY

Ammar, Michael. *A Manual of Magic Psychology: A Search for Pure Magic*. Bluefield, W. Va.: Author, n.d.

Andrus, Jerry. *Card Control* Vol. 2. Albany, Oreg.: J. A. Enterprises, 1976.

Bessent, Trent E. "Senior Sorcery . . . Entertaining the Elderly." *The Linking Ring* 59, no. 11 (1979): 41–43.

Bruno, Joe. *Anatomy of Misdirection*. Baltimore: Stoney Brook Press, 1978.

Buckley, Arthur. *Principles and Deceptions*. Chicago: Author, 1948.

Burlingame, H. J. *Magician's Handbook*. Chicago: Wilcox & Follet, 1942.

Christopher, Milbourne. *Milbourne Christopher's Magic Book*. New York: Thomas Y. Crowell, 1977.

Davies, Robertson. *World of Wonders*. New York: The Viking Press, 1975.

Devant, David. *Secrets of My Magic*. London: Hutchinson, 1936.

Dorfay [Dorothy Wagg]. "Why Are There Not More Women Magicians?" *Genii* 47 (1983): 257–58.

Dyko, James "Educational Showmanship." M. Ed. thesis, University of Toledo, 1973.

Edmonds, I. G. *The Magic Makers: Magic and the Men Who Made It*. Nashville: Thomas Nelson Inc., 1976.

Evans, Henry Ridgely. *History of Conjuring and Magic: From the Earliest Times to the End of the Eighteenth Century*. Kenton, Ohio: William W. Durbin, 1930.

Fitzkee, Dariel. *Magic by Misdirection*. San Rafael, Calif.: San Raphael House, 1945.

———. *Showmanship for Magicians*. San Rafael, Calif.: San Raphael House, 1943.

———. *The Trick Brain*. San Rafael, Calif.: San Raphael House, 1944.

Galloway, Andrew. *Diverting Card Magic*. Ayr, Scotland: Author, n.d.

Ganson, Lewis. *The Magic of Slydini*. London: Harry Stanley's Unique Magic Studio, 1960.

———. *Magic with Faucett Ross*. Bideford, England: Supreme Magic, 1975.

Gill, Robert. *Magic as a Performing Art: A Bibliography of Conjuring*. London: Bowker, 1976.

Gloye, Eugene E. *Theatrical Magic*. Chicago: Magic Inc., 1979.

Hope, James. *The Holistic Approach to Magic: Seven Possible Ways to Perform the Impossible*. Shoreham, N.Y.: Presto Books, 1982.

Hopkins, Charles H. *"Outs," Precautions, and Challenges*. Philadelphia: Author, 1940.

Hull, Burling. *Gold Medal Showmanship for Magicians and Mentalists*. Seattle: Micky Hades Intl., 1971.

Jones, Jan, and friends. *The Magician's Assistant*. Sierra Madre, Calif.: Magical Publications of California, 1982.

Kronzek, Alan Z. *The Secrets of Alkazar*. New York: Four Winds Press, 1980.

Leech, Al. *Don't Look Now*. Chicago: Magic Inc., 1948.

Lewis, Eric C. *Magical Mentality: Creative Thought for Magicians*. London: Davenport, 1939.

Maskelyne, Jasper. *Magic—Top Secret*. London: Stanley Paul, 1948.

Maskelyne, John Nevil, and David Devant. *Our Magic*. London: Routledge, 1911.

Masoni [Eric Mason]. *Showmanship Out of the Hat*. Bideford, England: Supreme Magic, 1970.

Maurice, Edward. *Showmanship and Presentation*. Alcester, England: Goodliffe, 1946.

Moskowitz, Joel A. *The Sorcerer's Apprentice, Or the Uses of Magic in the Psychotherapy of Children* N.p.: Magical Mask Press, n.d.

———. "Why Are There . . . Sorceresses, Witches, and Wondrous Women?" *Genii* 47 (1983): 259.

Mulholland, John. *John Mulholland's Book of Magic*. New York: Charles Scribner's Sons, 1963.

Mulholland, John, and George M. Gordon. *The Magical Mind*. New York: Hastings House, 1967.

Nathanson, Leon. *Slydini Encores*. New York: Slydini Studio, 1966.

Nelms, Henning. *Magic and Showmanship: A Handbook for Conjurors*. New York: Dover, 1969.

Pecor, Charles J. *The Craft of Magic: Easy-to-Learn Illusions for Spectacular Performances* Englewood Cliffs, N.J.: Prentice-Hall, 1979.

Randal, Jason. *The Psychology of Deception*. Venice, Calif.: Top Secret Publications, 1983.

Reneaux, James. *The Professional Technique for Magicians*. Colon, Mich.: Abbott's Magic, 1968.

Samp, Timothy E. "Behold . . . the Mind Is in the Hand of the Magician." *The Linking Ring* 60, no. 8 (1980): 33–34.

Searles, Lynn. *The Card Expert*. Colon, Mich.: Abbott's Magic, 1938.

Triplett, Norman. "The Psychology of Conjuring Deceptions." *The American Journal of Psychology* 11 (1900): 439–510.

Weibel, Richard J. "An Annotated Bibliography of Conjuring Psychology." *The Journal of Magic History* 1, no. 3 (1979): 157–161.

———. *Conjuring Psychology*. New York: Magico Magazine Publications, 1980.

———. "Psychology of Misdirection." *The Sphinx* 49, no. 4 (1950): 84.

3

THE CREATION OF ILLUSION: MANUALS ON THE EXECUTION OF MAGIC

Many accomplished magicians were introduced to the secrets of the art through the printed page, because economics (one might not be able to afford individual lessons) and geography (there may not be a qualified teacher in one's immediate vicinity) have often militated against one being able to learn by personal instruction. In America, matters have improved somewhat during recent decades as magic courses have come to be offered by junior colleges, colleges, universities, and civic organizations such as the Young Men's Christian Association. But even if all would-be magicians were able to take lessons from an experienced practitioner, the magic textbook would hardly be obsolete. Only the sustained, book-length format can conveniently accommodate theoretical considerations, subtleties, and the elements of magic criticism and refinement that are all crucial to the proper execution of magic effects. The present chapter will discuss magic texts according to the following classification:

1. General studies (works that treat a wide variety of effects and may thereby serve as introductions to the field)
2. Card magic (studies devoted mainly or exclusively to close-up magic with playing cards)
3. Close-up magic (studies devoted to close-up magic with objects other than, or in addition to, cards)
4. Coin magic (studies devoted exclusively or mainly to close-up magic with coins)
5. Stage magic (studies devoted to magic effects that are intended to be presented at some distance from the audience—including magic that is designed for entertaining children)
6. Miscellaneous magic and related skills

7. Spiritualism and mental magic (studies devoted to demonstrations of psychic phenomena)
8. Bibliographies (studies devoted to bibliographical material)

Biographies and autobiographies will be reviewed in our final chapter on selected famous magicians.

GENERAL STUDIES

Of all the contenders for the title "encyclopedia of magic," Harlan Tarbell's *The Tarbell Course in Magic* is the unqualified winner. The seven volumes, totalling nearly three thousand pages, excel in both the quantity and quality of their contents. All categories of conjuring are represented in admirable depth. Contributors to this masterpiece of magical anthologies constitute an unprecedented pantheon of outstanding practitioners. Tarbell's gargantuan editorial service was supplemented by Ralph W. Read and, in the seventh volume, by Harry Lorayne. Quite plausibly, it has been observed that were all other magic books destroyed, the art could endure through this series alone. In addition to offering an incomparable compendium of magic effects, Tarbell educates his readers in matters of magic history, psychology, presentation, routining, patter, promotion, and publicity. Published over a period of three decades, the first volume appeared in 1941 and the last in 1972. Each volume is of uniformly high quality. Although Tarbell was an accomplished magician who specialized in ingenious rope magic, he will undoubtedly be best remembered as the greatest magic tutor of all times.

While less all-encompassing than Tarbell's opus, *The Mark Wilson Course in Magic* is an exemplary overview of the field by a talented professional who has had his own network television magic show, served as a magic consultant for other television programs, and frequently been honored by his peers for his contributions to the enhancement of magic. This encyclopedic one-volume text features over two thousand move-by-move illustrations that greatly facilitate learning the wealth of material that Wilson has thoughtfully selected. One passage from Wilson's prefatory remarks underlines the value of his enterprise:

> I only wish that a course just like this had been available when I was first learning to be a magician; it would have saved me countless hours of study, research, and practice. That's what I'd like to do for you; let the experience and knowledge that I have gained from many years as a professional magician guide you to the quickest, easiest way to perform some of the finest magic effects in the world (iii).

Readers who pursue Wilson's course of instruction will find that he succeeds admirably in realizing his announced goal.

Variations for some of Wilson's routines may be found in *Hugard's Magic Monthly: Book Editions,* edited by Jean Hugard (pseudonym for John Gerard Rodney Boyce), a nine-volume treasury of choice material for all performing conditions that has been culled from Hugard's magazine of the same name. With over a dozen classic books to his credit as editor, author, or coauthor, Hugard has established himself as a revered teacher of English-speaking magicians throughout the world.

Among one-volume reference works, John Northern Hilliard's *Greater Magic* has been hailed as the greatest single book ever written on magic. Although card magic is emphasized in this one-thousand-page text, virtually every variety of magic is lucidly represented. Widely regarded as a magician's bible, Hilliard's work is now a prized collector's item.

Recently, Martin Gardner has edited the *Encyclopedia of Impromptu Magic*, a diverting collection of games, stunts, and magic effects that one can play or perform spontaneously with everyday objects. Occasionally, Gardner's zeal for exhaustiveness leads him to include effects that are so banal as to be humorous. He himself has noted that it remains for others to provide a needed cross-reference index. After all, Gardner has done more than enough by compiling the always-entertaining data. This text is nearly six hundred pages long, allowing Gardner to catalog effect after effect with such mundane objects as apples, bricks, cellophane, doughnuts, and so on—all the way to an entry on the zipper. Gardner can be credited with bringing together a number of worthwhile mysteries from scattered books and periodicals. Perhaps most importantly, Gardner can be praised for assembling a large number of items, each of which, like the single potato chip, entices us to consume another.

Ottokar Fischer's *Illustrated Magic* is a sumptuous pictorial survey of the varieties of magic that features intriguing sections on optical illusions and the feats of Oriental fakirs. The so-called Indian rope trick is, for example, treated in Fischer's discussion of exotic mysteries. There is also a section on puzzles that would be alluring to the Rubik's Cube addicts of the 1980s. While Gardner's feats can be done with ordinary objects and little or no preparation, Fischer's material sometimes requires special apparatus and elaborate staging. The book has been faulted by Robert Gill and others because it is said to concentrate on exposing secrets rather than on the teaching of effects. In its defense, one might point out that the work has enthralled any number of budding magicians and encouraged them to seek out magic treatises that are more pedagogically adequate. This author was weaned on this text among others.

For a kaleidoscope of the elements that constitute the magic world, three recent books can be strongly recommended. Geoffrey Frederick Lamb's *Illustrated Magic Dictionary* is the only reference book of its kind with which I am familiar. Key terms in the vocabulary of magic are defined and illustrated. "Zombie," for example, is characterized as a standard effect in which a metal ball appears to float under a foulard. Lamb's fine lexicon can be a real asset in helping to demystify the beginner's introduction to the field.

The Blackstone Book of Magic and Illusion bespeaks excellence in its title, for, to many, Harry Blackstone not only billed himself as "the World's Greatest Magician," he actually lived up to the grandiose claim. This engaging book, written by Blackstone, Jr., with Charles and Regina Reynolds, contains a quick, exhilarating history of magic, with special concentration upon the Blackstones. Its attractively plain prose means that the work is as good in form as it is memorable in content. The two remaining parts of the book are a discussion of the principles of magic and instruction in such classics as the cups and balls. True to his own philosophy, Blackstone puts history and theory before practice. Ray Bradbury's foreword, in which he allies himself with magicians rather than science fiction writers, conjures up the "real magic" that only the best of magicians can produce. An outstanding annotated bibliography and lists of magic societies, conventions, magazines, and dealers round out an excellent introductory study.

William Doerflinger's *The Magic Catalogue* is a rich mixture that features a capsule history of magic from antiquity to the present, a fine general bibliography, advertisements for magic books and apparatus, and data on magic museums, societies, conventions, dealers, courses, and periodicals. Representative types of magic, from pocket tricks (those small enough to be carried in one's pockets) to stage illusions, are also explained. Overlapping material will be found in *The Catalogue of Magic*, by Jeffrey Feinman, which is an encyclopedic manual that acquaints the reader with card, coin, and silk magic, but also discusses escape feats and mentalism. Feinman has rendered the reader an additional service by describing selected dealer items, that is, pieces of magic apparatus that one can order from a dealer in magic props. Many a young person has mailed off his money for a magic effect and been sorely disappointed by what he received in return. One's disenchantment on such occasions is matched only by the discovery of the Santa Claus myth.

Those faced with the problem of buying magic apparatus by mail now have a one-volume solution. *Catalog of Magic*, written by Marvin Kaye, with illustrations by Al Kilgore, is an extremely valuable buyer's manual, which is justifiably subtitled "An indispensable guide to the apparatus and technique of over 250 tricks." Kaye concentrates upon dealer items that are available at magic supply houses; in an appendix, he gives the location of ten such concerns. Arranging effects under headings like productions and vanishes, transpositions, and restorations and transformations, the author accurately describes some of the best-known pocket effects, feats of mentalism, and stage illusions.

The multitude of readers who purchase magic through a catalog will find Kaye's candor refreshing; for example, in discussing a standard effect in which beads of two colors are mixed together and then inexplicably separated, Kay notes:

> A dealer description of 'Bead-Diffusion' states that this is an easy trick to perform, but don't believe it. The trick depends on one set of beads being permanently moored, so that a deft twist will toss the loose ones back in the glass from which they first came. This twisting movement is tough to get right, and if it is not perfect, the beads will spill all over the floor (143).

All but the most well-informed magicians will become more enlightened shoppers through consulting Kaye's treatise. But even the knowledgeable magician will find it fascinating to compare his own impressions with the views expressed by the author. In order to protect magic-shop dealers, he tends to give the general principles that are at work rather than a detailed explanation of the exact secret behind the various effects. But revealing the general principles is often enough to enable the reader to determine if a particular effect is suitable for him. When a prop is potentially dangerous, as in the case of the vanishing cane, Kaye warns the reader accordingly; by contrast, magic catalogs sometimes do not include an admonition.

Kaye rates each effect according to one of four cost categories that run from inexpensive to expensive. His merit ratings for each effect are apt to be somewhat more controversial. For instance, he gives only two and a half points on a four-point scale to the linking rings. Surely many magicians would accord this classic a full four points. But if Kaye sometimes underestimates the value of an effect, one can often count on the dealers' catalogs to err in the opposite direction by exaggerating the merit of their merchandise. Thus, Kaye's study may serve as a useful antidote to inflated claims and descriptions. While his concentration is upon dealer items, he sometimes takes time out to discuss long-standing devices that serve the magician; mirrors and black art (covering an object in black material in order that it be invisible against a black background) are two of the subterfuges upon which he elaborates.

His scattered insights touch upon psychology, aesthetics, ethics, and religion. His psychological speculation includes the thesis that children may feel cheated if a magician causes an object to disappear, but fails to later reproduce it. One of Kaye's critical criteria for a good piece of magic apparatus is its ability to be adapted, modified, or presented in a great variety of ways. This could be expressed in the form of an aesthetic dictum: The simpler the prop, the more creative uses to which it lends itself. Thus, it is not surprising that he finds the linking rings more versatile than the linking safety pins effect. The former relies upon simple circles of metal, the latter depends upon the relatively more complex form of the safety pin. Kaye raises germane ethical questions in his remarks on mentalists who give the false impression that they have special powers. In analyzing the illusion of sawing a person in half, he speculates as to religious underpinnings:

> Whether it is Orpheus, Dionysus, or Jesus, there is a primal myth in Western culture of a deity or near deity being destroyed in bloody fashion only to be restored into immortality. In this legend, there is a suggestion of personal continuity for all believers. Perhaps the graphic representation of the sacrifice of an innocent (usually a comely women), and her survival of a process, awakens a dim, respondent spiritual chord in the onlooker (211).

Kaye's thought-provoking comments that enliven this practical guidebook are simply one more reason why this study has enduring merit. Those who are about to purchase magic apparatus and wish to do so intelligently can hardly do without this repository of information. Moreover, Kaye's engaging, straightforward style and fascinating asides make it the sort of work that one often hears about but only rarely discovers, one that the reader can hardly put down until he has turned the final page.

Another sampler is well worth the neophyte's perusal. George B. Anderson's *Magic Digest: Fun Magic for Everyone* is an eclectic, highly enjoyable volume that begins with some "Ground Rules of Magic." Among them is the categorical imperative of all magic: Don't expose the secrets of the art. Another but somewhat less general admonition is that one keep his act clean, that is, free of vulgar or off-color content. Material surveyed in Anderson's delightful hodgepodge includes effects with handkerchiefs, sponges, and playing cards; selected secrets for escaping from restraints; illusions; excerpts from two magic catalogs; plus a chapter on famous magicians and their posters. In fine, if his book cannot whet one's appetite for learning more, then one can hardly have had any disposition for magic whatever.

Among the numerous reference manuals, the following are representative. Jack Chanin's *The Encyclopedia of Sleeving* is a valuable compendium of ways by which one can indetectably insert and remove objects from his sleeves. It is ironic that although spectators frequently accuse the magician of using his sleeves to conceal objects, very few contemporary magicians are adept at this practice. Thus, the magician who learns Chanin's material will, more than likely, be able to fool some of his fellow conjurers.

Two Hundred and Two Methods of Forcing, compiled by the illustrious Theodore Annemann, reveals various ways of influencing the spectator's apparently fair choice of a color, playing card, name, number, book page, and so on. As one can readily understand, this has become a standard reference work for magicians. Many prediction effects, for example, depend upon being able to control the spectator's choice of an object and an endless series of card effects culminate in the surprising revelation of the spectator's supposedly freely chosen, but actually forced card. Suppose that the magician reveals that he has discerned the name of the selected card by showing that there is a miniature of the very card under the crystal of his watch. Surely, forcing the card in the first place is the most economical means that one could employ.

In *Fifty Tricks with a Thumb Tip: A Manual of Thumb Tip Magic*, Milbourne Christopher introduces the reader to the fertile possibilities of the standard magician's gimmick that is known as the thumb tip. This is a flesh-colored tip that fits over one's thumb, but still contains enough space for the concealment of a small object. Thus, the device can be used to produce and vanish a silk or to vanish a lit cigarette butt. The gadget is such a utility item that Harlan Tarbell's seven volume course in magic begins with a discussion of its resourcefulness.

Thumbs Up! by John Kenyon, is also devoted to effects that require the magician's favorite utility item, the thumb tip. Kenyon's booklet reveals some of its author's favorite uses for the standard gimmick and may stimulate the reader to develop his own novel employments for this prop of seemingly inexhaustible potential. One admonition is in order; because the thumb tip can be used as a means in such a great variety of effects, it might be tempting to overuse this gadget. The novice is, therefore, well advised to vary his methodology as well as his effects; by doing so, he reduces the likelihood that a spectator will detect his secrets and, at the same time, he increases his ability to be magically creative, for the more methods one has at his command, the more likely he is to discover fresh combinations and permutations. *Tips Galore*, by two highly published magical authors, Ravelle and Andree, is still another booklet of effects and routines using the thumb tip.

Michael Ammar's *The Topit Book* is a study that illumines the utility of a standard magician's gimmick, the "topit" (a receptacle that is concealed inside one's coat and which may be used to vanish or produce a variety of objects). This cloth container can be exploited by either the close-up or stage performer and can be substituted for the use of the lap, which is only possible when seated at a table. Prestigious magicians like Dai Vernon have hailed this device as an invaluable asset; yet, relatively few magicians seem to employ it. Ammar's informative treatise may lead to a renaissance of interest in this gadget, for the publication of his book in 1983 coincided with his announcement of a lecture tour in the fall of the same year. On such a trip, one travels from city to city teaching his own magical creations to groups of magicians. Those for whom one picture is worth myriad words will be pleased to know that his text is illustrated with over two hundred drawings by the top-notch magician/illustrator Richard Kaufman.

Let's Make Magic is Gordon Howatt's invitation to magic for the home workshop hobbyist. Using only simple tools and this monograph, the magician with a do-it-yourself instinct can make or build over fifty items, ranging from trick decks of cards to a levitation of a human illusion. The plans are printed on large pages for ease of study. Props employed include liquids, silks, jumbo playing cards, and regulation (bridge or poker size) playing cards. The magical craftsman will be pleased to know that a related manual is available. In *Bill Severn's Magic Workshop*, the prolific author explains how to construct your own magic props using tin cans, cardboard, matchboxes, cards, and other ordinary objects. This unusual survey should please those who are interested in magic and handwork. The amount of actual construction is sometimes quite minimal; for example, card magicians will be intrigued by some of the startling card mysteries that are made possible by the use of concealed cellophane tape.

Several books that speak to the youngest of readers can be enthusiastically recommended. Works on children's magic (feats designed especially to entertain young people) will be discussed under the category of stage magic, but among the manuals for children who wish to learn magic, David Strong's *Magic Tricks* can be highly recommended. This is an appealingly illustrated book that will enable children to fool adults with such mysteries as "the Disappearing Lollipops." Aldo Bonura's *The Electric Company Make Your Own Magic Show*! is a good selection of simple magic stunts for its intended audience, youngsters who are new readers. The title trades on the popularity of the contemporary television series for children, "The Electric Company." Finally, *Magic for Non-Magicians*, written by Shari Lewis and her father Abraham B. Hurwitz, and edited by Leo Behnke, will serve the young reader well. The intriguing title speaks to the interests of youngsters who wish to learn simple feats of magic rather than to follow the rigorous path to becoming accomplished magicians. Illustrations actually occupy more space than text in this primer of magic with everyday objects. As one would expect, virtually no sleight of hand is required.

Five general works give the reader an introduction to some of the milestone publications in the field. Patently, *Modern Magic: A Practical Treatise on the Art of Conjuring*, "Professor" Hoffmann's (pseudonym for Angelo John Lewis) premier contribution to the literature of magic, towers above all other late-nineteenth-century manuals; in fact, it was more encyclopedic than any previous publication in the English language. Catering to those who favor magic with simple props, as well as those who prefer elaborate equipment, the text expounds effects and theoretical observations that have endured to this day. Literally hundreds of items are explained, from the simplest card mysteries to involved stage illusions that require the construction of machinery. Magicians are indebted to Dover Publications for reprinting an inexpensive edition of this book.

More Magic, the second part of Hoffmann's trilogy, is another lengthy text; taken together, his three books total over fifteen hundred pages. Again, his purview is wide enough to satisfy varied magical leanings. *Later Magic* is the final volume of a landmark trilogy by Professor Hoffmann. Attention here is directed toward manipulative magic with household objects. Like his other two volumes, this work is of lasting value for both historical and pedagogical reasons. Hoffmann, a professional writer, brought academic precision to his exposition of each effect; and, therefore, served as a model for subsequent authors in the field.

Jean Eugene Robert-Houdin's pioneering survey of magic, *The Secrets of Conjuring and Magic*, is largely of interest to the historian or biographer, for its author was the figure from whom Houdini derived his stage name. Robert Gill reports that this study is said to have influenced the monumental *Modern Magic*, which was written by Professor Hoffmann.

Reginald Scot's *The Discoverie of Witchcraft*, published in the latter part of the sixteenth century, is truly a landmark work in the history of prestidigitation. It is the first major book in English to treat magic as a natural phenomenon. Scot hoped to squelch prevalent superstitions by exposing the actual means and techniques employed by magicians. He treats feats with cards, coins, and other props that were popular as late as the eighteenth century. For a fine recent discussion of the significance of Scot's text, one should consult Edwin A. Dawes' *The Great Illusionists*.

Conjuring as a Craft, by Ian H. Adair, is a good collection of effects, including this English author's originations, variations, and refinements. Stage illusions (effects in which human beings, large animals, or large objects are involved), mind-reading mysteries, and sleight of hand are all thematic. Adair's book concludes with a helpful bibliography in which British books are emphasized. On a more elementary level, Harry Baron's *Magic for Beginners* can serve as a fine general primer. It will not only instruct the student through the elucidation of effects from the various categories of magic, but it will also lay the foundation for learning more sophisticated feats.

Similarly, *Blackstone's Secrets of Magic*, by Harry Blackstone, presents a collection of standard effects that are primarily intended for the beginner. Since its original publication in 1929, it has been one of the building blocks for numerous talented magicians of today. Mysteries revealed include such sleight-of-hand effects as producing a cigarette from thin air and such lavish illusions as the vanishing lady. Blackstone has also catered to the budding mentalist by incorporating a section on effects that simulate mental telepathy. Neophytes will most likely enjoy *This Is Magic!*, in which Loring Campbell sets forth a good variety of effects in an unassuming monograph. As a highly traveled American magician, the author offers practical, audience-proven routines.

Conjuring with Christopher is one of the early writings of its prolific author, Milbourne Christopher. His splendid contributions to conjuring history have already been noted in chapter 1. This monograph reflects Christopher's all-encompassing interest in the categories of magic. Because of his catholic perspective, there is something for virtually every reader's taste in this short study. This brief sampling is apt to whet one's appetite for more material by the author. *Milbourne Christopher's Magic Book* has already been considered in terms of its insights on conjuring psychology and showmanship. But the book is also noteworthy as a general introduction to the field, for it embraces all varieties of magic from simple card mysteries to sawing a lady in half. Mentalists should be delighted, for instance, with the ingenious book test that Christopher reveals. In a book test, the magician either discerns or predicts a word or passage that has been secretly selected by the spectator.

Tips on Tricks is a booklet in which Christopher offers practical advice on the performance of magic together with a small number of effects. *Varied Deceptions*, another offering by the talented Mr. Christopher, is a potpourri of suggestions, bits of business, and effects that can serve admirably as an introduction to the field. Milbourne Christopher and Hen Fetsch, two of the most fertile minds in contemporary magic, have coauthored the monograph *Magic at Your Fingertips*. Contrary to what the title might suggest, the contents are not limited to effects that require digital dexterity, for the writers have also included the categories of mentalism and stage magic.

Harry Clarke's *Magic* is an ideal introductory work due to its winning combination of ingredients: A synopsis of conjuring history, a thoughtful sampling of appropriate effects, and the author's refinements for standard items. Similarly, Paul Curry's *Magician's Magic* is actually a primer for the novice rather than a text for the informed magician as the title might imply. A sketch of magic history and a clear exposition of selected standard effects make this an inviting introductory work. Robert Gill has lamented the fact that Curry's classic card mystery "Out of This World" is divulged and is thereby made available to a wide audience. But Gill's concern may be misplaced, for only the seriously interested person is apt to read, comprehend, and master the material. Those of us who wasted time learning inferior effects, because authors withheld better material, are prone to champion writers like Curry who practice a version of the golden rule by publishing high quality effects of the sort that they wish were available to them as beginners.

Will Dexter's democratically entitled *Everybody's Book of Magic* is a suitable introduction to the art by an author who favored a pseudonym over his actual name (William Thomas Pritchard). Interestingly enough, Dexter is the author of an engaging biography, *The Riddle of Chung Ling Soo*, which traces another figure who preferred an Oriental pseudonym over his given name (William E. Robinson). Dexter's text combines conjuring history and instruction in some first-rate magic effects. *101 Magic Secrets*, also by Dexter, explains and illustrates basic feats of magic for the introductory level reader. As is true of the above text, this book can serve as a suitable preface to more demanding material.

Dunninger's Complete Encyclopedia of Magic is a highly graphic presentation of magic effects from all categories. Although some of the effects require elaborate, impractical, or obsolete apparatus, all of the mysteries make for entertaining reading. With fewer than three hundred pages, this book falls short of its announced title. But its political cartoon format makes it a delight to behold and browse through. In addition, many of the effects explained are still able to baffle.

The Best in Magic, edited by Bruce Elliott, who has distinguished himself by his keen eye for effective magic in all categories, is a fine compilation of varied effects from numerous outstanding practitioners. Elliott's *Classic Secrets of Magic* features a host of innovative ideas for presenting such standard effects as the cups and balls mystery. Here as elsewhere, Elliott draws upon the ideas, tips, and refinements of some of the most accomplished magicians in America. Whether one prefers stage magic or close-up conceits, he will be impressed with Elliott's ability to match an economical method with a strong effect. In the foreword to *Magic as a Hobby: New Tricks for Amateur Performers*, also edited by Elliott, Orson Welles, the actor and one-time professional magician, bemoaned the fact that magic of such professional quality should be exposed. Welles' perhaps tongue-in-cheek concern is certainly relevant, for a good many first-rate effects with cards, coins, ropes, and slates are revealed. The justification for disclosure rests upon the utilitarian grounds that a new generation of magicians will be inspired. Elliott's *Professional Magic Made Easy* is a thoughtful, well-illustrated introduction to all phases of magic—running the gamut from effects with small objects to mentalism and stage illusions.

Like Elliott, Walter B. Gibson has contributed both qualitatively and quantitatively to the literature for serious novices. His *Professional Magic for Am-*

ateurs is an excellent introductory book that offers the reader instruction in fifty basic feats; intimate magic with household objects, mentalism, and stage illusions (such as the vanishing girl) are all detailed. Gibson has been identified as the most prolific author of magic texts of all times. Not surprisingly, his services as a ghost writer were sought by such greats as Blackstone and Houdini. Gibson contributed to popular culture by inventing "The Shadow," a character who came to great prominence during the heyday of the American pulp magazine. In fact, writing "The Shadow" tales under the pseudonym of Maxwell Grant, Gibson modeled this detective hero after the real-life magicians Houdini and Howard Thurston. Like Houdini, The Shadow was able to escape from any restraints and like Thurston, The Shadow used dramatic illusions whenever they served his purposes.

Collected Writings of Glenn Gravatt features the varied creations that its author has invented for over a quarter of a century. *Glenn Gravatt's Treasure Trove of Tricks* is a refreshing miscellany that can serve as a useful primer for the beginner and as a suggestive resource for the advanced magician. *How to be a Wizard*, by Robert Harbin (pseudonym for Ned Williams) will serve the neophyte well as a selective survey of the varieties of magic. Harbin's treatment of classic effects is marked by the creativity which typifies this British illusionist's approach to the art.

For a commendable account of the state of magic in the first quarter of the present century, one may consult *The Magic Art* by Donald Holmes (pseudonym for Donald H. Aladorf). The author couples his survey of basic effects with insightful suggestions on routining. The latter is especially important because proper routining can transform a disconnected string of feats into an organic whole. Just as unity is often a criterion of excellence in the traditional arts, a unifying theme is usually the hallmark of superior magic. Those mesmerized by the name and deeds of Harry Houdini might enjoy his smorgasbord of magical offerings. *Elliott's Last Legacy: Secrets of the King of All Kard Kings*, edited by Houdini (pseudonym for Ehrich Weiss) and Clinton Burgess, is automatically of historical interest because of its celebrated editor. Despite its restrictive title, the book is actually a survey of the field, with a preponderance of card magic.

George Kaplan's *The Fine Art of Magic* is a justifiably famous text that was published in the middle of this century. It represents a cornucopia of methods and choice mysteries with cards, coins, balls, cigarettes, money, rope, and matches. Mind-reading is also covered in this superb example of editing by Jean Hugard. Similarly, Marvin Kaye's *The Complete Magician* is an outstanding survey of elementary magic by which the novice can acquire a good foundation for more advanced forms of conjuring. Materials on patter and showmanship enhance the value of this well-illustrated introduction to the field.

The different emphases of primers will be evident in the following selected readings. *Magic!* by Jack Langham features a bird's-eye view of magic greats and a fine survey of techniques and effects for close-up and stage performance. Variety characterizes the contents of Arnold Liebertz' alliteratively titled monograph, *Marvellous Mysteries of Marvillo*. The author is an outstanding European magician who moves comfortably from close-up feats to stage bafflers and mentalism. Props required include cards, coins, candles, balloons, records, and silks. *Magic Feats: A Miscellany of Practical Magic* by Majikans (pseudonym for Leo Burns) is a mid-century survey of magic that is of more than historic interest, since some of the material explained in this monograph can be effective today.

Routined Magic, a monograph by Senor Mardo, is devoted to choice standards for both the stage magician and the close-up specialist. For whatever reason, the egg bag routine, which is detailed by the author, is one of the most neglected classics of magic. Like most good magic, the plot is simple: an egg appears and disappears from a small cloth bag. Yet when properly presented, the routine can hold its own even when preceded by sawing a lady in half and followed by the levitation of a woman. Mardo's booklet insures that the egg bag is available to the contemporary magician, who is apt to be startled by its strong impact upon spectators.

Jay Marshall's *How to Perform Instant Magic* is a thoroughly enjoyable compilation of platform feats, table magic, and gag tricks. Impromptu items with household objects prevail among the host of amusing effects that the author has gathered together. Causing a borrowed light bulb to become illuminated in one's hand is just one of the chestnuts that merits resurrection by Marshall. Having an international reputation for excellence as an entertainer, Marshall is surely one of the most seasoned magicians of our era. His theatrical persona strikes a perfect balance between dignity and wit; he is the David Niven of the magic world. His excellent book, *TV, Magic, and You!* will be discussed in the chapter on magic in relation to other arts. Among his many achievements are television appearances on the Ed Sullivan program in America and on both London and Australian stations. His encyclopedic show-business interests and accomplishments surely qualify him as a Renaissance man among twentieth-century performers.

In March 1983, *The Linking Ring* magazine devoted a cover article to his exceptional interests and achievements. Among the former are his fascination with origami (the Japanese art of paper folding in order to create figures and designs), his devotion to the Laurel and Hardy society, "Sons of the Desert," of which he is a charter member, his remarkable collection of magic books and memorabilia—certainly his magic library is one of the most comprehensive in private hands—his sponsorship of seventeen annual meetings of the Magic Collectors Association, and his status as a founding member of the Punch and Judy Fellowship. Horology, dentistry, printing, computer planning, chess, and shadowgraphy (the creation of figures and designs by throwing hand shadows on a surface) have also competed for his attention. Among his credits are distinguished performances as a writer, editor, and publisher of magic texts. He has played in three Broadway shows, on radio, in night clubs, at conventions, in both vaudeville and burlesque, and at Radio City Music Hall. His roles have included that of an actor, musician (bagpipes), humorist, mimic, ventriloquist, and, of course, polished magician. We can only hope that Mr. Marshall will add an autobiography to his stunning list of feats.

"Mulholland" is as well known a name in magic circles as "Marshall"; and, *John Mulholland's Book of Magic* is a superb introductory treatise, which has previously been cited for the light it sheds on the philosophy of magic. In terms of the magic that is revealed, this book excels with regard to both form and content, for lucid instruction is coupled with a choice cross section of mysteries for every magical taste.

For a sweeping introduction to magic that inspired a number of contemporary performers, one should consult C. Lang Neil's *The Modern Conjuror and Drawing-Room Entertainer*. The great mentalist (a mentalist is a magician who uses trickery to simulate feats of mind-reading and mind-control) Joseph Dunninger considered this to be the best book on the art of magic. Both sleights and effects with cards and coins are detailed as well as classic mysteries like the linking rings. In the latter, metal rings link and unlink in the hands of the magician but stubbornly refuse to penetrate each other when held by the spectator. In addition to magic, Neil presents material on plate-spinning and shadowgraphy.

Bell's Magic Book, in which no author is cited but Patrick Page is credited as magical adviser, presents simple but effective magic with string, coins, cards, and handkerchiefs. One section of the book is devoted to the virtually extinct art of shadowgraphy. The vanishing water glass effect (sometimes a salt shaker is substituted), which is explained, has launched many a neophyte on the road to magic. Another enduring work has been contributed by Robert Parrish, whose *For Magicians Only: A Guide to the Art of Mystifying* is a good, basic overview of some time-tested effects. This work is enhanced by the author's expression of his philosophy of conjuring. Parrish's contributions to the literature of magic are not limited to exemplary books on general magic, for he has also edited or contributed to numerous specialized studies such as *Okito on Magic*, with Theodore Bamberg.

In *New Ways to Mystify: A Guide to the Art of Magic,* Parrish again caters to the neophyte by supplying more elementary feats of magic. *"You'd Be Surprised"*, coauthored by Parrish and John Goodrum, is another introductory survey of merit, but in the form of a monograph. *Do That Again!* coauthored by Parrish and Oscar Weigle is also a wide-ranging introductory work that takes the form of a monograph. A rich collection of material, which runs the gamut from false shuffles to stage magic, is available in Ellison Poland's *Wonderful Routines of Magic*. The effects are intelligently chosen, well illustrated, and reflect the author's interest in entertainment as well as mystification. *The First Addendum to Wonderful Routines of Magic*, also by Ellison Poland, is a worthy successor to the above work. Again, there is fine material for the beginner, but the varied contents can be most comfortably appropriated by those with an intermediate level of skill.

Wendy Rydell and George Gilbert have contributed a solid collection of general magic effects in their especially well-illustrated *The Great Book of Magic*. In the same vein, but with an emphasis upon intimate feats, *Scarne's Magic Tricks*, by John Scarne, offers a good sampler of magic effects for the beginner. Concentration is upon household objects such as newspaper, string, and rubber bands. The author is a celebrated authority on gambling as well as an expert sleight-of-hand artist. Because of his singular talent, he has been a consultant for the United States government as well as Las Vegas gambling houses.

Bill Severn's Big Book of Magic is a well-written general work that also includes nonmagical forms of entertainment. Using a commendable step-by-step teaching technique, the author leads the reader from card magic to effects with rope, money, and handkerchiefs. There is something here for the stage performer as well as those who favor intimate conditions. One chapter, "Things that Go with Magic," details two acts, paper-cutting (by which one creates figures and designs) and chapeaugraphy (in which one produces myriad types of hats and headpieces by folding a single piece of felt). Jay Marshall is one contemporary magician who has vividly demonstrated the entertainment value of a witty paper-folding act.

Sorcar on Magic: Reminiscences and Selected Tricks combines autobiographical material with an assortment of effects from the various categories of magic. P. C. Sorcar is the most celebrated Indian magician of the twentieth century; advertising himself as the "World's Greatest Magician," he had the distinction of being among the handful of illusionists who perpetuated the old-time full-evening magic show for audiences in the second half of this century. It is just possible that this text will infuse the reader with a relish for the flamboyant, spectacular magic that Sorcar favored.

J. Elsden Tuff's *Teach Yourself Conjuring* is a rich survey of the field that begins with simple effects using pencils, string, and cards. One chapter is devoted to novel paper-cutting stunts, including the well-known paper tree, which can be taller than the performer himself or herself. Other material covered includes preparation for a show, advanced card magic, card fanning technique, coin and ball manipulation, thimble and cigarette manipulation (with a discussion of helpful gimmicks), handkerchief magic, misdirection, the use of assistants, apparatus that one can construct, close-up effects, and tips on how to entertain children with magic.

In *The Collier Quick and Easy Guide to Magic*, Hal G. Vermes has compiled a good selection of effects for different performing conditions. As the title indicates, the novice is the target reader for this modest, little study. Finally, *Magically Yours*, by Verrall Wass, presents a choice collection of varied magic effects that can serve as a somewhat demanding but worthwhile introduction to the art.

For those who can take their medicine straight, a number of manuals on sleight of hand can be recommended as introductory texts. *It's Easier Than You Think*, by Geoffrey Buckingham, is a first-rate, well-illustrated treatise on manipulative magic with coins, balls, and thimbles. Buckingham featured the aesthetic sort of act that magicians themselves never tire of seeing. Those who aspire toward artistic technique will find this to be a demanding but rewarding work. As Robert Gill has aptly pointed out, the title is rather misleading, for there are no short cuts to becoming an accomplished sleight-of-hand artist. This modern classic was preceded by another sterling work, *The Art of Magic*, by the celebrated coin manipulator Thomas Nelson Downs. It is a milestone publication that many magicians would include among the ten best books on the fundamentals of magic. Downs favored sleight of hand with everyday objects and the beautiful manipulation that he taught and exemplified is a sufficient condition for regarding magic as an art form. Robert Gill has suggested that the actual author was John Northern Hilliard, who is credited with being the editor. But while the authorship may be questioned, it is beyond dispute that the contents have been and will continue to be an inspiration to legions of magicians who place preeminence upon magic accomplished by digital dexterity. The simple props that are thematic include cards, coins, balls, eggs, and ropes. Fortunately for the contemporary reader, Dover Publications has reprinted this turn-of-the-century handbook in an inexpensive, paperback edition. Downs supplements his explanations with suggested patter; this is an important consideration, for the present writer has found that his students of magic are often at a loss for what to say during the presentation of their effects. Certainly, each performer must develop his or her own unique line of patter, but one must begin with something and Downs' suggestions can readily be adapted to one's own personality.

By themselves, sleight-of-hand operations are like beads without a string. Thus, magicians seek to link, arrange, or routine their moves into a flowing continuum. *Routined Manipulation*, by Lewis Ganson, carries an accurate title, for he carefully details the necessary routining that underlies any successful manipulative act. Would-be manipulators will be thrilled by Ganson's superb collection of sleight-of-hand routines. These include the production of lighted cigarettes, apparently from thin air; the three shell game (in which a pea is placed under one of three walnut shells, the shells are then moved about, and the spectator is asked to bet on the location of the pea); and the linking rings.

Routined Manipulation, Part Two, also by Ganson, continues the work of the above book by offering more high-calibre manipulative magic. Among the items covered are a color changing knife routine, thimble manipulation, card sleights, a blindfold act—in which one appears to use extrasensory powers in order to see while blindfolded—and the author's deservedly acclaimed billiard ball routine.

Routined Manipulation: Finale, which completes Ganson's trilogy on expert manipulation, treats magic with cards, coins, and sponges. It is here that he divulges his favorite method for the the barehanded or gloved production of playing cards at one's fingertips; this is surely one of the most aesthetic acts in all of magic. All three of these companion volumes are illustrated with hundreds of photographs and studded with contributions by the elite of the magic world. As reviewers have noted, the careful perusal of Ganson's writings is the next best thing to personal instruction.

Camille Gaultier's *Magic without Apparatus* (a translation by Jean Hugard of *La Prestidigitation Sans Appareils*) continues to serve as a beautiful introduction to sleight of hand for readers of English everywhere. This classic text has been called the best book of its kind by magic authors such as Stanley Collins. Cards, coins, billiard balls, and thimbles are employed in lieu of elaborate equipment. Pablo Picasso is said to have remarked to the effect that if he wished to test the ability of an artist, he would give the person a pencil and a piece of paper. The resourceful artist would, then, be able to produce something noteworthy with only these simple tools. Surely, the aesthetic dictum less is more is substantiated by those magicians who become proficient in the sleights with simple, mundane objects taught by Gaultier.

The Amateur Magician's Handbook, by Henry Hay, is another classic introduction to the field that combines drawings and photographs in order to teach the essentials of manipulative magic. Originally published in 1950, this superb text has served to inspire many talented magicians of today. Various categories of magic, other than sleight of hand, are also well represented. The appearance of a fourth edition in 1982 underlined the enduring value of Hay's sterling text. Among the material in this expanded edition are an introduction by Milbourne Christopher, valuable comments for those who wish to entertain children, and a chapter by James Randi that explains the value of videotaping one's rehearsals and presentations. Fresh material on intimate magic, an updated biography/bibliography, and a clear glossary are further merits of this ideal work for the serious novice.

Cyclopedia of Magic, again by Hay, is an older but still valuable overview of the field in which a number of standard effects are set forth. Among general textbooks with an emphasis upon manipulative magic, Jean Hugard's *Modern Magic Manual* also excels. Nearly three hundred illustrations clarify the "moves" (magicians sometimes use the word "move" or "sleight" as a synonym for a sleight-of-hand operation), procedures, and props needed for this valuable collection of basic effects and routines. Coins, cards, silks, cigarettes, balls, ropes, and watches are thematic, but classic stage routines, such as the linking rings, and sound advice on misdirection are also included.

Wilfred Jonson's *Mr. Smith's Guide to Sleight of Hand: A Course of Instruction* is a standard primer that is written in the succinct, academic style that is the hallmark of this author's fine publications. In just under one hundred pages, Jonson sets forth elementary- and intermediate-level principles of manipulative magic. Edwin Sachs's *Sleight of Hand*, a classic in nineteenth-century magical literature, has passed through five editions and proved itself as a standard work on elementary manipulative magic. This book has the merit of suggesting the wide variety of magic that can be accomplished through sleight of hand, whether one is interested in coin magic or apparent demonstrations of clairvoyance.

Now You See It, Now You Don't!: Lessons in Sleight-of-Hand, by Bill Tarr and Barry Ross, is a wonderfully attractive introduction to the pure magic that can be accomplished by digital dexterity alone. Ross's copious illustrations lead the reader through the sleights necessary to excel in the area of manipulative magic. This treatise is surely one of the most graphically perfect presentations of sleight of hand ever published. As one would expect, ordinary objects such as cards, coins, balls, and ropes are used in lieu of special apparatus. Among the multitude of first-rate effects that Tarr reveals are the lit cigarette trick, the cups and balls mystery, the three shell game, the three card monte (these last two items are actually gambling stratagems in which the spectator is challenged to keep track of a pea that has been placed under one of three shells or to follow the position of one playing card that is moved about with two others), the cut and restored rope, and the miser's dream routine, in which the magician seems to pluck half dollars out of thin air.

Tarr also instructs the beginner in card flourishes that give a polished touch to the performer's act. Such flourishes are not intended to deceive, but merely as displays of finesse, as when one springs the cards from hand to hand or fans them with symmetrical precision. Actually flourishes have a psychological value, for they establish that the performer is adept at manipulation and therefore not apt to bore his audience with amateurish, lengthy, tedious, mathematical stunts. In short, prefatory flourishes can inculcate an attitude of receptivity in the spectator.

One of Tarr's pedagogical predecessors is Edward Victor, an inspiring British magician. *Magic of the Hands*, Victor's first in his series of three treatises on sleight of hand, surveys manipulative magic with cards, cigarettes, rope, coins, silks, billiard balls, thimbles, slates, and miscellaneous objects. Written nearly a half century ago, this text has launched many a beginner on the path to presenting magic as an artistic expression. *More Magic of the Hands*, Victor's sequel to *Magic of the Hands*, continues his excellent coverage of sleight of hand in a book that is somewhat longer than its famous predecessor. *Further Magic of the Hands* is the third and final work in Edward Victor's commendable series of sleight-of-hand manuals. Card work is emphasized in this survey of manipulative magic with household objects like coins, ropes, cigarettes, and balls.

Anthologies can serve as effective introductions to the field, for they encompass varied material and sometimes draw on over a hundred contributors. *The Ireland Yearbook*, published annually between 1934 and 1970 by the Ireland Magic Company, which is now Magic Inc., provides a rich array of effects, tips, gags, "bits of business," routines, and sage observations. Each of these anthologies, laced with illustrations, photographs, and bibliographical and historical material, presents a compact feast for magic lovers of every persuasion. For over half a century, Magic Inc. has served as one of the world's largest magic companies. It has also been and continues to be among the most active publishers of magic books and monographs. With frequent visiting lecturers of national and international prominence, workshops, seminars, and collector's conferences, this Chicago-based operation has long been a mecca for travelling magicians and thereby an unexcelled source of magical creations for its books, *Yearbook* series, and other publications. The proprietors, Frances Ireland Marshall and Jay Marshall, are deservedly among the most loved and respected members of the worldwide magic fraternity.

Milbourne Christopher's *Magic from M-U-M* is a compilation of diverse effects that have been drawn from *M-U-M*, the official periodical of the Society of American Magicians. The reader's only complaint is apt to be that the editor should have expanded this excellent monograph into book-length form. His longer work, *The Sphinx Golden Jubilee Book of Magic*, is a rewarding anthology of choice material that was previously published in the legendary *Sphinx* magazine. Christopher demonstrates his editorial acumen by selecting effective mysteries to suit virtually every magical preference.

J. G. Thompson's *My Best: A Collection of the Best Originations Conceived by Eminent Creators* is a rich treasury that features two hundred effects as executed by over a hundred leading magicians. Because a working knowledge of magic is presupposed, this excellent collection of material is recommended for only the determined beginner. The reader who is conversant with the rudiments of magic will find items to suit virtually every magical style. *Our Mysteries*, a monograph-length anthology in which no author is cited, consists of first-rate contributions by an eminent group of practitioners representative of various categories of magic.

For a brief sampling of magic as practiced by outstanding Canadian magicians, one can read *The Centennial Magic Book: By the Magic Wand Club,* which was edited by Bill James. The diverse offerings are best suited for those familiar with the rudiments of magic. *Unconventional Magic* is a valuable anthology that has been assembled by Lewis Ganson. It features miscellaneous magic which has been drawn from the acts of outstanding British magicians and is admirably suited for the novice or intermediate-level performer. George Johnson's *C-O-N-J-U-R-I-N-G* is an anthology that consists of material contributed to the prestigious British magazine, *Magic Wand.* The editor has been pleasantly catholic in his selection of effects, but again, some acquaintance with the elements of magic is required for full comprehension of this welcome book.

For additional material by British magicians, one may read Will Dexter's *Magic Circle Magic: A Tribute to the Memory of George Davenport and Lewis Davenport, Instituted by the Council of the Magic Circle*. This anthology is composed of contributions from members of England's most distinguished magic organization. The contents include effective magic and routines for the stage illusionist as well as the close-up performer. In *Masterpieces of Magic Number 1: Advanced Conjuring for Practical Performers*, the editor, Douglas Craggs, has compiled a fine set of diverse effects, which have been contributed by some distinguished practitioners of close-up and stage magic. This monograph was published by the Academy of Recorded Crafts, Arts and Sciences in London.

David Devant's *Secrets of My Magic* reveals not only the choice close-up effects and stage illusions of its author, but also a profusion of mysteries contributed by some his illustrious contemporaries. This British performer is widely regarded as one of the greatest exponents in the history of art. *Lessons in Conjuring*, also by Devant, (pseudonym for David Wighton), is an excellent introduction to time-tested, standard effects by one of the most insightful theoreticians in the history of magic. His philosophical acumen is nowhere more in evidence than in *Our Magic*, which he coauthored with Nevil Maskelyne and which is discussed in the chapter on magic in relation to other arts. *Magic That Perks*, by Harry E. Cecil, is another smorgasbord of magic with the emphasis upon humorous, entertaining mysteries.

Books focused on a single figure abound, for one way to approach the study of magic is through the repertoire of an acknowledged master. Each of the following works will serve as just such an introduction. In *Amadeo's Continental Magic*, two adept magicians and authors of magic texts, Frank Garcia and George Schindler, have presented an introduction to the exciting magic creations of the Italian magician, Amadeo Vacca. Biographical comments enhance this compilation of varied magic. Another European spectrum of sleights is available in *Ken Brooke's Magic: The Unique Years*, which features outstanding magic and valuable lessons on showmanship by a highly acclaimed British magician. A diverse table of contents encompasses effects with cards, coins, and silks and routines for such standards as the egg bag, in which an egg appears and disappears from a cloth bag, despite the fact that the spectator is in close proximity and is allowed to repeatedly reach into the bag himself.

Recently, a senior magician has thrown light on similar material in a capstone volume. Through *Gene Gordon's Magical Legacy*, the author compresses a lifetime of magical knowledge and experience with the result that the reader receives far more than an exposition of magic effects. Gordon's reminiscences have been acknowledged as historically illuminating by Steve Tigner, editor of *The Journal of Magic History*; his pointers on presentation have been lauded by David R. Goodsell, editor of *M-U-M*, the official monthly periodical of The Society of American Magicians; and, magician after magician has extolled the merits of the seventy effects and routines that are revealed. While he excelled at card magic, Gordon also incorporates his favorite stage mysteries, demonstrations of mentalism, and routines designed especially for children. Given the initial, effusive praise for this book, it will very likely find its place among the classics of conjuring literature.

In *The Roy Johnson Experience*, a talented British magician introduces some of his favorite, audience-proved mysteries for close-up and stage performance. He has been highly praised by American magicians for his polished manner, clear thinking, and ability to explicate material so that it is readily grasped. Robert Gill has asserted of this monograph, "this publication is a must for all working performers." That Johnson is an active professional is important simply because some magical inventors devise effects but fail to test them under the acid-conditions of presentation before an audience. *Second Time Around*, a companion volume to the above work, features further innovations by Johnson.

Among the items covered are his close-up sponge routine (in this classic of intimate magic, sponges appear and disappear—sometimes in the spectator's hand), a slate routine, and a most practical table to construct. The reader is encouraged to read this and other books by Johnson, for he draws his material from his own highly successful act for laymen and lecture tours before his fellow magicians. Hugh Miller has rendered the magic fraternity a distinct service by writing *The Art of Eddie Joseph*, a lengthy compilation of Joseph's creative contributions to the various branches of magic. Although he is perhaps best remembered for his fertility as a mentalist, Joseph turned his energies to virtually every category of magic—as Miller's laudable anthology clearly demonstrates. Material covered includes standard card and coin magic, a section of close-up effects with household objects such as wooden matches, and a section on cabaret magic. In the latter section, Joseph's version of the sympathetic silk mystery is detailed. In this classic routine, three unknotted silks appear to change places with three knotted silks. Because of Joseph's eclectic interests, the reader will find magic to suit nearly any preference.

The Magic World of Stewart Judah, the final book by its author, delivers a storehouse of practical material by one of the more articulate magician/writers. Cards, ropes, ribbons, children's material, and coins are all thematic in the nearly three dozen effects and routines that are explained. Judah's text is pleasantly punctuated by his theoretical observations and by rare, old photographs. For more polished material, *Al Koran's Professional Presentations* was Hugh Miller's first book devoted to the sterling feats of magic and mentalism by which Koran established himself as one of the most outstanding conjurers of recent times. *Al Koran's Legacy* is Hugh Miller's sequel to his tribute to the creative Al Koran. The latter's powerful brand of magic is best approached by those who have acquired some experience in the field.

Another tribute features two all-time greats in its title. In *Dai Vernon's Tribute to Nate Leipzig*, Lewis Ganson lovingly details the legendary magic of Leipzig as explained by his good friend Dai Vernon. Leipzig's brilliant stage and close-up magic, though demanding, will richly reward the efforts of any magician, whether he gravitates toward card, coin, or silk magic. Since other books by Ganson will be cited in this and future chapters and since the present writer shares Robert Gill's high estimate of Ganson as an author and editor, it is appropriate to quote at some length from *Magic As a Performing Art*, Gill's excellent statement concerning Ganson:

> It is with firm conviction that we regard Lewis Ganson as the finest and most influential magical writer of this century. He was for many years the editor of Harry Stanley's excellent *Gen* magazine . . . a noted performer in the field of manipulation and sleight of hand, he has been closely associated with the world's foremost authorities on magic. He thus brings a lifetime of experience and knowledge to bear on his work; the contents of his books are always of the highest quality, for his painstaking care for detail, together with his use of superb photographic illustrations, mark his writings as models of instruc-

tion. He will undoubtedly go down in the annals of conjuring history for his fruitful association with the premier American performer Dai Vernon; the merger of brilliant inventor-and-performer with scintillating writer and teacher produced classics of literature which stand among the most influential magic books of all time. Nobody who is in any way interested in the finer points of conjuring can afford to overlook Ganson's work (72).

As citations throughout the present study will indicate, only a handful of American magicians have made comparable contributions to the literature of magic. Another commendable feat of editorial service has been performed by Ganson in the form of *Malini & His Magic*. Ganson's text is based upon tape recordings by Dai Vernon. Malini's close-up and stage effects are revered by magicians everywhere, and this book will ensure that he is accorded his rightful place in the history of conjuring. Mastering Malini's material will enable one to excel in both intimate and stage conditions.

In *The Magic of Pavel*, Peter Warlock (pseudonym for Alec Bell) sets forth the distinctive effects of the internationally known Pavel. Residing now in Switzerland, Pavel won many admirers during his lecture tour for magicians in the United States. Warlock carefully explains over three dozen of Pavel's straightforward mysteries with silks, ropes, bottles, and cards. The would-be reader should approach this text with a general knowledge of the field.

While Pavel emphasizes theater magic, the following three writings place a premium upon intimate magic as well. *Magic with Faucett Ross*, by Ganson, presents Ross' unique creations for both the stage and close-up performer. Ross' anecdotes and astute suggestions on presentation complement the effective mysteries that are explained. *The Magic of Tenkai*, compiled by Gerald Kosky (a brilliant magical innovator) and Arnold Furst (a perceptive chronologist of magicians and their programs), offers a double attraction. On the one hand, it contains Tenkai's charming autobiography; on the other hand, it is an explication of the subtle close-up and stage magic that has earned this Japanese performer devotees among magicians themselves wherever Tenkai has appeared. His magic is marked by an exceptional beauty and elegance that will amply repay diligent practice. Over forty-five of Tenkai's distinctive creations are revealed; illustrative material is by Tenkai, Shigeo Futagawa, and Bob Wagner. In *Peter Warlock's Book of Magic*, the author gives his own twist to a fine collection of classic effects from both the stage and close-up categories.

Readers who want a variety of effects in compact form may choose from the following monographs. Ian Adair's *Magical Menu* combines three of the writer's previous publications on the topics of entertaining children, mental magic, and illusions. In another monograph, *Oceans of Notions*, Adair sets forth more of the fresh ideas that are the hallmark of his numerous writings. *Major Magic* is but one of several fine studies by the prolific British magician George Blake. Herein one will find a group of high quality effects that are representative of various branches of magic.

Best Magic Tricks, by Lu Brent (pseudonym for Boleslaw Lubrant), is a three-part work by a talented professional entertainer. These monographs are truly wide-ranging in both their contents and their appeal to magicians. This trilogy was begun in 1969 and completed in 1982. Props employed in Brent's routines include playing cards, cigarettes, pipes, cigars, milk, flowers, and matches. *Novel Magic*, a monograph by Brent, lives up to the promise suggested by its title. *Totally Refreshing Ideas & Carefully Kept Secrets* is another fine monograph by Brent, which preceded his above-mentioned trilogy.

E. G. Ervin's *Club Deceptions* is a work with wider-ranging contents than one might infer from its title. Its innovative author does not restrict his attention to magic that is intended for the stage of a nightclub, but also speaks to the interest of close-up or bar-room magicians. Tony Griffith's *An Invitation to Mystery* explores close-up and stage magic that has been audience-tested before magicians as well as laymen. At sixty-four pages, it is considerably longer than the lecture notes that are sometimes sold by magicians who lecture to their brethren. Here it is appropriate to note that lecture notes, which typically consist of one or two dozen mimeographed pages, are unavailable in all but a handful of specialized libraries (see the Appendix). Sometimes these notes are so succinct as to be nearly unintelligible unless one has witnessed the lecturer's demonstration of the effects being elucidated. Magic supply houses (see the Appendix) can supply one with a list of titles for lecture notes that are for sale. As one might suspect, they are normally modestly priced in relation to monographs and books.

Arthur Setterington's *Straight Line Mysteries* is a praiseworthy miscellany of magic in monograph length that capitalizes upon the author's gift for developing direct effects and routines. Finally, *Designs for Magic*, by Peter Warlock, is an engaging potpourri in monograph form by one of England's most prolific contributors to the literature of magic.

Readers who wish diversity of material in a book-length format may appreciate any of the following writings. In *Reading Is Believing*, Trevor H. Hall, the noted English bibliographer of conjuring literature, divides his attention between card magic and mentalism. This well-regarded book presents routines for both close-up and stage presentation. Hall's interest in mentalism, as well as other forms of magic, is shared by Al Baker, a magician whose writings were enthusiastically received at the close of the first half of our century. His *Magical Ways and Means* is a deservedly acclaimed work by a dean of American magicians. No well-informed magician is unaware of Baker's contributions to all varieties of magic. Both the neophyte and the advanced performer will profit from mastery of Baker's effects and routines. A decade later, Baker authored another classic in the literature of magic, *Pet Secrets*. Like its predecessor, this is a lean volume but packed with creative, diverse magic effects.

In a similarly ingenious vein, *Magicana of Havana*, edited by Marc Tessler, features remarkable manipulative magic with cards, coins, and ropes from the creative mind of Jose De La Torre. Widely praised by outstanding magicians, this book presupposes some familiarity with magic, say, an intermediate level of attainment, but the clear text and abundant illustrations will allow the assiduous beginner to master much of the material. De La Torre is especially adept at devising innovations for standard effects. His version of the "professor's nightmare" (a standard rope routine in which three ropes of different lengths assume the same length and then revert to their original condition) is a masterpiece of pure sleight of hand that is painstakingly explicated with step-by-step illustrations.

The amtitious beginner will also be rewarded by the varied offerings of another demanding work—*Expert Hocus-Pocus*—by the well-known Chicago magician Alton C. Sharpe, for it is a choice collection of sophisticated effects with a variety of objects; many items are intended for close-range presentation, but others are suitable for stage work. The student of manipulative magic will be favorably impressed by the photographic illustrations and the historian will be taken with the author's revealing anecdotes. Will Ayling's *Genie Presentations* runs the gamut from intimate, close-up mysteries to flashy stage effects. The author's philosophy of magic is pragmatic and will appeal to the magician who seeks to be a working professional or semiprofessional. Illustrations and photographs are used to supplement the text. *A Conjuring Melange*, by Stanley Collins, is largely a reprint of his publications in various magic periodicals and books. The contents are, indeed, richly varied, with some effects that will challenge the industry of the neophyte.

Richard Heineman's *Original Magic* is another potpourri of effects and routines that is also punctuated by pointers on the essentials of showmanship. In *Magic in the Modern Manner: A Unique Collection of Magical Gems*, Orville Meyer treats a wide gamut of magic effects and offers effective refinements and modifications. Perhaps the most general of all general studies on magic are those rare works that attempt to cast light on the creation of magic effects. Books such as Dariel Fitzkee's *The Trick Brain* are representative efforts and are discussed in chapter two of the present study. It has been suggested, rather plausibly, that most magic effects are invented by amateurs and semiprofessionals because professional conjurers are largely preoccupied with performing itself.

CARD MAGIC

A cursory glance at the literature of magic makes it manifestly clear that playing cards, more than any other object, have long fascinated and continue to inspire the conjurer. Probably because they are so readily available, portable, and rich in permutations, cards are the most popular prop of the magician and, for that matter, the gambler. Thus, the present section of writings on card technique will be of considerable length in order to be representative of the vast literature that has been given over to card conjuring.

Writings on prepared cards and accessories will serve the novice well, for it is on such principles that the unskilled must first rely. In the booklet *Magic with a Marked Deck*, Sam Dalal illustrates how marked cards (playing cards which contain secret markings on their backs that indicate their face value) can be employed for entertainment purposes. Because the use of marked cards is uncommon among magicians, the reader of this brief study may be able to fool magicians as well as laymen. While marked cards are included in many works on magic or gambling, we know of no other study devoted to marked cards alone.

Nearly as popular as marked cards are "stripper" packs; often the two principles are incorporated in one deck. *Miracle Methods: Casting New Light on the Stripper Deck*, by Jean Hugard and Frederick Braue, is a booklet that investigates the magical possibilities of a shaved deck in which all the cards have been made narrower at one end than at the other. If one or more cards are then reversed, end over end, these cards remain under one's control even when cut to the center of the pack, for their reversed, protruding edges allow one to cut them to the top or bottom of the pack. The authors provide instruction in how to prepare such a deck, tips, and impressive effects. One who acquires facility with a stripper deck can replicate feats that only an expert could accomplish with ordinary cards. But the secret of stripper cards is rather widely known; therefore, they tend to be used by only the neophyte. Card devotees are prone to experiment with stripper cards, tire of them, and then master the more challenging sleights that eliminate the need for gimmicked cards. Thus, the stripper deck often serves as a stepping stone to more advanced card magic. But interestingly enough, the most adept card handler can also use stripper cards, precisely because those who know of his dexterity are prone to think that it precludes the need for such prepared cards. Thus, the cardician who uses the stripper principle sparingly is apt to baffle his equally talented peers. Beginners will readily discover that there is one crucial disadvantage in using stripper decks, since the spectator may challenge the performer to use a borrowed pack. When the rookie is confronted with this kind of challenge, one can only hope that she has read Charles H. Hopkins' *"Outs," Precautions, and Challenges: For Ambitious Card Workers*.

Miracle Methods: Prepared Cards and Accessories, also by Hugard and Braue, is a booklet devoted to gimmicked cards and basic accessories for the card worker who does not limit himself to pure manipulation. Cards with faces or backs on both sides are representative of the specially prepared cards employed in these feats. Used skillfully, these devices can yield strong, clean effects. Props discussed include magician's wax (a substance that causes cards to adhere to each other) and daub (any substance that can serve to mark cards, as in the case of lipstick or rouge). Related material will be found in the booklet *Double Double Magic with Cards*, in which Burling Hull explores the magical possibilities of specially prepared cards that have either faces or backs on both sides.

Appropriately enough, the substance responsible for some of the most impressive card feats is itself invisible. *Roughingly Yours*, by Al Aldini, is a monograph devoted to card magic that is made possible by use of a liquid known as "roughing fluid." This clear liquid, when applied to the surfaces of playing cards and allowed to dry, causes one card to adhere to another. The cards can be separated by a slight pressure, but will again become bonded to each other when they are placed in alignment. This simple principle has been applied in a host of ingenious card effects and "trick" decks. In some cases, roughing fluid is undoubtedly the most economical means for accomplishing a dramatic effect. *Rough Stuff*, by Joe Berg and Aldini, explains how one may make his own "trick" decks by treating cards with roughing fluid. Berg's reputation rests largely upon his flair for devising trick decks, and this monograph stood as the main work on its topic until the publication of *Roughingly Yours* by Aldini. He and Berg may encourage the reader to try out his or her own ideas by experimenting with this substance.

In addition, Trevor H. Hall's *Nothing Is Impossible* is a richly informative monograph that is devoted to startling card magic that is based upon the use of roughing fluid. As has previously been noted, the gems of magic tend to be both simple in their plot and simple in their methodology. A typical spectator has little chance of figuring out such mysteries precisely because he or she usually frames hypotheses that are so complex as to obfuscate the elementary factors that are actually at work. *The Testament of Ralph W. Hull*, also by Trevor Hall, explicates the artistic card technique for which Hull was noted; his variations on standard sleights will engage the adept of sleight of hand; and, those who favor no-skill effects can benefit from Hull's discussion of roughing fluid. *Rough and Smooth Possibilities*, by Hock Chuan Tan, is still another booklet of sophisticated card magic that depends upon the use of roughing fluid.

In *Sixteen Card Index Gems*, Max Andrews explores the potential of a gimmick by which the magician can, for example, extract from his pocket any card called for by a spectator. Used in a subtler manner, as part of a routine, this device can contribute to a startling impact upon the spectator. Moving from an unseen gimmick to a freely displayed prop, Don Tanner's *Fifty Ways to Use a Card Box* concentrates upon the resourcefulness of a gadget common among magicians. The card box is a container with a secret flap, sometimes a locking flap, which allows the magician to produce, vanish, or change a flat object. Tanner's imaginative booklet may very well encourage readers to obtain a card box and move those who already own one to begin experimenting with it.

Beginners who want a nonintimidating introduction will appreciate the following contributions. *Card Tricks Without Skill*, by Paul Clive, introduces the beginner to over one hundred card feats. Although the effects become progressively more complicated, virtually no skill is required due to the author's clever methods. Somewhat more technique is needed to master the material in one of the best-known manuals on card magic. *Blackstone's Modern Card Tricks*, published in the first half of this century, has served as a primer for many leading card specialists of today. Harry Blackstone, while famous for his spectacular stage shows, enjoyed intimate card magic, and his text clearly elucidates both basic sleights and the author's refinements. In one subtle form of card control, a card is secretly transported from the center of the deck to the top under the guise of a showy, cutting-the-deck flourish.

For the novice who wishes to focus upon a short list of effects, Howard P.

Albright's *Advanced Card Magic* is a collection of ten effects that can be done with an unprepared deck of playing cards. Despite a title that would alarm some readers, the book focuses upon mysteries which can be accomplished without difficult moves. Among the feats divulged is "The Persistent Card," in which the magician makes it appear as though all the cards in a borrowed deck are alike.

Theodore Annemann can claim credit for several engaging introductory works. *The Book without a Name* is a modern classic in the annals of magic, for it was in this monograph that Annemann established his reputation for straightforward card magic and mentalism. The author has an extraordinary flair for whittling away all that is extraneous in order to strengthen a given effect. *Card Miracles and Mental Mysteries* again demonstrates Annemann's ability to devise clean, direct effects that rely upon subtleties rather than the performance of difficult sleights. Annemann's *Full Deck of Impromptu Card Tricks* derives its name from the fact that he has gathered fifty-two card effects that can be done at a moment's notice with a borrowed deck. Again, as in other writings by him, psychological ploys often supersede the need for digital dexterity. *Miracles of Card Magic* is another fine compilation of card magic by Annemann. Sixty effects are explained for both the stage performer and the close-up specialist. In *Sh-h-h! It's a Secret*, Annemann offers forty feats that are a combination of card and mentalism effects. It is, like his other works, the sort of book that can be recommended to the beginner, but only with the following admonition: Just because great manual skill is not required is not to say that no skill is needed. The presentational skills of delivering patter, timing, and exploiting psychological ploys must all be practiced and honed to insure successful performance.

Card Tricks for Beginners by Harry Baron, is a photographic introduction to elementary card magic. Unlike some simple feats, those explained herein are both baffling and entertaining. *My Best Card Trick*, also by Baron, is a compilation of favorite card mysteries from Baron and other notable British magicians. It is an apt follow-up to *Card Tricks for Beginners* in that the material increases the neophyte's knowledge, but is not especially demanding.

In *Fifteen Star Card Effects*, Lu Brent sets forth audience-pleasing magic that requires only a minimum degree of skill. Among the plots explored is one in which the spectator unknowingly locates his own previously selected card. In *The Card Expert Entertains*, one of the supreme tutors of conjuring, Dariel Fitzkee, develops and illustrates his philosophy of magic through a careful exposition of nineteen effective card mysteries. This work goes beyond a pedagogical primer on presentation in that the author includes an additional thirty of his favorite effects.

What Fitzkee or Annemann were to an earlier generation, Karl Fulves is to the contemporary beginner. *Notes from Underground* is a monograph by Fulves that will appeal to the novice or to the magician who does not specialize in card magic. The effects that he has selected exploit mathematical principles and other subtleties rather than difficult sleights. Fulves' *Self-Working Card Tricks* is a collection of card feats that demand little or no dexterity because a prearranged deck or some other stratagem has replaced the need for skill. Unlike too many self-working effects, those selected by the author tend to have genuine entertainment value. In fact, even the experienced card specialist may benefit from Fulves' refreshing assortment of mysteries. The sequel, *More Self-Working Card Tricks*, has an opening ESP effect, in which the spectator seems to do all the work, that may disarm a seasoned magician; at the end of the trick, randomly chosen cards match the magician's prediction. In a similar vein, *Magic with Cards*, coauthored by Frank Garcia and George Schindler, caters to the needs of the neophyte. Unlike some rudimentary works that contain tedious material, this book features card magic that is genuinely appealing.

Martin Gardner is another very successful popularizer of card magic. In *Cut the Cards*, he offers a booklet of engaging card effects that can be readily mastered by the beginner. This author is especially adept at substituting clever stratagems for difficult sleights and has written or edited numerous books for magicians and math lovers. He is something of a Renaissance man in that he has also edited annotated editions of *The Rime of the Ancient Mariner* and *Alice's Adventures in Wonderland*. Gardner is perhaps best known as editor of the *Scientific American* magazine. Gardner's *Twelve Tricks with a Borrowed Deck* contains impressive feats that can be done spontaneously, using the spectator's own pack of cards. The minimal skill that is required is amply repaid by the entertainment value of the material. For a veteran's guide to card magic, one can read *Popular Card Tricks*, by Walter Gibson. It is a delightful monograph that is packed with subtleties and basic principles for the beginner. Often a prearranged deck or specially prepared cards are employed rather than sleight of hand.

Beginners and experienced magicians alike may profit from specialized studies. *Twenty-Five Rising Card Tricks*, a booklet by Ulysses F. Grant, offers various methods for accomplishing the classic rising card effect in which one or more selected cards mysteriously rise from the deck. Grant provides a good variety of techniques to suit different tastes and circumstances. In *50 Modern Card Tricks You Can Do!* Glen G. Gravatt, who is an expert on self-working card effects, presents mysteries that do not depend upon set-ups, sleights, or specially prepared cards. Gravatt has drawn from many outstanding magicians to assemble this collection. *Griff on Cards*, by Tony Griffith, is a worthwhile monograph featuring the card capers of one of England's leading cardicians. The beginner will need to learn only one sleight to master this material and that sleight is used only once.

The Encyclopedia of Card Tricks, edited by Jean Hugard, is a well-known work of over four hundred pages in which virtually self-working stunts are explored. Many of the effects in this vast collection have been contributed by outstanding cardicians. Beginners will appreciate the fact that subtleties and natural misdirection replace the need for dexterity. Prearranged cards, mathematical principles, and key cards (known cards which enable one to locate cards that are unknown) are among the dodges employed in order to avoid difficult sleights. Nikola's (pseudonym for Walter J. Obree Smith) card system, one of the standard set-ups for a deck of cards, is also revealed.

Stewart James' *Case for Cards: In Which You Will Find Twelve Self-working Miracles* will appeal to the beginner, since the material presented is truly easy to assimilate. Nonetheless, some of the author's wily ruses will also delight the more experienced card worker. *First Call to Cards*, also by Stewart James, is a booklet of good card magic that is based upon clever principles rather than sleight of hand.

That Edward Marlo (pseudonym for Edward Malkowski) has made a uniquely prodigious contribution to the literature of card magic will be noted when more advanced books are surveyed, but his *Amazing Isn't It?*, an early booklet, may serve as an inviting introduction to his distinctive brand of card magic. While none of Marlo's creations is self-working, doing any of them well should enhance one's self-esteem. *Discoveries*, also by Edward Marlo, offers the beginner suggestions for how to dramatically reveal that one has discerned the name of a spectator's card. This brief booklet helps facilitate one's transition from the status of an amateur, who concludes a "pick a card" feat by simpling naming the spectator's chosen card, to that of the polished performer, who identifies the selected card in some startling, entertaining fashion. Marlo's *Let's See the Deck* is a succinct presentation of fourteen entertaining effects that can be done impromptu and with a borrowed deck. Items like "Age Old Card Control" and an impressive blindfolded poker deal have made this a popular booklet. Only a modest degree of skill is required; therefore, one may wish to read this work in order to become acquainted with Marlo's style. *Pasteboard Presto* is a fine sampler of the card magic originated by Marlo during his early years in the field. This booklet is especially well suited for the relative newcomer to the field of card magic.

Abbott's Anthology of Card Magic, edited by Gordon Miller, is a genuine blessing for the magician who wishes to do card magic without becoming a card expert. This three-volume work has several obvious merits, not the least of which is a concentration upon specially prepared cards, arranged cards, and other subtleties that obviate the need for great dexterity. Some effects rely, for example, upon the "one-way principle," which permits the magician to locate a specific face down card among many others that are also face down. Detection is made possible because even cards with symmetrical back designs tend to be printed with irregularities that make these cards asymmetrical. Thus, if a given card is turned end for end among a group of cards that are all similarly oriented, one can readily identify it by its assymetry. A second virtue of the work is that it contains great variety, for over fifty card authorities have contributed material. Finally, it should be noted that many of the effects were previously sold as separate items; thus, the buyer of these three volumes receives a large number of secrets at a small fraction of what they originally cost when purchased individually.

For vintage material, A. Roterberg's *New Era Card Tricks*, a standard work in the field, was published nearly a century ago. Its age, however, should not prejudice the potential reader, for frequently the card worker of today finds material of value in the so-called dated studies of previous generations. As noted in its introduction, *Scarne on Card Tricks* has been regarded by many magicians as "the standard book on non-sleight-of-hand card tricks." As an authority on gambling and a virtuoso sleight-of-hand artist, John Scarne has enjoyed an enviable reputation among gamblers and magicians alike. In the present work, he has gathered together a large number of card feats that can be performed without mastering basic card moves. His "Traveling Aces" effect epitomizes how misdirection can sometimes supplant the need for physical dexterity. Scarne's book is valuable in itself for the nonspecialist and as a stepping stone for the would-be cardician.

"I Wouldn't Like to Play Cards with You!" by Harry Stanley, is a self-working routine in booklet form, which gives the spectator the impression that the performer is an accomplished card handler. A prearrangement of the cards substitutes for the considerable degree of skill that seems to be at work. Since spectators sometimes attribute more skill than is deserved to the performer, one might as well exploit this tendency. The card buff and collector of card feats W. F. Rufus Steele's *52 Amazing Card Tricks* is an excellent anthology of self-working card effects that were devised by such renowned figures as Carmen Di Mico, Paul Rosini, and Audley Walsh. Given the fact that no manual skill is called for, these effects have a surprising impact on the spectator. In *The Last Word on Cards*, Steele again shows his flair for selecting effective card items that require little or no skill.

James G. Thompson's *The Living End: Over 200 Different Impromptu Take-a-Card Endings* is a compendium that belongs in every card worker's library. Once the spectator selects a card and the magician knows its name or position in the deck, he or she must disclose or reveal the chosen card in some striking manner. Unless the card has been chosen and returned to the pack under very demanding conditions, simply naming the card will not be a sufficiently remarkable conclusion. In fact, to do so will usually relegate the performer to the level of a rank amateur. The author's myriad suggestions will insure that the cardician is never at a loss for entertaining climaxes to pick-a-card feats. In *Magic to Delight*, Thompson presents a fine assortment of close-up mysteries in which card effects prevail. Other props used include coins, balls, rings, and ropes. Thompson's magic has been praised because of its impact, but also because it relies upon subtleties instead of demanding sleights. Both photographs and illustrations will facilitate one's progress in mastering the material. In fine, this work can serve as an attractive introduction to the field of intimate magic. Bill Turner's *The Card Wizard: An Easy Course of Tricks*, which was written at mid-century, remains an informative, elementary survey of the rudiments of card magic.

One recent dictionary defines sleight of hand as "skill in card tricks." While patently too narrow a view, this definition does underline the preeminence that sleight-of-hand artists place upon cards. Readers who share such an interest will find essential material in the following books. *The Expert at the Card Table*, by S. W. Erdnase (pseudonym for E. S. Andrews), written at the turn of the century, is a milestone publication in the literature of expert card technique. It continues to be reprinted and is an established bible for card cheats and card magicians. The text is divided into three sections, the first of which concentrates upon card-table artifice. Bottom dealing (secretly dealing from the bottom of the deck while appearing to deal from the top) is just one of the gambling procedures that is painstakingly explained. A second portion of the book concentrates upon magical practices such as forcing a card (causing a spectator to choose a predetermined card while leaving the impression that his selection was random and free), indetectably transforming one card into another, and glimpsing (secretly peeking at the face of a card). The third and final part of the book is an exposition of classic card effects like the four ace assembly in which the four aces are placed in four different packets of cards, but somehow manage to reassemble in the same packet.

In the eight decades since Erdnase flourished, magicians have devised easier alternatives for a number of his sleights, but some of his techniques are still of great value and have hardly been superseded. Thus, his treatise remains essential reading for all who aspire to become expert practitioners of card manipulation. Erdnase's preface is perhaps the most candid and amusing that has ever been written for any book of its kind:

In offering this book to the public the writer uses no sophistry as an excuse for its existence. The hypocritical cant of reformed (?) gamblers, or whining, mealymouthed pretensions of piety are not foisted as a justification for imparting the knowledge it contains. To all lovers of card games it should prove interesting, and as a basis of card entertainment it is practically inexhaustible. It may caution the wary who are innocent of guile, and it may inspire the crafty by enlightenment on artifice. It may demonstrate to the tyro that he cannot beat a man at his own game, and it may enable the skilled in deception to take a post-graduate course in the highest and most artistic branches of his vocation. But it will not make the innocent vicious, or transform the pastime player into a professional; or make the fool wise, or curtail the annual crop of suckers; but whatever the result may be, if it sells it will accomplish the primary motive of the author, as he needs the money (ii).

Card Magic is another classic compendium of selected basic sleights together with some effects in which they are incorporated. The author of this well-regarded monograph is the famous British sleight-of-hand artist Victor Farelli. *Hofzinser's Card Magic* is a translation by Ottokar Fischer of Hofzinser's pioneering treatise *Kartenkunststucke*, which was published in 1910. Hofzinser's treatise exercised a profound influence upon subsequent writings in the literature of card magic, for he perceptively identified sleights and routines that continue to animate the card magic of today.

More contemporary works abound, for recent decades have seen an unprecedented boom in the publishing and dissemination of magic literature. Andrew Galloway's *Diverting Card Magic*, which has already been noted for its contributions to conjuring psychology, features straightforward, appealing card magic that runs the gamut from simple to advanced effects. By authoring the three-part work *Cy Enfield's Entertaining Card Magic*, Lewis Ganson has introduced lovers of card magic to a first-rate exponent of the art. Beginners will benefit from Ganson's lucid exposition of basic card sleights as executed by Enfield; and, advanced card men will profit from Enfield's distinctive refinements and renderings of such classics as "cards to pocket," in which playing cards vanish one at a time from one's hands and appear in one's pocket. Among the sleights described is the biddle move in which a card that has been counted off into one's hand is secretly returned to the deck in the act of counting off another card. Other sleights explained include the slip cut, in which an apparent cut changes the position of only one card, and the double lift, in which two cards are treated as though they were one. Instruction in showy flourishes such as card-throwing round out this excellent survey of card technique and effects.

Walter Brown Gibson's *The Complete Illustrated Book of Card Magic*, a beautifully photographed survey of virtually every phase of card conjuring, has already won the status of a standard work. Despite its considerable length (nearly 500 pages), the work is modestly priced, since it was printed by a commercial press rather than a specialized publisher of magic texts. Of course, the latter fact does have one possible disadvantage. Robert Gill has expressed regret that such professional card magic has been made available to the general public. One can only hope that the merely curious will not have sufficient initiative to absorb the wealth of secrets that are disclosed. John Northern Hilliard is responsible for another more established overview. His *Card Magic* is a reprint of the card material that first appeared in his encyclopedic *Greater Magic*. A wide variety of card magic is surveyed, and the contents are of the highest order.

Since the sleight-of-hand artist's risk of making a mistake is somewhat like the juggler's risk of dropping an object, one manual is highly germane. *"Outs," Precautions, and Challenges: For Ambitious Card Workers*, by Charles H. Hopkins, has already been discussed in chapter 2 of this present study. Magicians in general and card specialists in particular will benefit from the author's advice on how to save face when a mistake or spectator's challenge interrupts one's performance. A careful reading of this classic monograph will enhance one's self-confidence by preparing one to deal with the unexpected contingencies that can mar a presentation.

Jean Hugard's writings on magic in general and card magic in particular have been consistently exemplary. *Card Manipulations Series 1–5*, by Hugard, is a compact primer of basic sleights and variations for the would-be cardician. Contents include palming, flourishes (showy displays of card finesse that remind us of the magician's link with the juggler), and peeking (secretly glimpsing the face of a card). Like its sequel, this book has earned the status of a classic in the field. *More Card Manipulations, Series 1–4*, is Hugard's sequel. Like its predecessor, this study is essential reading for the card specialist. Dozens of good effects and refinements for standard sleights are succinctly set forth. Among the latter are palms, changes, and glides (when executing the glide, the performer appears to remove the bottom card of the deck, but actually takes the second card from the bottom instead; in effect, it is second dealing from the bottom rather than the top of the deck).

Hugard and Frederick Braue collaborated on *The Invisible Pass*, which is certainly one of their most fundamental additions to the literature of card magic. This monograph focuses upon an excellent version of the sleight that is known as the pass and which was once considered indispensable to the card worker. By this maneuver, one attempts to cut the deck indetectably. Thus, for example, a card that was at the center of the pack can be brought secretly to the top in preparation for second dealing, palming, or some other sleight. Because it is nearly impossible to perform a flawless pass, a number of stratagems have been devised as alternatives. Nevertheless, the card worker who is a purist will surely want to learn one version or another of this foundational sleight. Hugard and Braue concentrate upon an underhanded approach in which the lower half of the deck is moved upward rather than the conventional pass in which the upper portion is moved downward and below the original lower half. Their version, although hardly angle-proof, is a significant step toward the criterion of invisibility. In general, the regular pass relies upon speed to deceive, but a blur of motion is apt to arouse the suspicion of the astute perceiver. Larger body movements are sometimes employed to mask the flicker of motion, but these larger movements can themselves arouse suspicion. Underhanded passes, like the one elucidated by Hugard and Braue, depend less upon speed than upon covering the crucial movement by obstructing it with the back of the hand that is holding the upper half of the deck. In fine, the type of pass which they explain is probably the best that has ever been developed.

In *Miracle Methods: Miracle Shuffles and Tricks*, Hugard and Braue present a brief treatment of various false shuffles and a number of effects that rely upon these special shuffles. *Miracle Methods: Tricks and Sleights* is still another in the series of booklets by Hugard and Braue. Here the authors turn to mysteries that can be performed with ordinary cards because sleight of hand is employed. Among the sleights discussed is the top change, a move that demands perfect timing and a measure of courage, since it involves indetectably exchanging a card held in one hand for the top card of the deck, which is being held in the other hand, and doing so under the very noses of the spectators. It is indeed regrettable that so few magicians elect to employ this powerful weapon in the arsenal of the well-rounded cardician. Since this move can hardly be rendered invisible, the exchange of cards must occur at a moment when the spectator's attention has been misdirected. Although a classic in itself, *The Royal Road to Card Magic*, by Hugard and Braue, is an ideal preface to their classic post-graduate level text, *Expert Card Technique*. Quite wide-ranging in scope, the authors' primer introduces the reader to shuffles, flourishes, sleights, routines, and even stage effects such as the popular "Three Cards Across" feat in which three cards invisibly travel from one place to another. Serious students will glean satisfaction from acquiring the requisite skill, but will not be overwhelmed by an excess of extremely difficult material.

But Not to Play: A Practical Course of Instruction in the Fundamentals of Conjuring with Cards, by Wilfred Jonson, is a standard introduction to card manipulation by one of England's most articulate writers. Students who are learning basic sleights from other manuals may profit by consulting Jonson's presentation of these moves. *Card Conjuring* furnishes the reader with Wilfred Jonson's later thoughts on the elements of card magic. Line drawings facilitate the beginner's introduction to the field. One may wish to compare Jonson's writing with Al Leech's booklet, *Handbook of Card Sleights*, a manual of basic card moves that is as good as it is short. He describes each sleight in a step-by-step fashion and thereby coaxes the beginner toward successful execution. For the reader who wants all meat and no fat, this is the most compact work of its kind. It and the more expansive one that follows contain only sleights, no effects. *Basic Card Technique: A Textbook for the Student of Card Magic*, by Anthony Norman (pseudonym for Norman Binns), furnishes the novice with an admirable survey of fundamental card sleights. In addition to teaching essential card moves like the pass and the glide, Norman instructs the reader in the flourish of fanning the cards and offers patter suggestions.

Handle with Care, by Robin Robertson, features the author's distinctive refinements for a number of standard card sleights. Card workers will enjoy experimenting with Robertson's variations, but the conscientious beginner can also profit from this monograph. Hailed as a deserving successor to Erdnase's *The Expert at the Card Table*, Lynn Searles' *The Card Expert* manages to compress a great deal of important material into four dozen pages. Among the items are comments on the psychology of the card expert, false shuffles, false cuts, false deals, miscellaneous moves, and selected effects. Searles' one-hand shuffle is illustrative of the sort of feat that is not often found in print. His multiple card force and poker deal demonstration round out this valuable monograph. The democratically entitled *Card Tricks for Everyone*, by Ellis Stanyon, is really only suited to those who are willing to master the fundamentals of sleight of hand with cards. Given such a commitment, the reader will find Stanyon's primer to be an attractive introduction to the field. Finally, *Sleight Intended: Expressway to Playing-Card Expertise* is a monograph-length primer in which James G. Thompson sets forth selected basic card sleights. The novice will profit most if he compares Thompson's favorite handling for each sleight with the treatment it receives in one or more standard manuals on card technique.

Since card manipulation is so frequently associated with cheating, students of magic naturally seek out texts that treat gambling subterfuges. Russell T. Barnhart's *Two Second Deals* is a clear explication of two ways by which to execute the second deal, a standard gambler's stratagem that magicians have adapted to their own purposes. It consists of dealing the second card while appearing to deal off the top card. The card cheat who knows the top card of the deck (because the cards are marked or he has secretly peeked) can retain it on top and deal it whenever he pleases by employing the second deal. A magician who uses this deal can cause, say, the ace of spades to appear at any number down in the deck that a spectator chooses. Proper execution of the sleight entails that one's second deal perfectly simulate his normal mode of dealing. Even a visually perfect second deal can sometimes be detected by the auditorily acute spectator, for there is often a tell-tale swishing sound. Unlike thc magician who masters numerous sleights in order to increase his versatility as an entertainer, the successful card cheat may need little else in his arsenal other than a polished second deal.

Rather than cultivate the great skill that is required for a perfect second deal, one may turn to gimmicked apparatus. In *Marked Cards and Loaded Dice*, Frank Garcia, one of America's finest sleight-of-hand artists, divulges the principles behind two of the most common props of the professional cheat. Obviously the reader has the option of applying these secrets to the creation of magic effects or of utilizing them to bilk the uninitiated. Because magicians rarely use marked cards, those magicians who incorporate marked cards in their routines are likely to disarm and fool their fellow cardicians. Concerning marked cards, two points are noteworthy. First, it is possible to mark cards while a game is being played; small nicks or gouges can, for example, be made with one's thumb nail. Second, one method for detecting marked cards consists in riffling through the pack and looking for any marks that would then appear to be jumping around on the back designs of the cards. Of course, the best policy is not to play cards with anyone whose motives are suspect.

Card Mastery: With Which Is Combined the Expert at the Card Table, by Michael MacDougall, combines a monograph by the author with the full text of Erdnase's classic treatise, *The Expert at the Card Table*. MacDougall's contribution is two-fold, for he presents card magic together with his own refinements of procedures as described by Erdnase. Given that the techniques explicated by Erdnase are some of the most deceptive but most demanding ever devised, commentaries like MacDougall's are especially welcome. Card sleights must be "customized" or adapted to the individual; and, the reader may find that MacDougall's adaptations fit him or her better than Erdnase's original maneuvers.

B. W. McCarron's *The Gambling Magician* provides the reader with routines that demonstrate how to cheat at cards. Since laymen are both intrigued and entertained by exhibitions of card-cheating techniques, this is highly commercial material. Section two of this text explains such card sharp stratagems as the crimp (bent corner of a card that allows one to cut to the card), short card (a card that has been shaved a bit shorter than the others and which may be located by riffling the cards and cutting to it), deck switches (methods of secretly exchanging one deck of cards for another, often because the latter is specially arranged), and the mirror ring (as the name implies, this is a ring to which a small mirror has been attached in order to read the faces of face down cards).

Containing material from the inner circle of practitioners, *The Phantom of the Card Table: The Real Secrets of . . . Walter Scott*, by Eddie McGuire, is a detailed description of selected moves as employed by the master card mechanic Walter I. Scott. The cheating techniques revealed, such as the second deal, are among those most cherished by the card sharp. Prepublication copies of this professional manuscript are said to have been sold for fifteen times the price of the published version. Card workers who emphasize gambling subterfuges will not want to neglect this short, specialized study. Other sorts of cardicians will also profit from this work, since gambling stratagems are readily transferable to magic routines. Card magicians, as has been noted, frequently wish to force the spectator's choice of a playing card; this can readily be accomplished by placing the force card on top of the face down deck and asking the spectator to say ''stop'' at any point as cards are ostensibly dealt off the top of the deck. Using a second deal will insure that the force card remains on top of the pack and is, therefore, apparently the very card at which the spectator requested the magician to stop dealing.

Gerard Majax' *The Secrets of the Card Sharps* is a lavishly photographed exposé of card cheating techniques and gimmicks. Among the items covered are marked cards, mirrors (used for secretly peeking at cards), false cuts, and false shuffles. This fascinating study also includes a discussion of the cheat and the law, psychoanalysis of the card sharp, and the card sharps of the year 2000. Magicians who specialize in giving lectures to the public on the techniques for cheating at cards offer the laymen what other types of magicians never do, an exposé of the actual secrets of card manipulation. Because some of the secret principles of card cheats are also employed in the presentation of card magic, strong justification is required for breaking the magician's first commandment: Thou shall not reveal the secrets of magic. Of course, those who do so in their lectures usually defend themselves on ethical grounds; in short, they assert that the duty to protect an unwary public supersedes one's obligations to protect professional secrets. Since such lecturers are sometimes handsomely paid for their services, it is not always obvious that secrets are revealed for moral rather than economic reasons.

Magicians who are interested in the false deals of the card sharp will find Edward Marlo's *Revolutionary Card Technique; Chapters Eight, Nine, and Ten: Seconds, Centers, & Bottoms* to be an invaluable treatise. Dealing from the center or the bottom of the deck, while apparently dealing off the top, is extremely difficult; a majority of magicians have written about the second deal instead. Thus, the author has helped fill a noticeable gap in the literature on false deals. Less specialized than Marlo's manual, Floyd Moss' *Card Cheats—How They Operate*, is a compact, first-rate exposition of some of the card sharp's favorite stratagems. Since works of this kind are far less common than books devoted to card magic, the would-be card expert should not overlook Moss' monograph.

Audley V. Walsh's *John Scarne Explains Why ''You Can't Win!''* is a photographically illustrated exposé of the three card monte con game in which the sucker is asked to bet on the position of one card after it has been moved about with two others. It is a rare large American city in which three card monte operators cannot be found throwing their cards on some busy street. Lewis Ganson's *The Three Card Monte as Entertainment* is a richly photographed compendium of many of the sleights, ruses, and subterfuges by which the card cheat continues to make a healthy profit at the sucker's expense. As the title suggests, the routines may be presented as a demonstration for entertainment purposes only.

The following works contain intermediate-to-advanced material, which, not surprisingly, emphasizes variations and refinements for basic sleights and themes. *The Esoterist* features the novel but demanding card routines of Alan Ackerman. The reader's mastery of this sophisticated material is facilitated by the inclusion of both photographs and line drawings. In a similar vein, *Novel Concepts with Cards*, by Al Aldini, draws together refined presentations from the author's repertoire and that of other celebrated cardicians. *Andrus Deals You In: Advanced Card Magic*, by Jerry Andrus, is a remarkably original contribution to the field by a cardician whose work was created, as it were, in a vacuum. Put differently, Andrus had an unusual apprenticeship in that he did not depend upon classic texts on card handling. Instead, he devised sleights, effects, and flourishes on his own. When this work was first published, the considerable difficulty of the material caused some magicians to assert that no one could execute the requisite moves. Live demonstrations by the author at magic conventions soon dispelled any such assertion and won Andrus the esteem of his peers. Some of his sleights require that the spectator perceive from a certain angle or perspective and others require that the magician be seated at a table. Andrus' card magic is marked by his integration of flourishes and effects. In other words, showy displays or juggling feats are not presented as mere exhibitions of skill, but actually integrated into his routines.

Canadian Card Control, by the leading Canadian cardician Tom Batchelor, is described by its author as "an investigation into card controls, locations, discoveries, and revelations." Full appreciation of this material requires that the reader be familiar with basic card sleights. To control a card is to be in physical command of it when it has apparently been lost somewhere in the deck. Batchelor's fan control, for example, will give the reader an alternative to conventional techniques. His monograph strikes a good balance between sleights and effects or routines in which they may be incorporated. Leo Behnke's *Entertaining with Cards* presents twenty effects by a close-up performer who enjoys the reputation of being one of the best card handlers on the West Coast of the United States. Not surprisingly, he has frequently performed at the Magic Castle in Hollywood, where the audience consists of fellow magicians and ardent lovers of magic. Arthur Buckley's *Card Control* is a masterful, photographically illustrated, compendium of sophisticated sleights, effects, and routines intended for those who excel at elementary sleight of hand with cards. Much of the material presented here has itself been absorbed into the category of standard moves in the cardician's arsenal. Proficiency in the myriad sleights explained would stamp one as an expert card man, for the sweep of this volume is encyclopedic. Gambling sleights of the professional card sharp are also explored in illuminating detail. Original editions of this classic treatise are rare and highly prized; it surely can be regarded as one of the ten preeminent books in the field.

Farelli's *"Lend Me Your Pack"* is a monograph devoted to card magic that is impromptu and can be done with any deck of cards. This collection of sleights and routines makes a good follow-up to the author's *Card Magic*. Although both studies were written in the first half of this century, the contemporary reader can benefit from Farelli's distinctive approach and presentation. In *Thanks to Leipzig: The Cleanest Method of Passing Three Freely Selected Cards from One Pack to Another . . . and a Convincing Mental Effect*, Farelli offers a monograph that concentrates upon a standard transposition routine in which three cards disappear from one packet of cards and reappear in another. The title acknowledges Nate Leipzig, who excelled in his presentation of this popular mystery. Its versatility is evidenced by the fact that it can be equally effective at close range and on the largest of stages.

In *The Tahoe File: Card Magic by Terry Lagerould*, Bruce Florek has disclosed the fresh card routines of an active professional who entertains at Caesar's Palace in Lake Tahoe. This monograph is marked by an unusually clear step-by-step mode of instruction that also incorporates suggested patter. Not only are the items novel, but the accent is on amusement as well as amazement. In one routine with a mouse-catching theme, a playing card that represents a piece of cheese mysteriously becomes riddled with real holes. Such comedy is the stamp of the contemporary magician, who can rarely elicit awe in an era of moon shots and lasers. *Comedy a la Card*, by Karrell Fox, offers the commercial card magic of a professional entertainer who is internationally known for his highly visual, humorous brand of prestidigitation. In the twenty-three effects that are covered, novel and amusing ways to disclose the spectator's selected card prevail.

Karl Fulves' *The Book of Numbers* is a monograph-length compilation of card magic for the intermediate-level cardician. This prolific author brings a scientific precision to his elucidation of all levels of card magic. Fulves' *Methods with Cards* is an enormous, three-volume treatise on card sleights and routines that will delight the experienced cardician. *Riffle Shuffle Set-Ups*, also by Fulves, is a specialized study of some largely self-working effects that depend upon prearranging the deck and the use of one or more riffle shuffles. With a prearranged deck, a fair riffle shuffle will redistribute cards according to a predictable order; it is this little-known principle that is at work in these effective card mysteries. Fulves' *Riffle Shuffle Technique* is a two-part introduction to the multiple applications of the riffle shuffle for card magic. *Transpo Trix*, again by Fulves, provides engrossing material for the advanced card performer. Concentration is upon transposition effects in which two cards or two packets of cards change places.

Dai Vernon's Further Inner Secrets of Card Magic, by Lewis Ganson, is the third of four classic works on card conjuring as practiced by the inimitable Vernon. In all of these writings, Ganson sets forth the expert card techniques of a genuine master without whom contemporary card magic would be significantly impoverished. Vernon's impeccable card work has become a yardstick by which progress in the field of card manipulation is measured. The monograph under consideration offers material for a wide range of tastes. Among the items that are explained, through a lucid text and beautiful photography, is a card that travels to the magician's pocket effect and a three card monte routine. Of course the card is never where it appears to be, since imperceptible sleights are at work. In fact an accomplished "thrower" of monte can deceive the eye of a fellow charlatan. Here one is reminded of Mark Twain's insightful admonition to the effect that one should not bet against the proposition that a gambler can make the jack of hearts jump out of the deck and squirt cider, for the doubter will surely end up with a face full of cider and an empty wallet. The cliché that one should not try to beat a man at his own game is surely sage advice for one who is tempted to play three card monte. If, however, one insists upon playing, he can generally improve his chances by ignoring the card that seems to be correct and betting on one of the remaining two. Other sections of this study detail palming (secretly removing cards from the deck and concealing them in the palm of the hand) and second-dealing (dealing the second card from the top of the deck while appearing to deal the top card).

Dai Vernon's Inner Secrets of Card Magic is the first work in the quartet by Ganson. A painstaking exposition of the classic color change effect is included. This consummate feat of sleight of hand involves causing the face card of a deck to change after passing one's hand in front of it. *Dai Vernon's More Inner Secrets of Card Magic* is the sequel to the above highly acclaimed monograph. Unlike some sequels, which are pale postscripts, this work contains sleights and routines of the highest calibre. *Dai Vernon's Ultimate Card Secrets* is a fitting climax to Ganson's four-part graduate course in the fine points of card control. While the other three works in this series are monographs, this final contribution is a book-length exposition in which Vernon shares the secrets of some of his notable fellow cardicians as well as his own insights.

Million Dollar Card Secrets, by Frank Garcia, is a collection of strong card effects for the performer who is already comfortable with basic card sleights. Among the fifty mysteries revealed by the author is the "Chicago Opener" in which the spectator's freely selected card is suddenly discovered to have a different back design from the other fifty-one cards. Nearly one hundred illustrations facilitate learning the commercial card magic that has helped establish Garcia's enviable reputation as an entertainer. *Super Subtle Card Miracles* is Garcia's precursor to the above work. Although perhaps no book could live up to such superlatives (magicians have always felt comfortable with hyperbole), this treatise is definitely worthy of the card worker's attention. In addition to the effective routines that are detailed, there is considerable concentration upon variations and refinements for standard sleights such as the peek and double lift.

With the former, the magician is able to secretly glimpse a card; with the latter, the magician treats two cards as one. Given the frequency with which the card magician resorts to the double lift, alternative handlings are always welcome. Just as most magicians avoid repeating an effect because they fear that the secret might be detected, some magicians eschew using exactly the same sleight more than once during a single performance. Thus the cautious magician will master several versions of the same sleight in order to insure that his methodology is beyond detection.

Cliff Green's *Professional Card Magic* consists of top-flight material that is intended for the adept cardician. Great dexterity is required to present many of the routines such as the interlocked-hands card production. This much-neglected sleight enables the performer to interlace the fingers of both hands, turn his empty palms to the spectators, and then proceed to produce one playing card after another. Green incorporates excellent contributions from his peers, as is exemplified in a stunning four-ace effect by Henry Christ. Equally choice material is found in *The Card Magic of Edward G. Brown*, an English text that was written by Trevor Hall after Brown's death. The contents include six lectures on card magic that Brown delivered at the Magic Circle Society in London and seventeen of Brown's favorite card effects. Some skill is needed in order to properly execute much of the material, but the reader is rewarded by Brown's originality. Whether one adopts his themes and handlings will be a highly individual matter.

Close-Up Entertainer, by Paul Harris, details the distinctive card magic of one of the most prolific inventors and writers on the American magic scene today. Some coin magic is also thematic in this study, but the emphasis is upon card sleights, refinements, and effects. His card force, for instance, will appeal to some magicians because of its straightforward nature. "The Immaculate Connection," one of Harris' marketed magic routines that can be purchased through a magic dealer, has been justifiably heralded as just short of miraculous. In this routine, the magician tears holes in the centers of three playing cards in order to create three "frames." The illusion consists in causing the frames to link and unlink without damaging any of the cards. At the conclusion, the cards may be passed for inspection and no extra cards or gimmicks are employed. Magicians as well as laymen have been deceived by the ingenious principle that underlies this remarkable mystery. Fans of this work will want to acquaint themselves with the author's earlier writings. *Close-Up Fantasies: Book I* is the first in a series by Paul Harris, one of the most off-beat, unique entertainers in Las Vegas. Effects such as his "Tuning Fork" will warm the heart of the jaded cardician. His *Close-Up Fantasies: Book II* offers more novel magic as exemplified by his floating deck of cards effect, which requires no extra gimmick. *Close-Up Fantasies: Finale* completes Harris' trilogy and again the accent is on unusual card effects. Among the mysteries treated is how to tear and restore an entire deck of cards. Those who share Harris' sense of humor and his flair for the melodramatic are apt to become addicts of his material.

In *Paul Harris Reveals Some of His Most Intimate Secrets*, the author delivers what some have called his best book. One effect in which a card mysteriously and visually reverses itself is representative of the twist he gives to standard themes. Beside his own important writings, Jean Hugard has coauthored a number of significant works with Frederick Braue. *Expert Card Technique*, upon which they collaborated, is a landmark contribution to the field of sophisticated card control. No cardician who seeks to polish and perfect his art can afford to overlook this rich storehouse of first-rate information. Hugard and Braue have culled sleights, effects, and routines from a who's who of outstanding card practitioners. While assiduous effort is required to master much of the material, the author's precise, academic explanations do make such mastery possible. With its superb illustrations and lucid text, this treatise stands as a masterpiece in the literature of sleight of hand with playing cards.

For a more compact anthology, the reader may see *Showstoppers with Cards* by Hugard and Braue. This booklet which contains advanced sleights and effects for the true devotee. Charles T. Jordan's *Thirty Card Mysteries* features the creative card work of one of America's most innovative cardicians. This monograph includes a number of effects that require mastery of the faro shuffle in which one cuts the deck exactly in half and then weaves the two portions together perfectly so that the cards from each alternate with those from the other. Such material is best approached by the seasoned cardician. Additional material on the faro shuffle is thematic in *Another Card Session with Peter Kane*, a booklet for the intermediate or advanced card worker. Kane's distinctive sleight-of-hand routines have impressed card men in America as well as card specialists in his native London. *A Card Session with Peter Kane* introduced its author's exemplary card control to readers of English everywhere. The contents of this monograph consist of eleven feats for the real sleight-of-hand buff. *Off the Beaten Path*, by Wilbur Kattner (pseudonym for Howard Holden), is a worthwhile booklet devoted to some of the author's favorite card routines for various performing conditions.

Card Magic, edited by Richard Kaufman, is a compilation of material from contemporary cardicians that reflects the state of the art in the late part of the 1970s. Already recognized as a classic text, the book contains over five dozen contributions and includes over 700 excellent illustrations by the author-editor. Novelties like the "vanishing deck" are apt to arouse even the blasé cardician. *Cardworks*, also by Richard Kaufman, contains excellent card routines contributed by the author and other top-notch card workers in America. The novel effects and principles presented will challenge and, perhaps, inspire card specialists. As one might suspect, this work presupposes a thorough understanding of basic card magic. Kaufman sets high standards as writer, editor, inventor, and superb illustrator of this stimulating anthology. He includes intriguing correspondence with other card experts; in these letters, we see the posing of card problems and the exciting struggle for successful resolutions. *The Complete Works of Derek Dingle*, written and illustrated by Kaufman, sets forth the stunning, original magic of the man whom *Time* magazine described as "the greatest card manipulator extant." Sophisticated sleight of hand with cards prevails, but there are also some sterling coin and cigarette effects. Dingle's refined brand of sleight of hand and his ingenious, bewildering routines have elevated him to the top category of close-up performers throughout the world. His material is typically far beyond the reach of the average neophyte.

Good but less demanding material will be found in the following five books. *Off-Color Card Tricks*, by Milton Kort, is an engaging monograph that has nothing to do with the salacious; instead, its title refers to the fact that all the feats described are linked by a single theme, the colors of the cards. Kort's varied effects have a refreshing quality and are illustrated by Nelson Hahne, one of the most prominent illustrators of magic texts. *Card Man Stuff*, by Al Leech, again shows the author's knack for varied, crisp card magic. Magicians are usually as pleased by his economical methods as they are by his effects. *Cardmanship* exemplifies Leech's flair for clean, direct card work with genuine entertainment value. His prose is just as sparse as his magic, for he packs over a dozen items into just two dozen pages. Leech's "No Crimp, Ace Cut" will appeal to magicians who like to demonstrate gambling skills. A crimp is a bent corner of a playing card that enables one to cut to the card. Leech's *For Card Men Only* received great reviews in magic periodicals, perhaps partly because he avoids the well-worn "take-a-card" plot. Contents include surprising card reversals, transpositions, and card controls. His *Super Card Man Stuff* offers twenty-five fresh mysteries for the magician who is conversant with basic card sleights. Over two dozen large photographs assist one in learning the material.

Paul LePaul's *The Card Magic of LePaul* is a beautifully photographed masterpiece that sets forth one powerful effect after another. It is unquestionably one of the finest books on sleight of hand with cards that has ever been published. In addition to instructing the reader in routines of the highest calibre, LePaul discloses his own favorite handling for standard sleights such as the side steal (this involves indetectably removing a card from the center of the deck and palming it, all in a single smooth operation). In one representatively strong effect, the four aces, which have previously been lost in the deck, literally jump out of the deck as the performer shakes it. In *LePaul Presents the Card Magic of Bro. John Hamman, S.M.*, also by LePaul, a dozen outstanding card mysteries by another ingenious card worker are presented. Hamman's routines, all with ordinary cards, are punctuated by original touches that please laymen and often startle magicians themselves. The false count that is explicated in this monograph has already become a standard sleight among card specialists.

Afterthoughts features new card sleights, effects, and routines by Harry Lorayne, a New York cardician with a long list of books to his credit as author or editor. Those who enjoy novel magic may want to master a torn and restored stick of gum mystery that is detailed herein. Effects like the "Instant Three Card Location," which was contributed by Richard Kaufman, will add flash and a professional touch to a card worker's presentation. Lorayne's detailed elaboration of each item strikes some as highly commendable and nearly the equivalent of personal instruction, but others are put off by Lorayne's style and judge it to be verbose; in any case, the card specialist cannot afford to ignore Lorayne's writings. *Best of Friends*, also by Lorayne, is a treasury of card magic which gains its title from the fact that the first two-thirds of the contents is contributed by some of the most outstanding contemporary card workers. The balance of the book contains original material by the author himself. With over one hundred items beautifully illustrated by Joseph Wierzbicki, this anthology caters to a wide range of tastes. While some of the cffects can be learned by the beginner, most of the material consists of refinements and variations for the adept, well-read card worker. Those who learn effects like Phil Goldstein's "Ascension" will be able to fool many of their fellow cardicians.

The Card Classics of Ken Krenzel, again by Lorayne, is another compilation of valuable material that is designed for the somewhat accomplished card handler. Appreciated by hundreds of magicians themselves, the card work of Krenzel is superbly illustrated by Richard Kaufman. Effects like the "Magic Bullet" are representative of simple, forceful magic at its best. But the reader gleans more than effects or routines, for Lorayne describes Krenzel's handling for the double lift, false deals, and other fundamental sleights such as the pass. For Lorayne's early writing on card magic, one should consult *Close-Up Card Magic*, an outstanding reference work on card magic for everyone from the novice to the expert. Contributors to this collection of subtleties and effects include such illustrious performers as Dai Vernon, Frank Garcia, Alex Elmsley, and Herb Zarrow. In advertising literature for this text, one encounters a common claim to the effect that just one of the mysteries revealed (in this case a routine called "Out of this Universe") is worth the price of the entire volume. It is a pleasure to report that such a claim is, indeed, fully justified by the exceptionally high quality of the magic that Lorayne discloses. Yet another book by Lorayne is *Deck-Sterity*, a fine sequel to the above-mentioned book in which the author reveals strong effects such as his "Flying Aces" and idiosyncratic sleights like his "kick" double lift.

My Favorite Card Tricks is a highly praised monograph in which Lorayne sets forth varied ideas ranging from innovative transposition methods (techniques for causing cards to change places) to an impromptu version of "Out of this World," which is surely one of the most impressive feats in mentalism. *Personal Secrets*, by Lorayne, is a monograph-length addendum to the author's well-received classic, *Close-Up Card Magic*. Readers of the latter are treated to material that Lorayne chose to leave unpublished until now. *Quantum Leaps*, by Lorayne, is a rich collection of sixty effects, routines, and tips, all devoted to card conjuring. Among the unique sleights treated is the author's "Illogical Double Lift," which some will adopt as a utility move. Lorayne's substitute for the conventional faro shuffle will appeal to those who have not been able to master this precise mode of shuffling, which is required in numerous card feats. This volume also includes an early version of the linking cards routine that can be done impromptu. Although superior routines have since been developed, Lorayne's is marked by special ease of handling.

Reputation Makers, one of Lorayne's longest books, runs the gamut from routines with a gambling or card sharp theme to refinements of basic sleights and startling effects like Paul Curry's color-changing deck. Some of this material was previously closely guarded and is finally being released. Finally, *Rim Shots*, also by Harry Lorayne, is a book of sleights, effects, and flourishes that is intended for the knowledgeable card man.

The Cardician, by Edward Marlo, is a generous sampler of card magic in the Marlo manner. It is best approached by one who is familiar with basic card magic, for in addition to dozens of effects, Marlo introduces many new or refined sleights. Those familiar with the move known as buckling (using a finger to bend the bottom card of a small packet of cards so that all those above may be removed as though they were a single card) will be inspired by Marlo's eleven effects that rely upon this principle. There is something here for every sort of card specialist—including those who emphasize mental feats. Theoretically inclined magicians will be delighted with Marlo's chapter on the evolution of card effects, in which he scrupulously accords credit to all those who stimulated his own innovations. In *Future Reverse*, Marlo presents his technique for secretly reversing a card, that is, indetectably turning it face up or face down in the deck.

In *The Magic Seven*, a booklet by Marlo, the author details a complex, bewildering routine in which the number seven is thematic. His exposition of the five cumulative phases is itself a veritable mini-course in some of the fine points of card handling, but absolute beginners will be at a disadvantage in grasping the material. *Marlo in Spades*, one of Marlo's monographs that helped establish his preeminence in the field of card conjuring, is clearly designed for the genuine card specialist who seeks a fresh array of subtleties and sleights. Contents run the gamut from a new false cut to a masterful routine like "Aces, Kings, Ten," in which two very baffling card transpositions occur. Marlo's *Marlo Meets His Match* presents simple, straightforward effects based on the theme of sympathetic magic. As is true of good magic in general, the plot is simple: The magician and the spectator each select a card from their respective decks, yet the cards match. Typical of his thoroughgoing approach, Marlo sets forth over a dozen methods and suggestions. *Marlo's Objectives* represents the author's variegated contributions to a classic card problem, how to indetectably separate the twenty-six red cards from the twenty-six black cards in a standard deck. Students of card magic will be duly impressed by Marlo's resourceful investigation of possibilities and ramifications—all in less than two dozen pages. *Off the Top* is a booklet of choice Marlo material with ten sleights and fifteen effects and routines. Some items require extraordinary skill, as in the case of his "One Hand Double Turnover," which entails turning two cards face up and face down on the top of the deck as though they were one, using only the hand that holds the pack.

Other moves, such as his "One Hand Palm," are less demanding, but still beyond the range of a typical beginner. Routines like "Card to Pocket Surprise" exhibit Marlo's flair for devising unexpected climaxes for standard presentations.

Addressed to an earlier generation, Jack Merlin's ". . . *And a Pack of Cards*," edited by Jean Hugard, has passed through two editions and has acquired the status of a standard work in the field. The reader should bring a firm grounding in card magic to his or her study of Merlin's favorite sleights, variations, and routines. Excellent illustrations expedite one's mastery of this truly professional material. For a more recent perspective, the student may turn to Jerry Mentzer, one of the most prolific writers on the contemporary magic scene, who has delivered a major work on card magic in *Card Cavalcade*. In this exciting anthology, Mentzer supplements his own contributions with those of over two dozen other card experts. Contents cover new sleights, effects, routines, and fancy juggling feats. Most of the material is devoted to items with an ordinary deck, but one chapter treats magic with specially prepared cards. All in all, there is something to suit virtually every cardician's temperament. *Card Cavalcade 2* is an even larger treasury of contemporary card magic than its predecessor. Mentzer's concentration is upon sleight of hand as exemplified by a host of famous contributors. In addition to outstanding card effects and routines, one will find an explanation of new card sleights like the Ascanio spread; this is a useful move that enables the performer to display four cards in a fan while concealing the presence of a fifth. *Card Cavalcade 3* continues Mentzer's sweeping survey of recent additions to the field of card manipulation. Contents include strong, quick, spectator-pleasing effects as well as more esoteric material for the true specialist. A number of utility false counts are explained, including what is perhaps the most deceptive of all modern false counts, the Elmsley count. This smooth maneuver allows one to count four cards as four cards, but the spectator actually sees only three cards during the count. *Card Cavalcade 4* and *Card Cavalcade—Finale* add still more material in the same vein as their predecessors.

Magician Nitely: The Magic of Eddie Fechter, also by Jerry Mentzer, features audience-tested, close-up magic with the accent on cards. Fetcher's "card on ceiling" mystery is a genuine reputation-maker in which the spectator's chosen card is discovered by throwing the deck at the ceiling. Upon impact, 51 cards flutter to the floor, leaving the spectator's card adhering to the ceiling and staring him in the face. One of the chapters is given over to magic utilizing the sleight known as the peek, one which can be used to control, force, or glimpse a card. For a more recent study on the thoughts of a single cardician, one may consult Miesel's *The Creative Card Magic of William P. Miesel*. The author gives special attention to the double lift and the buckle sleights and is especially concerned to show how the latter may be rendered invisible. His interesting version of "Oil and Water," in which red and black cards refuse to remain mixed, and other innovations have not previously been in print. Some magic texts lack this distinction, for they are a compilation of items that were previously published in a variety of sources.

Ever So Sleightly: The Professional Card Technique of Martin A. Nash, which is the first book of a trilogy by Stephen Minch, gives considerable attention to the double lift and various ways of replacing the two cards as though they were one. A challenging one-handed double lift is also revealed. Other contents include Nash's version of basic sleights like the multiple shift and twenty strong routines that have endeared Nash to magicians and laymen alike. *Any Second Now: Part Two of the Professional Card Technique of Martin A. Nash* is the second installment by Minch. Among the contents is an extensive discussion of double-lift handlings, including an instant version in which the deck is resting on the table. Cardicians are also introduced to novel moves like the Hathaway change. Card changes in which the magician appears to change one card into another are among the most remarkable feats in the eyes of the spectator. Such transformations can be appreciated by audiences of all ages and background; moreover, the changing of one card into another immediately establishes the fact that the performer has a professional touch, for the average layman, who knows "a few card tricks," rarely masters such moves. Instead, he or she is prone to present painfully boring tricks that depend on mathematical principles. Minch's study features a good variety of card routines as well as a valuable analysis of key sleights. *Sleight Unseen: The Professional Card Technique of Martin A. Nash* completes Minch's stimulating trilogy on the card control of the illustrious Mr. Nash. This talented cardician, who has lectured before police officers and university audiences, is also a recognized authority on cheating techniques. Among the contents are Nash's professional gambling routines, the kind of highly commercial material that has enabled him to earn a full-time living in a field where skillful amateurs and semiprofessionals abound. Minch has compiled a goldmine of information for the card specialist in the nineteen sleights and twenty-five routines that are explained. As one might expect, the sleights covered include false deals. Under the category of second deals, one finds the scissors deal, a one-handed spinning deal, and others; under the heading of center deals, three methods are given for a one-handed version. Nash's thoughts on false counting, the multiple shift, and other card controls are also detailed. Only the adept card handler need apply for Minch's mini-course in the card work of Nash.

Two representative anthologies cater to the intermediate-level performer. Ned Rutledge and J. G. Thompson, Jr., have collected some attractive card mysteries in the monograph *Card Party: A Sparkling Assortment of Card Chicanery;* those with an intermediate level of skill will be best able to appropriate and appreciate the contents. *Expert Card Conjuring*, by the well-known Chicago magician Alton Sharpe, is an excellent anthology, drawing as it does from such stellar cardicians as Edward Marlo. Those versed in basic card technique will be amply rewarded by a study of the inner secrets that the writer has disclosed.

Bill Simon's *Controlled Miracles*, illustrated by the master magician Frank Garcia, is an engaging booklet of close-up magic in which card effects and routines prevail. Among the items that receive the deft Simon twist is the classic card in cigarette effect in which the spectator's chosen card is discovered to be inside a cigarette. Simon also discusses a cut control, a stab force, and an interesting card change. With the publication of *Effective Card Magic*, its author, Bill Simon, took his place among top-quality card workers who have flourished during the second half of this century. Edited by the knowing eye of Jean Hugard and illustrated by the late Dr. Jaks, this volume is a rich storehouse of subtle and original card magic. Had this clever New York cardician never written again, he would have already earned a position in the annals of card conjuring. In *Sleightly Sensational*, Simon delivers more of his clever originations for the close-up performer. Although predominately devoted to card magic, the author includes routines with sponges, a coin, and a ring on a wand. The latter is a classic in which a ring penetrates a wand and both articles can be passed for inspection. In one of Simon's most impressive card mysteries, a spectator cuts the deck into four piles and then discovers that there is an ace on the top of each.

Another prolific contributor to card magic was J. Stewart Smith. From 1954 to 1974, he published fifteen booklets on card magic; his eclectic taste insured considerable variety in his material. All of these writings have now been bound in a single book, *The Collected Works of J. Stewart Smith*. Not only is this one-volume edition of straightforward card magic a convenience, but it is also the occasion for incorporating additional material by Smith, for it contains a reprint of *The Top of the Deck*, which was previously distributed only to the author's closest friends, and an unpublished manuscript, "A Direct Approach to Real Card Magic." For equally professional material, one may turn to the routines of Rosini. In *Paul Rosini's Magical Gems*, W. F. Rufus Steele pays tribute to the sterling sleight of hand practiced by Rosini. With an emphasis upon card magic, Rosini imparts his touch to timeless effects and routines.

Steranko on Cards, by John Steranko, presents exciting originations that immediately captured the attention of the author's fellow cardicians. Some may find this material too idiosyncratic for their own use, but all will surely concede that Steranko's conceptions are thought-provoking. Contents include various controls, a lateral palm, a reversal (a method for secretly reversing a card, that is, turning it from face down to face up), and the author's own gambling demonstration. The text is well illustrated by the author himself who is a widely known American illustrator.

Going from the contemporary to the classic, Choon Tee Tan's *Variations on 2 Card Classics* is devoted to two time-tested mysteries, the "six card repeat" and "cards to pocket." In the former, which can be thought of as a magical "running gag," the performer repeatedly discards three cards from a packet of six, but the remaining cards always total six in number. In the latter, several cards travel inexplicably and individually from the performer's hands to his pocket. Since fresh suggestions for the classics are always received with pleasure, Tan's booklet is welcome reading indeed. Similarly, *Kardyro's Kard Konjuring*, by Senor Torino (pseudonym for Tony Kardyro), details the author's streamlined techniques for false deals, forces, peeks, controls, and other sleights. A total of eighteen sleights and one dozen professional effects are explained. This photographically illustrated monograph is best appreciated by those with a general understanding of card magic. *The Complete Walton*, by Roy Walton, is a one-volume collection of the striking card plots and routines that have garnered the author great acclaim in America as well as in his native England. Among the modern classics disclosed is "Card Warp," in which a card that has been folded lengthwise and face outward mysteriously turns back outward while encased by another card, which is folded widthwise. Walton's highly original turn of mind is evident in both the fresh themes that he conceives and the baffling methods that he devises. Only those with a solid grounding in card technique should undertake learning this material.

Warren Wiersbe's *Action with Cards* is a well-titled booklet, for it consists of fast-moving feats with genuine audience appeal. Card workers will be especially intrigued by Wiersbe's "New Ace Control" and an instant four ace transposition. Philip Willmarth's *Jim Ryan Close-Up: (3) Classic Card Routines* is one of four booklets devoted to the outstanding "bar magic" of one of Chicago's legendary figures. A bar magician specializes in performing intimate magic for the patrons of bars and restaurants. Ryan's highly commercial routines have been honed through hundreds of performances, and they serve as a mini-course in the fine points of how to simultaneously entertain and deceive an audience. In addition to his exciting card routines, Ryan's preferred method for palming cards from the top of the deck is explained. When properly executed, it is an impeccable way to steal cards from the pack. *Jim Ryan Close-Up: (2) Entertaining Card Quickies* is Willmarth's second booklet in the above-mentioned series. Here the concentration is upon short, bold, startling feats. Card buffs can enrich their education by studying how Ryan condenses a relatively lengthy routine into a far shorter, more direct presentation.

The books remaining to be discussed are illustrative of the innovative shuffles and sleights that animate contemporary card magic. *Faro & Riffle Technique*, by Karl Fulves, is a sophisticated exploration of the card magic that can be accomplished through the faro and riffle shuffles. Although proper execution of these shuffles requires a considerable degree of practice, one's efforts can be justified on the grounds that the shuffles render possible some of the most startling effects in all of card magic. In a faro shuffle, the deck is cut exactly in half, then the twenty-six cards of each portion are butted together and interlaced so that the cards from each alternate perfectly. Although the shuffle is scrupulously fair, it has myriad applications for card magic. For example, if a deck of cards has been arranged in a particular sequence, eight faro shuffles will restore the deck to its original order. The far more commonplace riffle shuffle, in which cards are interlaced by riffling their corners together, is also analyzed by Fulves in some detail. He reveals, for instance, how it may be employed as a means of card control. Mastery of these two shuffles is a hallmark of the expert cardician.

Edward Marlo provides perhaps the clearest available instruction on the execution of the faro shuffle in chapter 6, "Faro Shuffle," of his brief booklet,

Revolutionary Card Technique. This shuffle has recently become popular among card magicians. Herein, the author presents various handlings, including how to perform the shuffle with the cards resting on the surface of a table. Once one has mastered the rather difficult faro shuffle, he or she can be rewarded with some thirty effects and tips in chapter 7, "Faro Notes," of *Revolutionary Card Technique*.

Paul Swinford's *Faro Fantasy* is another collection of routines that may stimulate the reader to master the faro shuffle. Swinford explores possibilities with a borrowed, shuffled deck and with prearranged cards; he also explains procedures by which the magician may more readily follow what is occurring during one or more faro shuffles. Those card workers who have not satiated their appetite for magic based on faro shuffles will find still more material in Swinford's thoughtful sequel to the above book, *More Faro Fantasy*. Marlo's *Riffle Shuffle Systems* is one of the works that are only available by permission of the author. In this lengthy, two-volume study, advanced card workers are presented with an exhaustive exploration of the principles and applications of the riffle shuffle. Again, Marlo has broken new ground, for although the riffle shuffle is the prevalent way to mix cards, its rich potential for conjuring purposes had not previously been thoroughly investigated. Fulves adds further to the literature on special shuffles in *Gene Finnell's Card Magic*. Mathematics plays a role in the Klondike shuffle and some of the other effects devised by Finnell. Only the card specialist is apt to undertake learning most of this material.

Advanced Fingertip Control, by Edward Marlo, is a sophisticated elucidation of card control when the pack is being held at the fingertips so as to seemingly preclude the manipulative possibilities afforded by the conventional mechanic's grip. With the latter grip, the fingers wrap around the deck and may, for instance, be used to hold breaks or separations between sections of the deck. Not only does Marlo richly explore his announced topic of fingertip control, but he explains related effects. One classic feat of card magic involves having the spectator's selected card rise mysteriously from the shuffled deck; myriad methods have been devised; to these, Marlo adds his own fingertip handling. This manuscript, like some others by Marlo, cannot be purchased over the counter in a magic shop; instead, one must secure the author's permission to buy it. Those interested in such highly protected material can contact Magic Inc., of Chicago, Illinois, for further details. Marlo's achievements in card magic, like Picasso's in painting, are nothing short of awe-inspiring. He is a magician's magician in the best sense of the phrase, for only those versed in the most advanced expressions of card handling are in a position to recognize his inestimable contribution to the field. Marlo's fecundity as a writer on card magic is unprecedented; no one has written more often and more knowingly on the topic. A recent writer reported that Marlo's publications now stand at over 1,500. For nearly half a century, his superb writings have enriched the domain of expert card technique.

Like the historian who can trace major currents in twentieth-century art through Picasso's various stages, the informed cardician can follow the very evolution of contemporary card magic through Marlo's still-continuing stream of books, monographs, and articles. Indeed, it is as inconceivable to think of twentieth-century card technique without Marlo as it is to imagine the art of our century minus Picasso. It is certainly fitting that Marlo himself coined the term "cardician," for no one has better demonstrated the inexhaustible potential of a homely deck of cards. His brilliant creativity is matched by his penchant for meticulous exposition. Aesthetically speaking, he has set new criteria of excellence by which to judge one's finesse with playing cards. Any magician who has witnessed Marlo's sublimely flawless execution of the most exacting and refined card sleights realizes why he has been apotheosized in his own lifetime.

Card Control, by Marlo, is another of the books that can only be obtained by permission of the author. Its contents break new ground in the control of one or more playing cards during the course of shuffles and cuts. *Peek and Shuffle Controls* is another of Marlo's books that can only be secured with his approval. It offers a probing analysis of the peek technique by which a spectator can select a card and multiple methods for controlling the chosen card while the pack is subjected to shuffles.

Revolutionary Card Technique: Chapter Three: Finger Tip Control is a fastidious manual on card control in which Marlo depends upon such stratagems as jogging (bringing about the concealed protrusion of part of a card from some part of the deck), stepping (keeping one portion of the pack separate from another by not allowing them to come into perfect, squared alignment) and holding and transferring breaks (a break is a gap between cards that is maintained by inserting the fleshy pad of one's finger tip). Only the serious card handler has the prerequisites for mastery of this refined material. In *Revolutionary Card Technique: Chapter Eleven: The Multiple Shift*, Marlo scrutinizes the popular card sleight that is usually credited to Dai Vernon. This maneuver involves controlling several cards that are protruding from various parts of the deck and then apparently lost during the course of one or more cuts. As usual, the author has manifold versions and variations; in fact, some of Marlo's handlings are calculated to fool magicians who are familiar with only the standard procedure.

Jerry Mentzer's photographically illustrated *Multiple Push-Through Control* is a sophisticated work that the reader may wish to compare with Edward Marlo's lengthier study, *Revolutionary Card Technique: Chapter Eleven: The Multiple Shift*. Both works enable the cardician to do that which strikes the layman as almost impossible: control two or more cards at the same time during the course of cutting or mixing the pack. In *Sleightly Miraculous: A Treatise on the Panoramic Shift,* Jerry Andrus concentrates upon a sleight by which several cards can be controlled while seemingly being lost in the deck. Only diligent practice will enable one to perfect this deceptive maneuver. *Steals and Palms*, also by Andrus, details techniques for secretly removing cards from the pack and then concealing them in the palm of one's hand. The indetectable execution of these sleights marks one as an accomplished cardician of the highest order.

Revolutionary Card Technique: Chapter Two: The Action Palm distills Marlo's reflections on how to palm cards from the deck while it is in motion. Because it is a well-known principle of magic that a larger motion can help camouflage a smaller motion, Marlo focuses upon how to execute the lesser motion of palming a card while performing the larger one of shuffling the deck. His bottom palm, which is executed during the final phase of a riffle shuffle, may be one of the most deceptive palms extant. *Revolutionary Card Technique: Chapter Four: The Side Steal* gives Marlo's fresh perspective on the performance of a standard sleight by which one can indetectably abstract and palm a card from the center of the deck. Three dozen methods and suggestions are explored—surely enough to satisfy and probably surpass any cardician's needs. *Revolutionary Card Technique: Chapter Five: The Tabled Palm* is Marlo's highly specialized study on the art of palming off cards from the deck while the pack is resting upon a table.

In the booklet *Sleeving from the Deck (At the Table)*, Jerry Andrus explores ways to secretly remove cards from the deck and insert them in one's sleeve while seated at a table. Most magic effects do not depend upon sleeving; hence, magicians as well as laymen are apt to be deceived by those who acquire this skill. In *Mexican Monte & Other Tricks*, Karl Fulves explains a useful false count by which four cards can be made to appear as only three. This count is especially deceptive because of the casual way in which the cards are handled. The balance of the monograph details varied effects that are based on the count. Fulves' *Packet Switches*, which is intended for accomplished cardicians, details various techniques for switching one packet of cards for another. Fulves carefully explains how to secretly add or subtract cards from such small groups. Those interested in more material may obtain further installments from a magic dealer.

Revolutionary Card Technique: Chapter One: Miracle Card Changes is the first in a series of eleven monographs by which Marlo greatly updated the cardician's basic skills. This particular installment is devoted to novel ways for causing one card to be invisibly changed to another. Sometimes the move being explained requires special conditions like the use of a table or careful attention to the spectator's angle of perception. In *Revolutionary Card Technique: Chapter Twelve: Card Switches*, Marlo concentrates upon a somewhat untapped subject, the art of indetectably exchanging one card or packet of cards for another. These switches are to be distinguished from the card changes that were thematic in the first volume of the series, for with card changes the effect is usually the straightforward transformation of one card into another. Card switches, by contrast, can be employed, for example, in a prediction effect. Marlo's final entry in this distinguished series is *Revolutionary Card Technique: Chapters Thirteen and Fourteen: Estimation*. This is a trail-blazing investigation of estimation processes by which, for instance, one can calculate the number of cards cut from the deck or cut to a card that is in the middle of the deck. Natural as well as mechanical estimation is surveyed. Because the methodology of estimation is so little-understood, the effects it renders possible are extremely perplexing to the uninitiated.

Counts, Cuts, Moves and Subtlety, by Jerry Mentzer, is a much-needed primer which photographically illustrates some of the most popular sleights that have been devised in recent decades. Many of the moves taught herein are required for the ''packet trick'' form of card magic that is currently popular among magicians. In such effects, the performer dispenses with most of the deck and uses only, from, say, three to twelve cards. Even though this monograph is written for novices, advanced card workers will find it to be a refreshing review of material that is usually scattered throughout other books. Experienced cardicians, who have not kept up with recently developed card sleights, will find this to be a welcome distillation of some of the more versatile maneuvers that now prevail in card routines. It would surely profit the general reader to master the contents of Al Leech's *Handbook of Card Sleights* prior to undertaking the material which is so ably explained by Mentzer.

CLOSE-UP MAGIC

For reasons of convenience and economy, the vast majority of magic performances are of the close-up variety. The following works focus upon close-up magic that is not restricted to the use of cards. Although card effects often appear in these writings, a wide variety of other props are also represented. Harry Baron's *Close-Up Magic for Beginners*, illustrated with line drawings and photographs, is a modest but above-average introductory work that can be highly recommended for its intended audience. Novices may also want to acquaint themselves with some of the writings of Samuel Berland. For a lively monograph, with the accent on varied close-up magic, one may consult his *Berland 1970*. The author has distinguished himself by inventing numerous magic effects that are sold by magic dealers. *Berland's Portfolio of More Exclusive Tricks* offers more close-up mysteries by one of Chicago's most creative magical minds. *Berland's Tricks and Routines, Mark III* is a third monograph by the prolific Berland in which he explains close-up feats that call for basic skills rather than extreme dexterity.

Newcomers to close-up magic will not want to neglect the standard work *Magic with Small Apparatus* by Jules Dhotel. This is a somewhat demanding but commensurately rewarding text. Karl Fulves speaks to the novice in *Self-Working Table Magic: 97 Foolproof Tricks with Everyday Objects*, an excellent primer on close-up chicanery with such household objects as eggs, dice, rubberbands, balloons, coins, match sticks, silks, and safety-pins. Even the veteran magician will be refreshed by Fulves' refinements and additions to standard effects and stunts. Any experienced magician knows that there is great impact whenever the climax of an effect seems to take place in the spectator's hands. Fulves furnishes one such effect in his chapter on safety-pins. The title is not to be taken literally, for a modicum of skill is sometimes required. As has been noted in our discussion of texts on card magic, Fulves has contributed prolifically to contemporary literature for cardicians.

An even more prolific author, Walter Gibson, has written *The Complete Il-*

lustrated Book of Close-Up Magic, a beautifully photographed, superb introduction to sleight of hand with coins, billiard balls, cards, and other small objects. Other fine books by Gibson abound, and his *What's New in Magic*, written thirty years ago, has become a standard reference work for close-up magicians.

Close-Up A-Ginn, by David Ginn, is a booklet of good, varied material for the devotee of small magic. Part one contains coin and bill magic, part two explains seven changes and transpositions with small objects, and the third section furnishes sixteen novel ways to disclose a spectator's chosen card. Ginn, who specializes in entertaining children, places the accent upon comedy as well as mystification. In a related vein, *"Winners All"*, by David Howarth, is a booklet of close-up mysteries with cards, coins, and other small items. The author's feats are marked by their directness and relative ease of execution.

Three works from the thirties can be recommended for their enduring value. *Close-Up Magic for the Night Club Magician*, by Jean Hugard, collects effective close-up feats as explained by one of the truly great contributors to the literature of magic. Coins, cards, cigarettes, sponges, and handkerchiefs are thematic in this classic monograph. L. L. Ireland's *Ireland Writes a Book* is a refreshingly eclectic work that contains a brisk treatment of the cups and balls. A number of the other professional mysteries explained are close-up effects or they can be adapted for close-up performance. Sleights with silks, coins, cigarettes, thimbles, and cards prevail. The author's "Card and Mousetrap," in which the selected card is discovered by catching it with a mousetrap, exemplifies his fresh approach to conjuring. This thirty-five page booklet, with one hundred and fifty illustrations, breathes new life into the cliché that good things come in small packages. *Impromptu*, by E. Brian MacCarthy, gathers together quick, spontaneous feats with small objects and makes a suitable short introduction to the field of close-up entertainment.

Another half-dozen texts, which dramatize the prosaic, can be recommended for the amateur. Clettis Musson's *Minute Magic* focuses upon effects and stunts with such pedestrian props as popcorn, bread, sugar, olives, string, money, salt, pepper, and goldfish. This monograph of three dozen items will be especially attractive to beginners. Charles J. Pecor's *The Craft of Magic: Easy-to-Learn Illusions for Spectacular Performances* provides good instruction on basic sleights with cards, coins, ropes, and other ordinary objects. In *Thanks to Pepys*, Bob Read sets forth his amusing brand of close-up magic with a wide array of household objects. The fine material in this monograph has been well received by magic critics as well as laymen. *Bill Severn's Impromptu Magic* is the talented Severn's latest publication. Emphasis is placed upon "spontaneous" magic, effects that can be done with little or no preparation and with ordinary objects. Richard Kaufman, who has recently become recognized as one of the finest illustrators of magic texts, provides the excellent pictures for this collection of effective mysteries. Even the seasoned magician will be impressed by the author's fresh effects and direct methods. Some of Severn's fellow magicians are bound to be disturbed because he has divulged such choice material in the form of a widely available trade book. His "Gaze into My Crystal Ball," for instance, is surely a professional quality feat of divination. *Magic across the Table*, by the prolific Severn, is an inviting introduction to magic feats that are intended to be performed under close-up conditions. Step-by-step instructions on presentation and patter make this an ideal primer. Severn's *Magic from Your Pocket* enables the performer to carry the materials for an entire act in his pockets. Items used are either household objects or can be purchased at modest prices.

Since the basic elements of magic are rather stable, more writings are devoted to the intermediate and advanced performers than to beginners. *Close Up Time with Don Alan*, by Don Alan, features the author's distinctively polished and commercial brand of intimate magic. His achievements include hosting his own weekly magic show on a Chicago television station, performing at a great many smart supper clubs, and graduating from the celebrated Chavez School of Magic, which is the Juilliard of conjuring academies. Alan served his apprenticeship by entertaining at the world-renowned Schulien's magic bar in Chicago. His booklet treats magic with a sponge, pencil, orange, and the most ubiquitous prop of magicians, playing cards. One card item, Alan's riffle force, has been widely adopted by contemporary cardicians.

In *Pretty Sneaky*, Don Alan divulges more of the professional prestidigitation that has given rise to his enviable reputation. The props used in these effects and routines include cards, balls, a ball point pen, flash string (a chemically treated string that disappears in a flash of fire when ignited), and a lump of coal. All of this material has passed the acid test by winning Alan lucrative bookings. A general knowledge of magic is again presupposed in this monograph. Bert Allerton's *The Close-Up Magician* contains the varied routines of one of Chicago's most successful cafe entertainers. In his prime, Allerton performed for such celebrities as Helen Hayes, Kate Smith, Loretta Young, Pat O'Brien, and Ray Milland. Contents include his comical broken and restored scissors mystery, jumping flower effect, and a knife-swallowing illusion. Card workers are rewarded with an explanation of the author's speciality—cutting the deck to any card called for. Finally, Allerton's rules for the close-up magician deserve the scrutiny of every newcomer to the field. Moving from the Midwest to the West, *Entertaining Close-Up*, by Leo Behnke, consists of sixteen fine effects by a leading West Coast magician. Since this booklet has fewer pages than effects, some background in magic is required to fully assimilate the material.

Bennett's Best, by the Virginian Horace Bennett, contains the exemplary routines of an award-winning magician who has inspired such talented close-up specialists as Woody Landers. In one representative routine, Bennett's gentle, deliberate actions leave the spectator completely unprepared for each successive climax as a pearl appears, disappears, changes colors, multiplies, and becomes enlarged. Coins, cards, and other small objects serve as props for his beautiful and bewildering magic. Serious students will detect that there is a book within a book in this and other writings by Bennett, for each of his publications contains implicit, unannounced lessons on misdirection that are of inestimable value. At times Bennett's moves require that one be seated at a table in order that objects can be concealed in one's lap. In *Bennett's Fourth Book*, the author places the accent on his own adaptations of classic card and coin themes. As fans of his would expect, he adds a unique climax to Al Schneider's ''Matrix,'' in which three coins travel mysteriously to join a fourth. Bennett's card to pocket routine incorporates his own brand of situation comedy in another standard plot. Jaded magicians will surely be refreshed by the ingenuity with which the author draws upon the inventions of others and makes them his own. A basic familiarity with coin and card sleights is assumed throughout the text. For a more recent collection of close-up capers by Horace Bennett, one can read his *Alternative Handlings*. Once again familiar material is improved and enlivened by his deft touch.

The Best of Benzais, by John Benzais, features the reputation-making magic of another fine close-up worker. Thirty routines with cards, coins, and other items are explained, including the author's version of ''Coins through the Table,'' a classic plot in which the magician causes several coins to apparently penetrate the top of an ordinary table. Thanks to Benzais' ingenuity, only modest skill is required to master this gimmick-free material.

Sleight of hand with cards, coins, and cigarettes, plus a lesson on the art of sleeving, figure importantly in Ross Bertram's *Magic and Methods of Ross Bertram*. The author also contributes his fine versions of such gems as the egg bag, the blindfold act (in which a blindfolded performer reads, fires at a target, or even drives a car in order to demonstrate his ''psychic'' vision), the thumb tie (in which the performer's thumbs are tied together and he is still able to pass his hands through solid objects like the leg of a chair), and the cups and balls. At the climax of his cups and balls routine, Bertram produces live chicks from the cups.

J. B. Bobo's *Watch This One!: A Collection of Choice Magical Effects with Small Objects* delivers exactly what is promised in its subtitle, close-up magic of the highest order. The author, who is one of the most respected sleight-of-hand artists of our century, turns his attention to intimate magic with cards, coins, and other household items. *Phoenix* is a six-volume storehouse of excellent magic in which close-up, impromptu, professional material prevails. Literally thousands of items are offered in this reprint of material from Bruce Elliott's prestigious periodical of the same name. E. G. Ervin's *Club Deceptions* is a monograph in which four of the author's previous booklets on pocket magic have been reprinted. Fifty clever items are included for the performer who wants to carry an entire close-up act in his pockets. Coins, bills, cards, matches, watches, paper, and needles all figure in the intimate mysteries detailed by Ervin. Douglas Francis' *Right under Your Nose* is a booklet in the same vein as Ervin's, for again choice, direct close-up feats are thematic.

The name ''Slydini'' has long been a hallmark for excellence in intimate magic and stage subtleties. Karl Fulves' *The Magical World of Slydini* is a recent and monumental contribution to the literature of close-up conjuring. All parties involved deserve the highest commendation. First, Slydini himself has held nothing back from his breathtakingly pure routines. Second, Fulves devoted six months to the task of clearly elucidating the magical stylings of a man whose unique approach to sleight of hand has inspired countless magicians. Third, over twelve hundred photographs by Arthur Manfredi will endear him to every magician who has ever struggled to grasp material that has been inadequately illustrated. Finally, the publisher, Louis Tannen Inc. of New York, is to be congratulated for its lavish, two-volume production of this opus. One volume consists of text and the other of photographs. Coin specialists will be transfixed by Slydini's versions of "Coins through the Table." His impeccable feats with silks are also divulged, including "Splitting the Knots," in which two silks are tied together and instantly pulled apart only to reveal that each still possesses a knot at its end. Visually it appears as if the knot has undergone a process of fission.

While the close-up worker is the chief beneficiary of Slydini's artistry, a number of his items are equally suitable for stage presentation. Others, in fact, are intended to be done on stage, as in the case of his stunning version of the "Sympathetic Silk" mystery, in which he seemingly transports the knots from three tied silks to three loose ones. Card specialists will be challenged by Slydini's "Invisible Pass," his ace routine, and other subtleties. Three ingenious effects with a destruction-restoration theme feature, respectively, a rope, a newspaper, and a cigarette. Only those with an artistic commitment to magic can hope to master the superb contents of this study. Lewis Ganson's *The Magic of Slydini* was the first substantial compilation of the moves, effects, and routines by which Tony Slydini has achieved international prominence as a master sleight-of-hand artist. Sponges, coins, and other small objects prevail in the flawless table magic of this one-of-a-kind performer. Even the seasoned magician will be challenged by the sophisticated magic in Leon Nathanson's *Slydini Encores*. Stratagems like the "revolve vanish" prove that Slydini's hallowed reputation is fully warranted.

For a European counterpart to New York's Slydini, one can turn to John Ramsay. *The Ramsay Legend*, by Andrew Galloway, is the author's first tribute to the illustrious magic of the late John Ramsay. Contents include his coin specialties (transpositions, vanishes, and penetrations), sleights, a complete routine for the production of ten thimbles, a cut and restored rope effect, Ramsay's deft touch with selected classics of card conjuring, and a brief biography. In *The Ramsay Classics*, Andrew Galloway presents a superlative sequel to the *Ramsay Legend*. Both books feature the extraordinary sleight of hand of the world-renowned John Ramsay, whose work had previously been published in the form of small booklets. Galloway, a fellow Scotsman and close friend of Ramsay, has gathered together some of Ramsay's finest presentations in this one-volume format. His cups and balls routine, coin magic, and thimble manipulations (which Galloway has lovingly rewritten for this edition) are all truly timeless in their appeal. Ramsay's ideas on misdirection and on the utility item that is known as the thumb tip enhance the value of this fine text. Finally, the reader is rewarded with numerous photographs and anecdotes that had not been previously published.

Three of Lewis Ganson's writings illustrate his enrichment of the literature on close-up conjuring. Ganson's *The Art of Close-Up Magic* is a two-volume treasury of outstanding material that includes hundreds of illustrations in its over six hundred pages. Among the eminent contributors to this anthology are Slydini, Dai Vernon, and Horace Bennett. Those with an aversion to card magic will be pleased to learn that no card effects are included in this huge collection of intimate feats with such small objects as cigarettes, silks, yarn, pens, paper clips, matchboxes, and knives. Conscientious beginners will be able to master the contents and will surely profit from Ganson's opening chapter on the topic of presenting close-up magic. He offers suggestions on the presentation of close-up magic for a single spectator, small group, or somewhat larger gathering. His advice on the appropriate length of a close-up routine should be considered by all close-up workers. Lewis Ganson's *The Dai Vernon Book of Magic* has been hailed by Robert Gill as one of the most significant and influential books in the last century. Vernon's excellence as both a creator and performer of sleights has earned him the affectionate nickname of "the Professor." He would certainly be on any magician's list of the top ten greats of the twentieth century. In short, the student of intimate magic could do no better than to acquaint himself with the diabolical gems of Vernon as explicated by Ganson. *Unconventional Magic*, also by Ganson, is a monograph that deserves the close-up worker's attention, for it features gems like Marconick's "Gypsy Thread," in which a piece of thread is broken and restored under seemingly impossibly conditions.

In *Griff on Close-Up*, Tony Griffith, one of England's leading cardicians, reveals some of his favorite close-up feats. This thoughtful author has a flair for devising magic that is relatively easy, but nonetheless deceptive. For a sometimes zany American counterpart, *Las Vegas Close-Up*, by Paul Harris, contains magic with cards, coins, and even a full, unopened can of beans. His twenty-one mysteries (an apt number for a professional who performs in Las Vegas) are anything but conventional. Prestidigitators, who are unfamiliar with the magical fertility of Scottish conjurers, will enjoy *Fifty Years Later: Produced by the Scottish Conjurors Association to Celebrate Their Half Century*. Edited by A. S. Hodson and S.A.S. McMillan, this monograph of varied items emphasizes small magic.

The Roy Johnson Experience, Johnson's first work in a four-part series, introduces the practical, effective magic of one of England's most clever and talented contemporary magicians. Fourteen routines, sometimes with the accent on amusement, are detailed. While different small objects are employed, the cardician will be intrigued by the mentally selected card that travels to the performer's wallet and Johnson's card and chewing gum comedy routine. In *Second Time Around*, Johnson's second entry in the series, sponges, slates, cards, and even a table knife are among the items needed. Each mystery is from the author's highly successful shows and reflects the refinements that only extensive experience can yield. *Third Dimension* is Johnson's third work in the series and one that explains his favorite close-up effects, such as an impressive dice cup routine in which dice are shaken into a balanced stack, appear, or disappear, and so on. More than twenty routines have been revealed, including a practical book test for the mentalist. Close-up workers, who seek material that has not been overexposed, will profit from the author's engaging ring and rope routine. *Final Call* is Johnson's fourth and final entry in a series of monographs that concentrate upon entertaining close-up magic, mentalism, and cabaret effects. If one values variety, Johnson's employment of such little-used props as lipstick, a powder puff, and nail polish will be especially attractive. The sixteen fresh, diverse, well-illustrated effects will appeal to a wide range of magicians.

Rick Johnsson's *Practical Impossibilities* contains inventive close-up magic of a high order by an unusually articulate author whose fine sense of humor is always at work. Some knowledge of elementary magic is presupposed by this delightful text. The same uncommon intelligence and wit inform the author's column in *The Linking Ring*. *Kort Is Now in Session*, illustrated by Steranko, who is a creative cardician and professional illustrator, presents the originations of one of America's best known close-up entertainers, Milton Kort. The author's varied conceits include a boomerang card effect, magically bending a penny, coin manipulations, and a miniature version of the cups and balls. Only those with sufficient knowledge of magic will fully appreciate Kort's novel turn of mind. *The Magic of Gerald Kosky*, by Gerald Kosky, sets forth the innovative close-up conjuring of a first-rate cardician who also excels at magic with other small objects. Among the four dozen valuable card items explained is the author's "Invisible Card Change," a slow, smooth move that can defy even close scrutiny. Coin magic, mentalism, and miscellaneous magic are treated in chapters 6 through 12. Kosky's tip on the unlinking of safety-pins is representative of his helpful suggestions for all lovers of intimate magic. This volume is a collector's edition that was limited to five hundred copies. Harry Lorayne's *Reputation Makers*, by a New York magician whose reputation rests largely on his card magic, is worth citing here because it does include strong impromptu close-up feats for those magicians who shun card work. Properly presented, the broken and restored rubberband is a clean, baffling close-up stunt that can give a sense of real spontaneity to one's act. Lorayne's instant magic square is tailor-made for impressing the intellectual spectator. Fortunately, mastering these effects is not especially demanding.

In 1973, the outstanding Canadian magician Sid Lorraine was honored in America by the publication of *The Early Stuff* in Chicago, Illinois. Close-up workers will be introduced at once to fifteen fine effects and the distinctive humor of Lorraine, which enlivens them. Those interested in a booklet of effects and bits of business that are especially suitable for the bar performer can read *Magic for Bartenders*, by Señor Mardo. *The Book of John*, by John Mendoza, sets forth the commercial, close-up specialties of a successful professional. In a section on card magic, Mendoza gives his own handling for the card in wallet mystery in which a spectator's signed card inexplicably travels to the performer's wallet; in a section on coins, the author concludes one routine by producing a drill bit that is over a foot long and weighs more than eight pounds. Miscellaneous items include routines for the cups and balls and a dove production. Given that the author earns his entire living by performing, it is not surprising that his routines are both baffling and entertaining. Since Mendoza has generously shared his choice material with all members of the magic fraternity, his readers can return the favor by not presenting Mendoza's mysteries until they are perfectly mastered. *John: Verse Two* is a further collection of excellent close-up feats by Mendoza.

Close-Up Cavalcade, complied by Jerry Mentzer, is part of a well-regarded trilogy. This installment features effects with ropes, cigarettes, coins, and other household objects by such accomplished sleight-of-hand artists as Jack Chanin, Tony Kardyro, and Horace Bennett. The "Matrix" coin routine, which was invented by Al Schneider and is explained herein, has become a classic of modern coin magic. In *Another Close-Up Cavalcade*, again edited by Jerry Mentzer, British as well as American magicians share their feats of intimate magic with coins, knives, dice, rope, and so on. Effects like Fiedler's cigarette through card mystery demonstrate that the creative cunning of magicians is inexhaustible. *Close-Up Cavalcade—Finale* completes Mentzer's series of works for the close-up specialist. Again, choice secrets have been revealed for routines with such objects as table salt, dice, and coins. The three-shell con game is also treated.

Cards, coins, and rings are thematic in Earl Nelson's *Variations*. His high caliber sleight of hand has been praised by such luminaries as Dai Vernon. In the final pages, the author comments on the presentation and theory of magic, making the much-needed observation that too many magicians try to justify their sloppy technique with the claim that their magic is entertaining—as if the performer were not supposed to mystify as well as entertain. Similar props are thematic in a fine Japanese text. *Tokyo Trickery*, by Takeshi Nemoto, is the first book of Japanese magic to be published by an American publisher, Magic Inc. of Chicago, Illinois. The author studied under Tenkai, inventor of the Tenkai palm, by which a card can be concealed in the hand even though the fingers are spread apart. Nemoto's polished sleight-of-hand routines employ coins, cards, cigars, ropes, rings, Japanese cups and balls, and other miscellaneous props. *Fingertip Fantasies*, by Bob Ostin, acquaints the reader with one of England's finest close-up specialists. Props other than cards figure most often in the thirty-one effective items that are explained. Ostin has a flair for clean, direct magic that reflects years of honing and perfecting his material. Experienced magicians will especially enjoy Ostin's versions of "the coin in the bottle" and "the card to wallet."

For related material, *An Evening with Charlie Miller*, by Robert Parrish, features the magical stylings of a top-notch magician and teacher. Card workers will surely profit from Miller's advice on how *not* to palm a card. Magicians of every persuasion will appreciate the approach and subtleties that Miller brings to a number of standard mysteries. Jon Racherbaumer's *The Lost Pages of the Kabbala* features advanced sleight of hand with cards and coins, with contributions by some of the most adept contemporary magicians. With forty-five items, ranging from mentalism to a torn-and-restored card effect, this book will satisfy a diversity of appetites. In *The Complete Mike Rogers*, Rogers supplements his own original material with contributions by his friends. The result is a book of direct, commercial magic with cards, sponges, coins, dollar bills, and so on.

Jim Ryan Close-Up (1) Sensational Stunners, by Philip Willmarth, presents Ryan's treatment of classic sleight-of-hand effects with rings, ropes, and cards. Humor, audience-appeal, and simplicity are the hallmarks of Ryan's outstanding magic. Maurice Sardina's *The Magic of Rezvani*, translated from the French by Dariel Fitzkee, features the sleights, effects, ideas, and refinements of Rezvani, the Iranian magician who has been a sensation among the magicians of Paris. Particularly intriguing is the first complete explanation in English of the "Tomato Trick," as performed by Arabian magicians on the streets in cities of the Near East. This effect is a version of the cups and balls. *Controlled Miracles*, by Bill Simon, is a sampler of close-up feats as performed by a highly respected member of the magic fraternity. Illustrated by another famous magician, Frank Garcia, this monograph includes effects with cards, coins, cigarettes, and silks. Readers who know Simon only as a cardician are in for a refreshing surprise. *Sleightly Sensational*, also by Simon, contains the sort of card magic that earned him his reputation among leading card workers. In one routine, the spectator himself manages to cut to all four aces. Sponges, coins, and a finger ring are thematic in other routines. Ed Mishell's customarily clear illustrations simplify following the text.

Stars of Magic, edited by George Starke, contains polished sleight of hand by a who's who of twentieth-century magicians. This bound volume consists of eleven pamphlets, each devoted to a favorite gem of an outstanding magician, which were published by Louis Tannen Inc. under the same title. The prestigious "Stars of Magic" series of pamphlets continues to the present, with Paul Harris' "The Immaculate Connection" being a recent example. Meticulously photographed, step-by-step instruction is the hallmark of this exemplary series of feats with cards, coins, cigarettes and other small objects. Video-tape lessons are the latest addition. As in the case of his other books, James G. Thompson's *Magic to Delight: Pleasing Tricks in Abundant Variety* concentrates upon his favorite form of conjuring, small magic. Thompson's success as a teacher is demonstrated by the fact that his books have been big sellers. A half-century involvement with magic underlies his pedagogical skill. More of Thompson's fresh thinking and subtleties are evident in *The Miracle Makers*, a compilation of over six dozen close-up feats. Pocket items such as cards, coins, dice, rings, and ropes all figure in these miniature miracles. The three volumes that constitute J. G. Thompson's *Top Secrets of Magic: Routined Mystification with Small Objects* provide a wealth of information for the close-up specialist. His keen editorial eye invariably settles on first-rate material; his clear exposition insures that the reader can grasp the major and minor elements in an effect or a routine. Cards, the three shell game, safety pin magic, cups and balls, coins, silks, dice, and paddle routines are all treated in this outstanding compendium of close-up chicanery. *Dan Tong's Close-Up Magic*, by Danny Tong, presents tips and baffling effects for the veteran as well as the novice. Just as the traditional Chinese painter gives us only the bare bones of a landscape, Tong's writing style is refreshingly sparse. Where some would write pages, Tong writes paragraphs. Yet his explanations are clear, provided that one is familiar with the basics of sleight of hand. *Early Vernon: The Magic of Dai Vernon in 1932* collects the first originations of the superb sleight-of-hand artist, Dai Vernon. Like Edward Marlo, Vernon is held in the highest esteem by magicians throughout the world. Contents include modern classics such as the "Five Card Mental Force," in which the magician influences the spectator's mental choice of a card. Illustrated by Vernon, the text is peppered with nostalgic photographs of his evolution as a magician. In *Select Secrets*, another early monograph by Vernon, close-up magic of the highest order prevails. Props include coins, cards, silks, and dice.

Peter Warlock's *Come a Little Closer . . .* features professional feats by some of the finest contemporary sleight-of-hand artists. *The Magic of Matt Schulien*, by Philip Willmarth, contains the favorite sleights, effects, and routines of the legendary bar magician. Schulien's material is marked by its directness and by its strong effect upon spectators. Many magicians regard Schulien as the greatest close-up entertainer of this century; surely the countless patrons of his restaurant and bar, many celebrities included, would agree. While card magic is emphasized, there are spectator-pleasing items with coins, matches, a spoon, and other items. Items like his "Goldfish Eating" stunt reflect the fact that Schulien was just as interested in amusing his customers as he was in amazing them. Although Matt is dead, Schulien's restaurant and bar endures as a Chicago institution, with his son, Chuck, and grandson, Bob, performing the same brand of high-impact magic. No close-up specialist can afford to overlook this treasury of audience-tested feats, which represents Matt's lifetime of dedication to magic. But as much as he loved magic and as skillful as he was, it was probably Matt's love of people that elevated him over his peers. *Diverse Deceits*, by William Zavis, is a short and superb manual of close-up conceits. With his subtle, skillful routines, the author has established an international reputation among magicians. Cards, coins, and the cups and balls are all given the distinctive Zavis touch. A fiendishly clever one cup and one ball version of the cups and balls is also explained.

Frances Ireland Marshall's *The Sponge Book* is a compact treatment of magic with the sponges that have become part of the stock in trade of virtually every close-up worker. In editing this excellent monograph, Marshall has drawn upon such expert sponge ball manipulators as Al Goshman and "Senator" Clarke Crandall. The simple principle which underlies much sponge ball magic is that two or more sponges can be compressed so as to appear as one. Numerous illustrations facilitate mastering the professional routines which include productions, vanishes, transpositions, and transformations. Audley V. Walsh's *Sponge Ball Manipulation* is among the earliest explanations of the popular routine, in which sponge balls appear, disappear, and eventually multiply in a spectator's hand. Those seeking a relatively short, simple routine will be pleased with this booklet. It is no wonder that sponges have become a standard prop of the magician; like rabbits, sponges are silent and able to evoke instant amusement when produced. In the booklet *Dai Vernon's Cups and Balls Routine*, Lewis Ganson meticulously records every step in one of the most imitated presentations of a genuine magical classic. Small balls appear, disappear, penetrate solid cups, and multiply in a flowing series of moves that leaves the spectator completely perplexed and quite unprepared for the powerful climax—the production of three much larger objects from the cups. At one point in the routine, a wand-spinning flourish is instrumental in causing a ball to vanish; it is by such visual poetry that Vernon has assured himself immortality among magicians.

Ireland's Original Cups and Balls Routines, by Laurie L. Ireland, is another comprehensive monograph on one of the most impressive feats of close-up conjuring. Virtually all magicians learn a cups and balls routine at some point in their magical education. The author, one of the leading sleight-of-hand artists of his era, specialized in presenting this standard. The clearly written, generously illustrated text is a model primer, but experienced practitioners can also profit by Ireland's handling of a double load. Many performers climax their routine by producing three lemons, oranges, or large balls from the three cups with which they have been working; naturally, this entails that these objects be "loaded" during the course of the routine. Ireland's manual instructs the reader in how to load the cups twice so as to bring about a double surprise. *The Last Word on the Cups and Balls*, by Eddie Joseph, contains eighty-six fresh sleights, effects, and routines for the cups-and-balls specialist. Like Ireland, Joseph gives special attention to the final load and details how it can be a liquid production. In *The Cups and Balls*, Señor Mardo's scrupulous elucidation facilitates the reader's progress with a time-tested classic. Even those who have mastered other routines may wish to adopt one or another of Mardo's moves. Tom Osborne's *Cups and Balls Magic* is required reading for any magician who wishes to learn some of the endless permutations of this venerable classic. Material includes the historical background, advice on what cups to choose, basic sleights, and numerous refinements. Sketches, plus a comprehensive text, clarify the various productions, vanishes, multiplications, transpositions, and transformations.

In the nine-page pamphlet *Nick's Routine with the Cups and Balls*, Nick Trost sets forth a routine that depends upon subtleties rather great dexterity; thus, the presentation is especially suitable for those who are discouraged by routines such as Vernon's. *Jim Ryan Close-Up: (4) The Famous Cups and Balls Routine*, by Philip Willmarth, details Ryan's striking version of the standard. Ryan, a famous Chicago magician, found that this was the strongest item in his repertoire; for this reason, he used it as the climax of his close-up act. Mark Wilson's *The*

Chop Cup Book richly explores the possibilities of a one cup and one ball routine. This is the first book devoted exclusively to ideas for the gimmicked cup that contains a concealed magnet; the ball used has a metal core. These simple props can greatly enhance the sleight-of-hand routine in which a ball appears, disappears, and becomes a different object. Two hundred line drawings illustrate the eight complete routines and variations that are set forth. Those interested in the aesthetic and the history of the cups and balls should consult Kurt Volkmann's *The Oldest Deception (Das Becherspiel): Cups and Balls in the Art of the 15th and 16th Centuries*.

Ian H. Adair's *Paddle-Antics* is a welcome monograph on a subject that had not previously received sustained attention in the literature. Paddle effects are among the most popular of pocket items in the magician's repertoire today; magic dealers continue to market numerous props that depend upon the paddle-principle. The latter allows one to seemingly show both sides of a flat object, but in reality show the same side twice. Adair's probing analysis may very well inspire magicians to devise their own distinctive paddle routines. In color-changing knife routines, the paddle move is the essential sleight. *Ascanio's World of Knives*, written by Jose De La Torre, is a free translation of selected parts of Ascanio's Spanish work *Navajas y Daltonismo*, which was the first work solely devoted to routines with a pocket knife. Concentration is upon the theme of changing the color of the knife's handle, but other sleights enable one to vanish the knife and to transform it into a handful of miniature knives. Ascanio's battery of moves and variations will benefit the expert and the novice alike. His chapter on conjuring psychology contains insights that can be applied far beyond the limits of knife manipulation. Ascanio supplemented his own contributions with those of Lewis Ganson, Fred Kaps, Fu Manchu, and Slydini. Given the high quality of its contents, it is not surprising that sleight-of-hand artists have already recognized this as a classic textbook. *Merrill's Knife Book*, by R. D. Merrill, has the distinction of being the first such specialized study to be published originally in English. The author is widely regarded as the best manipulator of pocket knives in the field. Beginning with the simple paddle move, Merrill treats the reader to a postgraduate course in sleight of hand with pocket knives. His explanations for the various maneuvers and routines are usually quite detailed and lucid. Photographs of his hands and their reflection in a mirror enable the reader to see things from both the magician's and the spectator's perspective. Merrill's remarks on perception will prevent the performer from showing a flash of the second color when he executes the paddle move with a knife that has two different colored handles. A generous bibliography is one further merit of this fine overview of productions, vanishes, and color changes with pocket knives.

Because of the performer's arm's-length proximity, dinner-table magic can be especially startling. *After the Dessert*, by Martin Gardner, contains thirty quick feats with articles that can be carried in one's pockets or found at the dinner table. This standard booklet of largely impromptu items is suitable as an introduction to the art of table magic. *Over the Coffee-Cups* is another group of close-up capers that have been compiled by Martin Gardner. Contributors include such Chicago notables as Dorny, Matt Schulien, and Chic Schoke. Again props are of the dinner-table variety: sugar cubes, silverware, paper matches, napkins, and drinking glasses. Over a hundred quickies have been treated in fewer than three dozen pages. Eddie Joseph's *A Magician Goes to Dinner* is a third booklet of easy, largely impromptu effects with items commonly found at the dinner table. Among the props used are coins, a bottle, and matches. The latter have themselves been the centerpiece in several studies, such as David Ginn's *Matchbox Delights*, a collection of stunts, gags, puzzles, and magic effects that employ matchboxes and wooden matches. His "rattle box" version of the three-shell game is fun, deceptive, and easily learned. *Matchic*, an early booklet by Martin Gardner, also exploits the entertainment possibilities of a box of matches and some match books. Seventy effective mysteries and gag-items are explained. *Between Cocktails—With a Packet of Matches*, by Sidney Fleischman, again describes effects and sleights in which the performer employs a homely packet of matches. Interesting productions, vanishes, and other feats insure that the reader of this booklet will always be prepared to surprise his table companions. The author's clean, simple plots are "matched" by his direct methods.

Penetration effects, in which one solid object appears to pass through another without harm to either, have long been popular with stage magicians. But the close-up magician has his own versions of this staple. *Mohammed Bey's Routines for the Jardine Ellis Ring on Stick*, by Mohammed Bey (pseudonym for Samuel Leo Horowitz), presents the author's stunningly direct routines with the standard dealer item that is known as the Jardine Ellis Ring. This ring is sold with a close-fitting shell that makes it possible to perform remarkable penetration and transposition effects with a simple wand. Bey's masterful presentations have become inseparably associated with this classic piece of close-up wizardry. John Howie's *Routines with the Jardine Ellis Ring* features his favorite sleights and routines with this classic item of the close-up worker. This fine monograph provides a bibliography as well as the author's interesting tips for presentation. Since only a modest number of writings have been devoted to the Ellis ring, those who use it will certainly want to study Howie's contribution.

Effects in which a ring penetrates a solid object are emphasized in Hans E. Trixer's *Conjuring Trix and Jardine Ellis Ring Effects*. Using a Jardine Ellis ring (a ring on which a shell ring fits tightly in order to give the impression that the performer is working with only one ring), beautifully clean routines can be done at close range. Philip Willmarth's *The Ring and the Rope Book* explains forty-two effects with rings and ropes by the author and friends. There are twice as many photographs as there are pages in this excellent monograph. In the best known feat, a ring is threaded on a rope and then mysteriously penetrates the rope. The simplicity of the plot and the smoothness with which the ring appears to melt through the rope make the effect elegant as well as deceptive. Jerry Andrus' *Safety-Pin Trix* impressively exploits the magical possibilities of the mundane safety-pin. Methods for linking, unlinking, producing, and vanishing pins are presented in considerable detail. Some of Andrus' magic does rely upon using a gimmicked version of the seemingly innocent safety-pin, a ploy by which he disarmed a number of magicians themselves. Among the most innovative of American cardicians, the author has demonstrated his versatility in this specialized monograph. One can only hope that it will inspire others to seek out the magical applications for any number of other pedestrian objects. One earlier work is in the very same spirit. Ulysses F. Grant's *Clever Little Ideas Presented by U. F. Grant* explores the magical applications of the ordinary paper-clip, the one household item that can hardly wear out and is rarely thrown out. Grant examines the usefulness of the paper-clip both as a prop and as a gimmick. One of the more obvious examples of the latter consists in holding one or more cards with the clip and then using a safety-pin to attach it to the inside of one's coat where the cards can secretly be removed at will.

Readers who are interested in cheating techniques will find the following works to be enlightening. Close-up magicians may be inspired by John Nevil Maskelyne's *Sharps and Flats*, which is an exhaustive survey of the artifices and techniques that are employed in order to cheat at supposed games of chance. The secrets and principles that Maskelyne discloses can, as the saying goes, "be applied to magic, for entertainment purposes only." *Hello, Sucker!* is Jack Chanin's commendable exposition of the sleights and principles that underlie the classic three shell con game. Mastering this material will insure that the spectator never gets an even break in trying to follow the position of the pea as the shells are moved about. Because the pea is often not under any of the shells, but instead is in between the performer's fingers, the sucker scarcely has a chance. Magicians who present a three shell routine for entertainment purposes may not expose the actual techniques that are at work, perhaps because anyone who witnesses a baffling demonstration of this game and still wishes to play for money deserves to be taken. *All in a Nutshell* is Frank Garcia's famous contribution to the inexhaustible possibilities of the three shell game. Garcia's routine has the distinction of having been presented on numerous network television shows in America. His entire routine, with patter included, is set forth in a step-by-step fashion. This is the longest exposition in print to date. *Three Shell Games*, by Tom Osborne, furnishes explicit instructions for this popular con game. Intriguing historical material, the requisite sleights, and full routines make this a standard source book on its topic. *The Three Shell Game*, by Ralph W. Read, is a respected overview of one of the oldest practices by which to separate a sucker from his money. Robert Gill has described this relatively early manual as "the best work on the subject."

"Senator" Clarke Crandall's *How to Stack Dice* is a booklet that instructs one in a standard flourish of the dice handler, dice-stacking. This activity is not to be confused with a favorite practice of the card cheat, stacking the deck. For the latter involves arranging cards in a certain order during the course of a shuffle. But dice-stacking is merely a flashy display of skill in which the performer shakes four dice in a cup, abruptly stops this action, and then lifts the cup to reveal that the dice are stacked one on top of another in a column. Magical touches that Crandall incorporates in his routine include the production of a king-sized die from the cup. Readers will be treated to Crandall's W. C. Fields style of humor throughout this helpful manual. A more comprehensive introduction to dice magic and manipulation is available in Edward Marlo's *Shoot the Works*, which has become must-reading for the close-up performer who wishes to add dice to his list of props. Marlo explains flourishes, routines with dice and other props, dice controls (methods for throwing dice that allow one to get whatever total is desired when using legitimate dice), the varieties of gimmicked dice, and how to present a gambling demonstration. Whether one is simply interested in how to detect "loaded" dice or in how to switch them (secretly exchange them for fair dice), he will profit from Marlo's authoritative elucidation.

Close-up specialists, whose appetite for dice technique has not been satisfied by the above writings, should find ample material in *Scarne on Dice*, by John Scarne and Clayton Rawson. This is an encyclopedic study of dice manipulation and gimmicked dice, which does for its topic what Erdnase did for cards in *The Expert at the Card Table*. The authors survey the history of dice, the mathematics of gambling, the rules, and the most fascinating dice-related topic, cheating with dice. Two chapters are devoted to the various types of crooked dice; another chapter explores crooked moves with fair dice. Any thoughtful magician will perceive the applications of this material for close-up magic. Nick Trost's *Gambling Tricks with Dice: This is a Fifty-Dollar Book* reminds us that braggadocio is part of the stock-in-trade of magicians. Those for whom John Scarne's exploration would tell them more than they really wanted to know about dice will appreciate this digest. In this booklet of fewer than three dozen pages, Trost comments upon dice control, sucker bets, dice games and swindles, and crooked dice. *Dice Deception*, by Audley Walsh and Ed Mishell, features flourishes and sleight-of-hand maneuvers with ordinary dice. In the dice-stacking flourish, one of the most flashy juggling feats, four dice that are being shaken in a mouth down cup are snapped into a neat column. One may wish to compare the author's account with that of Crandall's, which is noted above.

As Americans eat more meals in restaurants than ever before, restaurant magicians are multiplying. *Tips on Table-Hopping*, by Kirk Charles, is an excellent manuscript for those who wish to enter the field of close-up entertainment as practiced in bars or restaurants. Charles offers valuable suggestions on how to approach a table, whether to work strictly out of one's pockets or from a close-up case, how to encourage tipping, the proper length of a table routine, the type of material that is most effective, how to deal with drunks or the obstreperous patron, and how to deal with the returnee. His thoughtful opinions are grounded upon years of successful experience and can save the neophyte from needless difficulties. What does the card worker do, for instance, when a customer spills a drink on the deck and thereby renders the cards useless? If the would-be cardician has read Charles' monograph, he will carry a spare pack in his pocket and not interrupt his performance in order to leave the premises and buy a new pack. In one perceptive section of his study, the author comments on the special intimacy that marks close-up magic. During the course of a routine, the typically male magician may touch a female spectator, hold her hand, or ask her to remove an article from his pocket. Even if all these actions are integral to the magic being performed, the magician runs the risk of inciting jealously in any male escort or his female assistant. Charles' prudent remarks can help one diminish the chances in favor of such a possibility occurring. This highly praised study also discusses how to sell your act to the restaurant or bar manager, what fee to charge, and how to promote or publicize your act.

Scott Hollingsworth's *Cashing in with Close-Up Restaurant Magic: A Personal Portfolio* collects the thoughts of an active performer who specializes in entertaining the patrons of restaurants. His discussion treats business cards, table toppers (small folders which are placed on tables to inform customers that table-side magic is available), flyers, lobby boards, selling points by which to win bookings, how to determine one's fee, how to approach a table, the length of one's presentation, and when to approach a table. Hollingsworth's intelligent, audience-tested observations are supplemented with copies of his own promotional material. Before one can profit from this excellent monograph, he or she must, of course, have an entertaining repertoire of well-honed effects and routines. Unfortunately, some beginners perceive restaurant work as a field for the practice and development of their skills, but only the seasoned magician is apt to succeed under the special conditions posed by the circumstances of a bar or restaurant. While the magician who walks on stage automatically receives the spectators' attention, the close-up worker must work to win initial attention. While stage magic is generally performed under rather controlled conditions (spectators are at a fixed distance from the magician and he or she decides which members of the audience may serve as assistants), close-up magic is performed under the spectators' noses and often provokes unsolicited audience participation.

Table Hopping, by Bruce Postgate, compresses a great deal of information in its monograph format. Drawing from his years of engagement as an entertainer of restaurant patrons, the author discusses the sort of magic and stunts that he used in going from table to table. Anyone who wishes to take up this lucrative form of conjuring (restaurant magicians can earn the hourly wages of a psychiatrist) will be delighted by the secrets and tips that Postgate presents. Restaurant or bar-room magic makes a strong impact on spectators, since it is performed under their noses and with everyday objects that the performer removes from his pockets. "I didn't realize that magic could be done so close-up" is a typical response of restaurant patrons. Of course, the magician must face and adapt to various challenges; not only is he or she performing at close range, but, at times, completely surrounded by spectators. In addition, the informality of atmosphere will sometimes prompt spectators to request that they be allowed to examine the magician's props—a demand that is rarely made of the stage performer. Despite these problems, a growing number of magicians has elected to take up table hopping. This is especially fitting at a time when people are investigating their roots, for the restaurant/bar magician is returning to the beginnings of the art, to street magic without the rain.

The "Himber" wallet is a standard prop among close-up magicians in general and restaurant workers in particular. *Richard Himber's Ideas in the $100.00 Book*, by Harry Lorayne, explores the possibilities of the Himber wallet, which can be obtained from a magic dealer. This gimmicked wallet allows one to switch a bill, card, or other thin, flat object for another such item. Given that the wallet appears to be disarmingly innocent, takes virtually no skill to use, and renders any number of great effects possible, Lorayne's enlightening study can be highly recommended. Val Andrews' *Gags in Close-Up* furnishes comedy material for the intimate conditions of the close-up specialist. In such circumstances, humor is particularly important, for without it, the performer runs the risk of being perceived as intimidating or challenging. Of course, American magicians will have to exercise discretion in drawing upon the comedy of a British entertainer. But reflecting upon Andrews' routines may help one develop his or her own comedic style.

COIN MAGIC

Compared to playing cards, coins are harder to manipulate, less malleable, noisier, and less rich in their permutations for magical purposes. But conscientious magicians still rise to the challenge of sleight of hand with coins; spectators are unfailingly drawn to these hypnotic trinkets. Thomas Nelson Downs' *Modern Coin Manipulation*, published in 1900, superseded all previous treatments of coin magic. Much of this material persists in the routines of the contemporary coin magician. Certain of the sleights set forth are so difficult that some magicians today doubt that even Downs himself could actually execute them. Among such sleights is the back-hand palm, in which a coin is secretly and repeatedly transferred from one side of the hand to the other as the performer apparently shows that both sides of his hand are free of any coins. Performing the sleight with one coin demands great skill, but executing the move with several coins is virtually impossible. Over a half century elapsed before the next substantial treatise on coins appeared. J. B. Bobo's *The New Modern Coin Magic* is unquestionably the finest and most comprehensive treatment of its topic extant. For most magicians, mastering its contents would probably be the work of several lifetimes. Bobo is a popular professional who specializes in entertaining college and university audiences. His life demonstrates that poverty can be responsible for excellence, for as a youngster, he could not afford to buy elaborate, self-working apparatus; this encouraged him to master the most exquisite elements of sleight of hand. Not since T. Nelson Downs' *Modern Coin Manipulation* at the turn of the century, has anyone attempted to write a definitive treatise on coin magic. Not only has Bobo matched Downs' unprecedented accomplishment, but Bobo has added greatly to the sleights, techniques, and stratagems of the coin specialist. With over five hundred pages, nearly seven hundred illustrations, and over four hundred sleights, effects, and routines, this book is fairly advertised as "The world's most complete text book on coin conjuring." Were all other books on coin magic to be destroyed, the art of coin manipulation could endure through Bobo's work alone.

In the tradition of Downs and Bobo, Richard Kaufman has greatly enriched the literature of coin conjuring in *Coin Magic*, a superb and stunning collection of moves and routines. With over a thousand illustrations and a sterling cast of contributors, this coin manual is simply in a class by itself. Naturally, only those familiar with earlier texts can fully benefit from Kaufman's treatise. Even more recently, David Roth's *Expert Coin Magic*, directed toward the seasoned coin manipulator, has taken the magical world by storm. Less demanding works include *Convincing Coin Magic*, by Victor Farelli. This anthology of coin sleights and effects represents the state of coin manipulation at the middle of this century. As in the case of Bobo's tome, a helpful bibliography is provided. Bibliographies are especially important with coin magic, since books devoted strictly to coin effects are not numerous, but other books, which carry no reference to coins in their titles, often contain valuable material on coins.

Coin sleights and routines are well-illustrated in Shigeo Futagawa's *Introduction to Coin Magic*, a shorter, less imposing work than Bobo's *The New Modern Coin Magic*. Contents include comments on the close-up mat (a cloth pad that serves as a working surface, facilitates picking up coins, and prevents any undesirable "talking"—sounds), three no-skill effects, some of his own trophy-winning close-up feats, and contributions by such expert coin manipulators as Dai Vernon, John Scarne, T. Nelson Downs, Slydini, and Tenkai. Futagawa also provides photographs and biographical remarks on a number of outstanding, contemporary coin workers. *Coin Magic*, a monograph by the prolific Jean Hugard, is an outstanding early primer of sleights, flourishes, and routines. "The Miser's Dream" (a classic stage item in which the magician seems to pluck an unending supply of coins out of thin air) is detailed in addition to a number of close-up feats. Dai Vernon has spoken of the Miser's Dream routine as the most impressive masterpiece in the realm of sleight of hand. This routine brings to mind Spinoza's dictum, "All things excellent are as difficult as they are rare." For additional versions of the routine, one may turn to Bobo's classic text. Edward Victor's *Coin Manipulation, in Six Easy Lessons* can serve the reader well as a brief primer on its announced topic. *Bullseye Coin Tricks*, by Laurie L. Ireland and Edward Marlo, is a booklet that caters to the beginner as well as the advanced practitioner. In addition to routines and effects with coins of various sizes, the authors present patter for the Miser's Dream. As Beam notes in his introduction to *Steve Beam on Coins*, far less has been written on coin magic than on card work. His study is a successful attempt to help balance the scales. Innovative sleights include the author's methods for switching coins. Would-be coin experts, who have mastered basic sleight of hand with coins, will be rewarded by Beam's pleasant wit as well as by his creativity. Those interested in the Okito coin box (a utility item for coin workers) will enjoy the author's treatment of this standard prop. The Okito box, named after its inventor Theodore Bamberg, who used the stage name "Okito," consists of an innocent-looking, circular pill box and lid, both made of metal. That the lid will fit the bottom as well as the top of the box is the simple principle which has given rise to an inexhaustible number of effects and routines. In the most basic employment of the box, a coin is placed in it, the lid is fairly fitted to the top of the box, yet the coin escapes. This is accomplished by indetectably moving the lid from the top of the box to the bottom at the same time that the box is secretly being turned upside down. The larger move of shaking and rattling the coin in the box conceals the smaller sleights that are at work.

Mohammed Bey's Routines with the Okito Coin Box, and More Mohammed Bey Routines, by Mohammed Bey, offers a medley of coin changes, transpositions, and penetrations with the Okito box. Distilling his forty years of experiments with and refinements for the box, the author gives the reader a postgraduate course on a masterpiece of modern close-up magic. In the booklet *Coining Magic*, Edward Marlo lends his own deft touch to standard themes in coin magic, including the Okito coin box. Tom Osborne's *Coin Tricks* is another clear presentation of basic coin material in booklet form. Jules De Barros' *The Coins of Ishtar* features excellent coin magic, with an emphasis on transposition routines. His utility move and one-page bibliography are further merits of this monograph. In *Downs' Palm Technique*, Horace Bennett renders the magic fraternity a service by resurrecting and underlining the value of the Downs' palm, a method for concealing a coin in one's hand. At a time when too many magicians are merely interested in what is new, Bennett reminds us that the best in magic often lies in reconsidering time-tested techniques. His version of "the expansion of texture" (an effect in which a coin penetrates a handkerchief), for example, vividly demonstrates the utility of the often-neglected Downs' palm.

Two works on gimmicked coins illustrate their multifarious possibilities. William E. Spooner's *Here's "Hoo" with Coins* is a pamphlet on a coin that has been gimmicked by attaching a hook to it. With proper misdirection, such a coin can be secretly attached to and detached from one's clothing, thus making possible startling coin vanishes and appearances. *Tricks with a Folding Coin*, published by Magic Inc., is a booklet of suggested uses for a folding coin, a standard gimmicked coin that has been cut and then reassembled with a rubber band. One classic feat involves borrowing a coin, switching it for a folding coin, and then inserting the latter into a bottle, the neck of which is obviously far too narrow to admit the coin.

STAGE MAGIC

Stage magic, with its ties to theater arts such as acting and pantomine, is clearly the most glamorous, although least performed, variety of conjuring. Loring Campbell's *Magic That Is Magic* can be recommended to the beginner who wishes to assemble a simple but effective stage act. However, those who want to earn the greatest accolades must master the more demanding sort of material that is presented by Arthur Buckley. His *Principles and Deceptions* is a remarkably good treatise on the manipulation of coins, cards, and billiard balls. Chapter 1, which contains Buckley's philosophy of conjuring, should be on every beginner's list of essential readings. In addition to close-up routines, a stage act with fifty-five silver dollars and one with eight billiard balls are also detailed. Only the industrious, who will be amply rewarded, need apply for Buckley's course in professional prestidigitation.

The following works represent three distinct approaches to stage magic by leading twentieth-century performers. With an introduction by Mrs. Harry Houdini, John Booth's *Marvels of Mystery* is a complete presentation of the author's effects, routines, and novel ideas. For the most part, he concentrates upon dramatic stage magic, frequently giving an original twist to items such as the vanishing bird cage. *Gene Gordon's Magical Legacy*, by Gordon, combines tales of his life with routines and patter for over seventy commercial items. Gordon was responsible for introducing "Fraidy Cat Rabbit," a classic sucker effect, to the magic fraternity. "Sucker effects" will be discussed in connection with texts on entertaining children. While some close-up feats are explained, platform magic is emphasized. This recent work has received the most laudatory reviews in various magic periodicals. *Lots of Lawton*, by Don Lawton, demonstrates the author's uncommon flair for revitalizing common effects. His excellence has been recognized by the Academy of Magical Arts and Sciences, which presented him with the Stage Magician of the Year Award in 1970.

Two very representative magicians place a special premium on comedy. *Topper's Mad, Mad Magic*, by Gene Anderson, consists of zany material drawn from the act of the very successful comedy magician Topper Martyn. Like Carl Ballantine, Martyn has made it manifest that the magician who intentionally fails can be more entertaining than the magician who blandly succeeds. *Kornfidentially Yours*, by Karrell Fox, contains sixty humorous items or bits of business by one of America's supreme comedy magicians. Material covered includes routines with rabbits, humorous magic props, and a pitch act. Fox's humor endears him to audiences at magicians' conventions as well as to laymen at trade shows. Moving to the serious or dramatic, *Okito on Magic*, by Theodore Bamberg, who favored the stage name "Okito," is a monumental contribution to the literature of conjuring. Bamberg's father served as court magician for King William III of Holland. Bamberg himself toured the world and entertained members of royalty on numerous occasions. While American magicians such as Blackstone were gaining fame in the United States, Bamberg flourished in Europe. For a time, he played a role in the illusion show of Howard Thurston in America. Bamberg's Oriental costumes and his props, which were decorated with Chinese characters, lent a special beauty to his act. Whether he was producing a stack of water-filled fish bowls or several live ducks, he performed with a captivating grace. Bamberg's text contains explanations for dozens of choice effects, but also includes individual chapters on "The Elements of Magic" (his philosophy of conjuring), "The Progress of Magic," "Classical Conjurers," "Romantic Magicians," and "The History of the Floating Ball." *The Magic of Ho-Yam*, by William Mayoh, is another of the relatively few books on magic as performed in an Oriental manner. Flowers, lanterns, doves, rabbits, rice, and confetti all figure in the attractive magical stylings of Mayoh. While the author is best known for his stage work, we would like to add that he once presented a most stunning color-changing knife routine for our enjoyment. *Oriental Conjuring and Magic* features a bibliographical section by S. H. Sharpe in which he gives a chronological list of books, pamphlets, and periodicals that discuss Oriental magic. In the remaining and much longer portion of the book, Will Ayling analyzes over one hundred of the methods employed in this variety of magic. Interestingly enough, each of the above books on Oriental magic is by a westerner.

Card fans and productions have long been a staple for the stage magician. In *Exhibition Card Fans*, by Goodlette Dodson, the accent is on flourishes in which the deck of cards is fanned into symmetrical arrangements. Such fans are usually incorporated in a stage manipulative act. Dozens of photographs assure the reader that he has the next best thing to personal instruction. Moving from flourishes to baffling feats, Lewis Ganson's *Expert Manipulation of Playing Cards* details various aspects of a manipulative card act in which the performer appears to pluck cards out of thin air. This beautiful form of card magic can be appreciated even by those who detest card tricks. The reader may wish to compare Ganson's excellent study with another by the consummate cardician Edward Marlo and one by Edward Victor. That Edward Marlo's *Card Fan Productions* has been reprinted twice testifies to its value for all who wish to master the production of cards at the finger tips. Marlo's bibliography identifies other writings that include some discussion of card-fan productions. In this elegant feat of manipulative magic, the performer produces fan after fan, despite the fact that he has shown the palm and back of his hand to be devoid of cards. Sketches of front and back views clarify the sleights that are at work, but extensive practice is essential to the flawless execution of such a routine. With his customary thoroughness, Marlo explains types of fans, gimmicks, and the use of gloves. Edward Victor's *Card Manipulation, in Six Easy Lessons* focuses on the production of cards at one's finger tips and should be compared with the preceding works.

Two representative works speak to the manipulator who wishes to produce coins instead of card fans. *The Interlocked Production of Coins*, by Richard Kaufman, can add novelty and beauty to any manipulative coin act. This production technique involves interlacing the fingers of both hands, turning the palms outward to show their emptiness, and then producing a series of coins from the supposedly empty hands. While this sort of approach has been used with playing cards, the procedure is easier and more angle-proof with coins. For the student who wishes to master the elements of a stage act with coins, Walt Lees' *Ron MacMillan's Modern Art of Coin Manipulation* provides ample information. Topics include the proper coins, palms, flourishes, and routining. Those familiar with coin magic can still profit from MacMillan's refinements and views on arranging a routine. The bare-handed production of billiard balls is another classic of stage magic. *Billiard Ball Manipulation, in Seven Easy Lessons*, by Edward Victor, succinctly explains the author's favorite moves and routines.

Another standard manual, *Expert Billiard Ball Manipulation*, by Burling Hull, is an outstanding compendium that contains over two hundred photographs to illustrate the text. For more recent material, *Ron MacMillan's Symphony of the Spheres*, by Lewis Ganson, explains MacMillan's superb routines for a billiard ball act. Most every novice has received a set of billiard balls in his first magic kit, but very few ever master the sort of sophisticated productions, vanishes, and transformations that have been devised by MacMillan and a handful of others. For another good booklet of similar length on billiard ball manipulation, the reader can consult *Frank Garcia's Billiard Balls*. Finally, Richard Kaufman's *Balls! Lessons in Side-Arm Snookery* offers a veritable postgraduate course in billiard ball manipulation. Simultaneous manipulations with two hands, color changes, and an eight ball routine are conveyed with nearly two hundred exemplary illustrations.

Cigarette manipulation, especially with lighted cigarettes, remains one of the most mysterious stage routines. Keith Clark's *Encyclopedia of Cigarette Tricks* is not simply a standard reference work but *the* standard work. All phases of cigarette magic (with and without sleights, with and without gimmicks) are covered in a volume that is over three hundred pages and includes three hundred photographs. Jack Chanin's monograph *Cigar Magic* presents a great variety of sleights and subtleties with cigars and/or cigarettes. Similarly, D. Deveen's *Cigarette Magic and Manipulation* describes cigarette vanishes, productions, and a sample routine. Gimmicks and the manipulation of lit cigarettes are also treated. *Expert Cigarette Magic*, also by Deveen, is a longer, more comprehensive analysis of its topic than its predecessor. *Producing Lighted Cigarettes*, by Edward Loyd Enochs, a brief but important study, describes productions, vanishes, variations, and switching a lighted cigarette for a dummy (one that appears to be lit). *Tops Treasury of Cigarette Magic*, edited by the distinguished American magician Neil Foster, contains sleights, ideas, effects, and joke items that have been culled from the famous magic magazine, *Tops*. This fine sampler should whet one's appetite for more material. *How to Do Cigarette Tricks*, edited by Don Tanner, contains sleights, routines by artists such as Ed Marlo, novel ideas, and an explanation of gimmicks for the cigarette worker. A great deal of useful information has been packed into this booklet.

Less exciting than a lighted cigarette, the simple thimble has, nonetheless, won its own set of advocates. E. Loyd Enochs' *Loyd's Master Manipulation of Thimbles* is a first-rate booklet that covers all aspects of sleight of hand with thimbles: vanishes, productions, penetrations, color changes, and others. Using slightly oversized thimbles, brightly colored ones, or proper spotlighting, magicians have performed thimble routines before large audiences. Given that magic with ordinary objects is especially impressive, it is regrettable that thimble acts are rarely seen today. Jean Hugard's *Thimble Magic* was the first manual to focus exclusively upon thimble manipulation. This excellent monograph leads the reader from finger exercises to simple sleights, advanced moves, variations, and a complete act. *Thimble Manipulation in Six Easy Lessons*, by Edward Victor, is an excellent treatment of various aspects of thimble magic. *Tantalizing Thimbles*, by the Chicago cardician Warren Wiersbe, features clean magic with unprepared thimbles and without gimmicks. Contents include productions, vanishes, color changes, transpositions, penetrations, and an impromptu routine.

For many magicians, doves rather than rabbits symbolize the magic art. *Encyclopedia of Dove Magic*, by the prolific British magician and author Adair, is a three-volume opus that exceeds a thousand pages. *Cagey Doves*, by Tom Palmer, explains and gives construction details for various versions of the vanishing cage of doves illusionette. The author has enhanced his manual by drawing from contemporary greats like Harry Blackstone, Jr. Since the above sort of feat is expensive when purchased from a dealer, the craftsman-magician can save considerably with Palmer's construction plans. Bruce Postgate's *Dove Pan-Orama* explains novel employments for a utility item of the stage magician, the dove pan. As usually performed, the pan is shown empty, its lid is placed on top, and a moment later the pan is opened to reveal the production of a dove or rabbit. This piece of apparatus is a first choice among amateurs, for it is self-working. The lid, which is never shown empty, contains a load chamber that is automatically released in the act of covering the pan.

Few props can lend such beauty to an act as variegated silks. Harold R. Rice's *Encyclopedia of Silk Magic*, a three-volume work, is the definitive treatise on every phase of silk magic. This all-encompassing labor of love contains nearly six thousand illustrations and the entirely hand-lettered text totals over fifteen hundred pages. *Silks Supreme*, a booklet by Keith Clark, sets forth a graceful routine in which silks are produced, multiplied, and magically unknotted. *A Rhapsody in Silk*, by Ade Duval, presents an audience-tested act in which the standard prop known as the "Phantom Tube" plays a central role. Its double-wall construction allows the magician to extract silks from an apparently empty container. *Marconick's Silk Magic*, by Lewis Ganson and Hugh Miller, details the highly creative silk magic of one of Europe's most brilliant magical minds. *Silken Sorcery*, by Jean Hugard, offers a mini-course in silk magic by a first-rate practitioner and author of magic texts. Sleights, effects, routines, and related apparatus are all discussed in illuminating detail. *Tips on "Soft Soap,"* compiled by Gordon MacDonald, collects ideas and patter for the standard soft soap silk effect in which several silks that have been stained or marked are magically laundered. Excellent magicians such as Milbourne Christopher have contributed fresh suggestions for this reliable "sucker" trick. The expression "sucker trick" will be explained when magic for children is discussed. Few magicians who use silks have been able to resist using Walsh's vanishing cane, a prop that can be used with one or more silks. *Walsh Cane Routines*, by Francis B. Martineau, presents over three dozen ideas and routines for the collapsible cane, which was invented by Russ Walsh and subsequently adopted by myriad stage and nightclub magicians. Vanishes, color changes, and transformations are all treated. The potential user of this cane should be aware that its metal construction and the speed with which it snaps closed can cause cuts and scratches.

From its legendary associations with Hindu fakirs to the present, the rope has figured importantly in magic acts. *Abbott's Encyclopedia of Rope Tricks*, edited by Stewart James, is the unrivaled omnibus in the field. With a thousand pages and over fifteen hundred illustrations, this three-volume work covers every facet of rope magic. Dozens of magicians have contributed their favorite rope effects and ideas, making this study the definitive treatment of its subject. Harold Denhard's *How to Do Rope Tricks* is an excellent compilation of rope effects as practiced by contemporary greats like Tenkai. Some of the forty-two items in this valuable manual are tying and untying knots without letting go of the ends, spinning a knot, one hand rope tie, and Adcock's rope restoration. *Hocus Pocus: Rope and Scarf Tricks*, by Ib Permin, contains good, basic material for the neophyte. Those who seek advanced material on rope magic will enjoy Hugh Miller's booklet, *Rink's Original Rope Mysteries*. Lewis Ganson's *Give a Magician Enough Rope—And He'll Do a Trick!* offers choice rope routines by the author and his friends. These effects and routines are best approached by someone familiar with basic rope technique. Dariel Fitzkee's *Rope Eternal* is a veritable graduate course on how to cut a rope and restore it. The six basic methods, with many variations, should satisfy nearly every performing style.

Rope Royale, by Keith Clark, features material from the author's polished and much-admired night club act. This booklet explains the restoration of a rope that has been cut into three pieces rather than the usual two. Colored ropes also figure in Clark's routine. In his booklet *Stretching a Rope*, Milbourne Christopher explains alternative handlings for a standard item in the repertoire of numerous professionals. *Sands' Improved Ropesational*, by George Sands, describes one of the most staggering rope routines ever devised. Diligent practice is required to perfect this bewildering sequence of moves in which a rope is cut and restored several times; the ends of the rope change places with the center; the rope is stretched, knots appear, slide, and disappear, and jump from one end of the rope to the other. Sands' prediction that this routine will become a classic is apt to be fulfilled, for I have never seen a more impressive rope routine. *On Your Feet*, by Horace Bennett, presents magic that is equally amusing and amazing for the stand-up performer. All of his writings, whether in periodicals or books, set forth thoughtful, professional magic of the highest order. Bennett's "Amazing, Jumping, Flying, Sliding Knot" exemplifies his flair for uniting mirth and mystery.

The linking rings, metal bands that seemingly interpenetrate each other in a bewildering series of unions and separations, constitute a paradigm of stage magic. Dariel Fitzkee's *Rings on Your Fingers* is a standard reference work on the linking rings. This book remains as a definitive treatment, collecting in a single volume the accumulated thoughts of decades and perhaps centuries. In one chapter, Fitzkee outlines the actual routines employed by over a dozen great magicians such as the world famous Blackstone. Instruction is also given on how to create representational forms by manipulating a configuration of rings. Another classic contribution on the topic is Laurie L. Ireland's *The Ireland Linking Ring Routine*, an audience-pleasing sequence in which two spectators assist the magician. Because some of the action takes in the volunteers' hands, this routine packs a punch. With a running time of four minutes, the magician avoids the tedium of some longer routines. Those who are just as interested in amusing as they are in amazing will appreciate a recent booklet: *David Ginn's Comedy Linking Rings*, by Ginn, places emphasis upon laughter rather than subtle moves. The author is a working professional who specializes in entertaining children and performs over four hundred school shows every year. A number of Ginn's humorous touches can be used in routines for adults as well as children. That this booklet has gone through six printings testifies to its value. No one who does magic for children can afford to overlook this and other writings by the prolific Ginn.

Dai Vernon's Symphony of the Rings, by Lewis Ganson, is a masterful linking rings routine that uses a half dozen rings rather than the traditional eight to ten. The student who masters Vernon's presentation will be in command of the most aesthetic of all versions. It should be added that Vernon's "unlinking a solid ring" maneuver is one of the most brilliant subterfuges ever introduced in a linking rings routine. Another sophisticated routine is available in a booklet by Bob Novak. *Jack Miller's Linking Ring Routine*, by Novak, is a photographically illustrated text that presents an uncommonly complicated routine, parts of which are calculated to fool magicians themselves. Virtually every magician will find some new move, sleight, or twist that is of value. Miller's deceptive false count of the rings is a gem that fools the eyes even when the mind is aware of what is taking place. Unfortunately, the instructions for this complex routine are not as complete as they could be; thus, readers have difficulty comprehending certain phases. Magicians who have struggled in vain to understand the instructions in Robert Novak's *Jack Miller's Linking Ring Routine*, will be encouraged by George Gore's *The Linking Rings of Jack Miller*. The latter, being over twice as long as the former, is a more detailed account of a truly wonderful routine. In *Horace Bennett's Prize-Winning Magic*, Bennett details the ingredients in his smooth, flowing routines, which have entertained laymen and garnered accolades from magicians themselves. Bennett's witty and perplexing rendition of the linking rings (a presentation that draws from Miller) is a sophisticated gem in which one subtlety succeeds another. Finally, *The Ring Routine*, by Richard Ross, a two-time Grand Prix Champion of Magic recipient, exemplifies the fertility of contemporary magicians in developing innovative routines with the classic linking rings. The text is written in English, German, and French, thus making an international contribution to magic.

Would-be levitators will find uplifting material in the following three studies. Ian H. Adair's *A la Zombie—Plus* features several versions of the floating ball mystery that was made famous by great magicians like Okito. The title of this manual refers to a one-person method that is called the Zombie and which was popularized by the distinguished American magician Neil Foster. Anyone who has witnessed Foster's enthralling, artistic presentation will be interested in Adair's work. *Floating Ball Magic*, by Roy Fromer, is a good, brief overview of its announced topic, including a floating, illuminated light bulb variation. This last mystery is currently being featured by Harry Blackstone, Jr., whose father first popularized the feat. Henry Bohlen's *Bohleno's Five Original Performance-Proven Mysteries* features award-winning, manipulative stage routines, including his "Impossible Floating Handkerchief."

Those interested in levitating women must consult manuals on stage illusions, that is, feats using humans, large animals, or large props. Burling Hull's *Encyclopedia of Stage Illusions* is a lavish volume that is regarded as one of the best of its kind. Hull, sometimes viewed as a curmudgeon by his fellow magicians, will surely be remembered for his innovative contributions to various branches of magic. In *The Great Illusions of Magic*, compiled by Byron G. Wels, classic feats, as presented by such greats as Jack Gwynne, are lovingly detailed. The publisher, Louis Tannen Inc., is to be congratulated for helping to preserve these choice mysteries in a lavish, two-volume format. Whether one is interested in the "Thin Model Sawing a Woman in Half" or the "Agra Levitation," he or she will be delighted with Wels' precise elucidation of all details. Historical data, construction tips, and professional draftsman's plans (an advertisement states that such plans are included for the first time in an illusion text) make for one of the most enlightening studies of this kind. S.K.V. Kumar's *Illusionsesame* is a lavish and well-received explication of some of the most popular contemporary illusions. As an advertisement for Neil Foster's *Tops Treasury of Illusions* notes, "There are very few books on magic dealing with the subject of stage illusions." Foster has compiled sixty illusions by drawing from over three hundred issues of *Tops* magazine. Contents include vanishes, productions, and the levitation of a human being. One strong point of this compendium is that many of the illusions can be constructed for a modest cost. Those who wish to buy the secret of one particular illusion can often purchase individual blueprints from a magic dealer. More recently, Micky Hades has edited a worthwhile collection of illusions in a monograph that is entitled *The Conjuror's Book of Stage Illusions*.

As in the above work and the two that follow, the magician with a limited budget will be rewarded. *Tricks and Illusionettes*, by Joseph Ovette, is a booklet of flashy feats and illusions that the performer can construct himself. Such apparatus is considerably easier to transport than the usual full-scale illusions. In a similar vein, Tom Palmer's *Modern Illusions* details how to construct eleven practical illusions that can be easily transported in the family car. In the first half of the century, illusionists like Kellar required a train to carry their elaborate paraphernalia. For those who can read Japanese, Hakufu Hiraiwa's *Stage Magic Highlights* will be of interest. Albert A. Hopkins' *Magic: Stage Illusions and*

Scientific Diversions, Including Trick Photography is even more absorbing than its title would suggest. Large-scale, stage magic and related tricks of the theater are emphasized in this well-illustrated study. Written just before the turn of the century, with an introduction by Henry Ridgely Evans—which is itself a valuable if tantalizingly succinct history of magic from antiquity to the nineteenth century—the work will appeal to all lovers of magic, the theater, and Hollywood special effects. The principles underlying the production, vanish, and decapitation of a human being are pictorially revealed; the dodges of the sham psychic are exposed; and, optical tricks, such as the visible transformation of a person into a skeleton, are explained. The last item continues to be a feature of sideshows at fairs and carnivals today. In fact, a good deal of the magic presented by Hopkins is still fully capable of mystifying contemporary audiences. In some cases, the method used has been superseded by modern devices that are simpler (as in the case in the levitation of a woman illusion), but sometimes the method is no more obsolete than the effect. Brief chapters are devoted to jugglers, sword-swallowers, fire-eaters, ventriloquists, shadowgraphy, and the verbal codes of mind-reading teams. Temple tricks practiced by the Greeks are explored and the back-stage effects of the nineteenth-century theater are discussed at length. Chess-playing automatons and curious toys are also given consideration. Hopkins' treatment of trick photography culminates in a final chapter on moving pictures. Considering the date of its publication, this work is as comprehensive as one could ask for. Moreover, no single volume has ever appeared to rival or update Hopkins' wide-ranging, landmark book. One footnote on ventriloquism is in order. Although not a magician as such, the ventriloquist relies on misdirection to carry off the illusion of throwing his or her voice. If the performer's lips do not move, but the dummy's do, the spectator attends to the latter and thereby, in his own mind, transports the voice of the ventriloquist to the ventriloqual figure. A last sample work, Harbin's *Magic of Robert Harbin* concentrates upon illusions and explains his brilliant "Zig-Zag" mystery in which a woman appears to be divided into three parts. This particular illusion, a twentieth-century version of sawing a woman in half, has become very popular because it can be performed surrounded, without any stage settings, and at rather close range.

Given that most magic is performed for children, the practical performer will want to read books on magic directed toward youngsters. This is not to relegate magic to the level of children, for entertaining children need not be only an end in itself; rather, it can also be the means for gaining insight into how to reach the child within every adult. Totalling six volumes, written and published over a period of two decades, Frances Ireland Marshall's *Kid Stuff* is the uncontested encyclopedia for magicians who entertain children. Marshall draws upon the experience of dozens of children's entertainers as well as her own extensive background. The result is a genuine treasury of material and ideas on virtually all aspects of performing magic for youngsters. Topics include magic and fire prevention shows, patter for kids, magic for kids in hospitals, birthday party magic, school shows, and routining. *Open Sesame*, by Eric C. Lewis and Wilfred Tyler, has been praised by Robert Gill as "the best work on children's magic ever written." While subsequent writings of the highest quality have appeared, this is surely one of the finest and most sustained elaborations of conjuring for children. *Conjuring for Children*, by William W. Larsen, is a booklet that has been a best-seller because of its straightforward, laugh-provoking material. Others who specialize in entertaining children, such as Sid Lorraine, have categorically recommended this collection of a dozen items.

The obvious appeal of the clown is sometimes wedded to that of magic. *How to Be a Magic Clown*, by Ernie Kerns, serves as an excellent introduction to the art of conjuring as a clown. Items discussed include clown names, make-up, costumes, gags, and bits of business. The author, a veteran of both live and televised performances, speaks to all would-be clown magicians, whether they wish to practice their skills for fun or profit. In *How to Be a Magic Clown, Volume 2*, Ernie Kerns examines wardrobe ideas, special props, and how to book one's act; Fred Olsen discusses clown magic, juggling, and other bits of business; and G. Elmer Jones offers further ideas on how to find work, gags, and costuming. *The Bongo Book*, by Ali Bongo (pseudonym for William Wallace), contains the creations of one of the best clown-magicians in the field. His act was judged to be the best of the year on a popular children's television show. *Professional Magic for Children*, by David Ginn, is a definitive treatise on all aspects of performing magic for children. He regards it as the best of his thirty-three publications. What the great children's entertainer Gene Gordon said about *Kidbiz* surely applies to the present book, "Anybody who can't get a raft of ideas and useful material from this book should have his head examined. Magic will thank you for writing this book." Just as valuable as his colorful, lively magic routines are Ginn's theoretical observations on topics such as the relation between children and magic, the mechanics of children's shows, and the psychology of handling child hecklers. Whether he is dissecting the nature of "sucker tricks" (effects in which the magician seems to have failed, but in the end, triumphs; or effects in which the spectators think they have detected the magician's method, but in the end, they are proved wrong) or describing his approach to birthday party shows, Ginn generously shares what he has learned by performing before millions in live appearances and on dozens of television programs. *Kidbiz*, another of Ginn's books that are devoted to entertaining children, contains over five hundred items (effects, routines, gags, bits of business) by the author and some of his magician friends. No pipe dreams or impractical ideas will be found in this audience-tested, professional material. *Children Laugh Louder*, also by Ginn, is an excellent sequel to his highly successful *Professional Magic for Children*. Ten routines direct from his shows before thousands of children are carefully detailed. One chapter, "Comedy Bits with Audience Volunteers," presents over fifty ideas for creating amusement with one's assistant; in short, the book is typically "Ginn" in its fusion of comedy and conjuring. Another well-regarded offering, *Doing Magic for Youngsters: Including the Art of Con-*

juring to Children, by Bert Easley and Eric P. Wilson, contains fine, child-pleasing magic as practiced by some of the best children's entertainers.

The following works treat such elements of stagecraft as routining, scenery and sets, costumes, and music. Señor Mardo's *The Act* concentrates upon creating an act rather than the mechanics of individual effects. Fifteen sample routines are given in order to stimulate the reader's thinking on the arrangement of an act. Most of the props discussed by the author are standard dealer items. Since art often involves uniting different elements into a commanding whole, attention to the organization of magic effects into a flowing act is of the utmost importance. In *New Look for the Magic Show*, R. E. Arthur offers suggestions for enlivening one's act through colorful scenery (including translucent backgrounds) and stage settings. This booklet of fresh ideas is a one-of-a-kind item. *The Magician's Assistant*, by Jan Jones and friends, will be of value to stage magicians, but armchair magicians and historians of magic will be fascinated by its many pages of rare photographs and anecdotes. Just as appropriate music enhances the impact of a film without distracting from it, good assistants improve the magician's presentation without diverting attention from him or her—except, of course, when misdirection is required. *Illusion Show Know-How*, by Ken and Roberta Griffin, discloses the inner workings that underlie the mounting of a large-scale magic show. Having toured worldwide with their own illusion show for over a quarter of a century, the authors draw from a wealth of experience. All aspects of an illusion show are treated including routining, showmanship, illustrated instructions for the construction of fifteen illusions, scenery, costumes, advertising, make-up, lighting, music, and manners for magicians. Whether one is interested in entering the illusion show field, a rare phenomenon these days, or one simply wants to vicariously experience a typical day with a touring magic show, the Griffins' book is a delight. Henry Hay's *Cyclopedia of Magic* covers some of the same features of stage magic that are discussed in the Griffins' book. Stage magicians may wish to consult George Armstrong's discussion of make-up in *Tricks of the Trade*. *Dorny on Trix* presents the often hilarious magical stylings of one of Chicago's favorite sons, Werner C. Dornfield. One chapter is given over to suggestions for appropriate music, a topic that is usually overlooked.

Other writings are devoted to utility techniques, props, and accessories. Eddie Joseph's *The Art of Body Loading and Production*, a one-of-a-kind manual, enables the performer to secretly load objects into the spectator's pockets, under his coat, and elsewhere and then create surprise and laughter by extracting these items. In recent years this hilarious form of conjuring has virtually disappeared. Perhaps magicians have discounted this variety of magic because the procedures employed are sometimes rather crude, but it should not be forgotten that it is the effect and not the means that counts. And, as it turns out, spectators tend to love being amazed and amused by body loads. Francis B. Martineau's *Victory Bouquet* is a booklet on how to make the highly compressible, feather flower bouquets that have long been employed by stage magicians. Given that such flowers command a high price in magic shops, the cost-conscious magician will appreciate this exposition. *Hold-Out Miracles*, by Ed Mishell, reaffirms the utility of the gimmick that is commonly known as a hold-out, a gadget that can invisibly pull an object out of one's hand and into one's sleeve or indetectably deliver an object from one's sleeve into one's hand. Mishell concentrates upon applying the hold-out to standard effects such as the cut and restored rope and the egg bag. *Black Art Well Tricks*, by Charlie Miller, cleverly explores the magical possibilities of a gimmicked table top in which a hole and pocket are invisible because the latter is made of the same black material as the surface of the table. Those who think this device is obsolete may change their minds after reading Miller's engaging study. *Reel Magic*, by Albenice, is a monograph devoted to effects that are made possible by the concealed gimmick that is known as a reel (a device that mechanically rewinds a length of thread). In addition to the classic mystery in which a knotted silk visibly unties itself, feats with cards, ropes, cigarettes, bills, and rings are detailed. In *Reelistic Magic*, Lewis Ganson further demonstrates the possibilities of the reel.

MISCELLANEOUS MAGIC AND RELATED SKILLS

Under the heading of "miscellaneous" are writings devoted to distinctive props, specialized audiences, sensational feats, science and math principles, pickpocketing, and con games. Because money is of universal interest, Jack Lamonte's *Stunts with Stage Money* features routines with built-in audience appeal. One witty American magician, Harry Anderson, has cleverly exploited the humorous possibilities of a torn and restored bill effect in a number of recent television appearances. The more homely paper on which news is printed comes into the spotlight in one outstanding work. *Newspaper Magic* by Gene Anderson and Frances Marshall, includes the outstanding "visible" or flash restoration of torn pieces, which was featured by Doug Henning on Broadway in the play *The Magic Show*.

Audiences of Christians and Jews are addressed in two recent discussions. David Allin's *Magic for the Master* caters to the clergyman who wishes to practice what is known as gospel magic, that is, magic that is employed in the service of religious instruction. Ministers who use magic to enhance their preaching or teaching do, of course, become vulnerable to criticism. It has been argued, for instance, that such activities degrade religion through guilt by association with mere trickery. Some psychologists would add that critics are disturbed by gospel magic because it brings to mind primitive societies in which religion and magic were interfused. Aldini's *New Concepts in Magic* is distinguished by its inclusion of material that is intended to be used at Bar Mitzvahs and other Jewish events. Those who enjoy do-it-yourself projects will be pleased that the plans for a rabbit vanish were drawn by an architect.

Those intrigued by sensational feats will enjoy the following quartet. In *Thrilling Magic*, by Leonard H. Miller, the author divulges the secrets of such sensational stunts as fire-eating, sword-swallowing, and "Driving a Spike into the Head." Why the public regards these feats of pseudo-masochism as vulgar, but does not feel similarly about sawing woman in half, is an interesting question for the psychologist. Clettis Musson's *Fire Magic* is a standard monograph on fire-eating and numerous other fire effects. It should be noted that virtually all fire-eaters have had accidents at one time or another. Gerald Taylor's *The Classical Technique of Fire Eating* is an authoritative manual that is frequently cited as the best book on its subject. Albert A. Hopkins' *Magic: Stage Illusions and Scientific Diversions, Including Trick Photography* contains short chapters on fire-eating and sword-swallowing. The former can be traced to the third century before Christ in ancient Greece, where it was practiced by some jugglers.

Escape artistry may be best approached through the stunts of its greatest achiever. *Houdini's Escapes: Edited from Houdini's Private Notebooks and Memoranda*, compiled by Walter B. Gibson, is a basic work on escapology as practiced by the world's most famous exponent. While magicians themselves distinguish between magic and escapes, the general public does not. In *Houdini's Fabulous Magic*, by Walter Gibson and Morris Young, a number of Houdini's favorite escape stunts and magic effects are explained. It is interesting that the nonmagician sometimes harbors the romantic belief that Houdini's secrets and those of other great magicians are still closely guarded. But, in fact, a great deal of all such material has been published in books that are to be found in any large public library. *Houdini on Magic*, also coauthored by Gibson and Young, details Houdini's technique for picking locks, escaping from a strait jacket, and his discussion of famous magicians and frauds. Harry Houdini's *Handcuff Secrets*, published nearly three-quarters of a century ago, remains an unsurpassed compendium on picking locks, gimmicked cuffs, and escape techniques. *Magical Rope Ties and Escapes*, also by Houdini, is another required treatise for all performers who aspire to become escape artists.

Scientific or mathematical principles are thematic in a number of recent studies. *Handbook of Chemical Magic*, by Earl Leamon, presents liquid color changes, smoke and fire items, invisible ink stunts, and other effects, all based on simple applications of chemistry. Walter Gibson's *Magic with Science: Scientific Tricks, Demonstrations, and Experiments for Home, Classes, Science Clubs, and Magic Shows* can serve as a fine introduction to magic for the scientifically inclined reader. *Magic with Electronics*, by Bud Morris, is a specialized study in which some fundamental principles of electronics are applied in the creation of several impressive effects. *Math Miracles*, by Wallace Lee, contains material on the magic square, mind-reading, cryptograms, and puzzles. This sort of material is well received by math lovers, but some sleight-of-hand specialists find it boring. In *Mathematical Magic*, Bill Simon, an accomplished sleight-of-hand artist, presents effective feats in which mathematical principles rather than dexterity, are at work. *Mathematics, Magic, and Mystery* is Martin Gardner's engaging survey of feats based upon mathematical principles and numbers. As one might expect, card effects are prominent, but the author also explains items with coins, dice, watches, and other household objects. One chapter discusses topological mysteries, and two others focus upon geometrical paradoxes. Readers will appreciate the fact that this book itself is a magic prop, for at the start of each new chapter, the fifteenth word is always ''of''; this fact, coupled with the performer's ability to force the spectator's choice of a number, permits the magician to perform a prediction mystery.

Some of the works that treat con games or criminal activities were once sold under the counter or surreptitiously. Today such writings may be purchased over the counter in any well-stocked magic shop. Eddie Joseph's *How to Pick Pockets* is one of the relatively few works devoted exclusively to its topic. The author begins with a statement on ''The Theory and Fundamental Principle of Pickpocketing.'' This is followed by instruction in the actual practice of stealing from both inner and outer pockets. Advertising by the publisher judiciously suggests that this material should be used in a stage act for entertainment purposes only. In *Pierre Jacques' Complete Course in Pickpocketing*, the subject is richly explored by one of Europe's most accomplished practitioners of the art. Contents include secretly removing watch bands, wallets, ties, belts, and even the shirt off a spectator's back. That pickpockets who limit their activity to performing on stage can sometimes earn more than those who use their skill to steal gives some credence to the cliché that crime does not pay. *The Pickpocket Secrets of Mark Raffles* is a book-length study of the techniques of pickpocketing, which some regard as the definitive text. Raffles, like Jacques and Eddie Joseph, treats pickpocketing as a form of stage entertainment. Limited to five hundred numbered and signed copies, this is a relatively rare book.

Houdini's *The Right Way to Do Wrong: An Expose of Successful Criminals* treats such engrossing topics as burglary, pickpocketing, tricks of the bunco men, famous swindles, and cheating Uncle Sam. *''Step Right Up, Folks!''* by Al Griffin, exposes some of the gaffs or cheating techniques of game operators at amusement parks and carnivals. In addition to obvious ploys, like rigging a roulette wheel, Griffin discusses such amusing rip offs as the ''Mouse Run'' in which the mark or sucker bets on which path a mouse (that happens to be male) will take when allowed to run free. The operator can control the mouse's direction by placing a drop of vinegar at the desired location, for the smell of vinegar approximates the scent of the female mouse. Ralph Mayer's *Short Changed* details the technique whereby one can short change the clerk at a cash register. Through a number of confusing procedures, the clerk is led to return too much cash in change to the operator. This sort of bilker can be thwarted by the clerk who insists upon slowing down the complicated transaction. *The Short Change Artist: Bullshit*, by W. M. Tucker, divulges the methods of the professional shoplifter as well as the short-change artist. The author's study achieves redeeming social value through its exposition of preventive measures by which the store clerk can protect himself or herself. For some related practices of the cheat, see the previously cited works on card magic (marked cards, three card monte, etc.) and on close-up chicanery (the three shell game, loaded dice, and other deceits).

SPIRITUALISM AND MENTAL MAGIC

In spiritualism and mental magic, the performer simulates demonstrations of supernatural phenomena and extrasensory perception. What makes these two forms of conjuring unique is that sophisticated, contemporary audiences, who naturally regard all other types of magic as trickery, are often quite gullible when it comes to the feats of the bogus medium or mentalist. Burling ''Volta'' Hull's *The Encyclopedic Dictionary of Mentalism* is a definitive overview of mental magic and related activities such as hypnosis. Hundreds of routines, effects, secrets, and principles are treated in this mammoth work. Volume two includes items like Robert Nelson's ''Miracle Prediction,'' a feat with which the adept performer can garner considerable publicity. Volume three features a practical form of so-called spirit photography in which the performer causes any symbol, message, or image to appear in a photograph that has been taken with a Polaroid camera. As a bonus, ten feats from Robert Nelson are also explained. In fine, this encyclopedia is essential reading for the mentalist who wishes to be thoroughly conversant with his art.

Tony Corinda's *Thirteen Steps to Mentalism: A Step-by-Step Course on Mental and Allied Arts* is an award-winning, lesson by lesson exposition of the gimmicks, principles, procedures, and secrets of a world-famous mentalist. The wide-ranging contents are as follows:

Step 1. The Swami Gimmick (nail writers of all kinds and their uses)
Step 2. Pencil, Lip, Sound, Touch, and Muscle Reading
Step 3. Mnemonics and Mental Systems
Step 4. Predictions
Step 5. Blindfolds and X Ray Eyes
Step 6. Billets
Step 7. Book Tests
Step 8. Two Person Telepathy
Step 9. Mediumistic Stunts
Step 10. Card Tricks
Step 11. Question and Answer Effects
Step 12. Publicity Stunts
Step 13. Patter and Presentation

In the October 1983 issue of *The Linking Ring*, Phil Willmarth in ''Starting in Mentalism—An Unorthodox View'' praises Marvin Kaye's *The Handbook of*

Mental Magic as an ideal primer. Since Willmarth's thoughtful remarks can be of real value, especially to the novice, we will quote from him at length:

> Newcomers to mentalism are often advised to begin their study with Annemann's *Practical Mental Effects* and Corinda's *Thirteen Steps to Mentalism.* The traditional list of "must" reading also often includes the major works of Robert Nelson, supplemented by such authors as Burling Hull and George B. Anderson. My feeling is that this is not a good way to start. Several of these works make for rather tedious reading, contain few routines a newcomer will actually use and, all in all, can possibly do more to discourage a budding mentalist than to encourage him. Also, they tend to give a false impression that mentalism must be based on billet switches, center tears, impression boards, verbal codes, nail writers, and other techniques that are somewhat passé nowadays . . . fortunately for the modern newcomer to mental magic, more recent writings provide a much better way to start out. By first reading the newer works, the mentalism novice can build a foundation on which to appreciate the books usually recommended. For a well-represented overview of the traditional techniques of mentalism, read Marvin Kaye's little-known *The Handbook of Mental Magic* (Stein and Day, 1975). You will find it to be a far better-written introduction to the field than is the Corinda volume (65–66).

Students of mentalism should read Willmarth's entire statement in the above-mentioned periodical for further reading suggestions. As its title would suggest, *Self-Working Mental Magic*, by Karl Fulves, contains material suitable for the beginner. Experienced magicians will, however, profit from Fulves' twists, refinements, and tips on presentation. Subtleties supersede the need for dexterity in this choice collection of direct, mental mysteries. *Close-Up Mental Magic*, also by Fulves, caters to the mentalist who prefers working under intimate conditions. Effects include a demonstration of psychokinesis in which the performer appears to change the position of a card merely by thinking about it. Effects with cards, sometimes gimmicked cards, prevail in Fulves' fresh look at mentalism. Knowledgeable magicians will be especially interested in Fulves' approach to "Brainwave," a dealer item that enables the performer to show that the spectator's mentally selected card is the only one reversed in a deck and has a different back design. Fulves has distinguished himself by the quantity, diversity, and quality of his writings, especially in the area of close-up card magic. Jack Yates' *Minds in Close-Up: A Collection of Mental Mysteries Using Small Accessories* has been hailed by Robert Gill as "a superb collection of mental items for close quarters." Readers will be impressed by Yates' direct methods and the entertainment value of his material. *Gems of Mental Magic*, by Arthur Buckley and John B. Cook, first published at mid-century, has become a standard text. The authors treat effects for small groups, stage audiences, and publicity stunts. Most of the feats require no assistant or confederate (a "confederate" or "stooge" pretends to be a member of the audience, but is actually the performer's ally). George Anderson's *It Must be Mindreading!* is a classic primer in the literature of mental magic in which the author gives his own twist to standard prediction, clairvoyance, and mindreading effects. Anderson concludes his monograph with a chapter on practical suggestions for the would-be mentalist and a short bibliography. In a sequel, *You, Too, Can Read Minds!* Anderson explains more professional material, from divination tests to a gimmicked blindfold in the same engaging style.

C. L. Boarde's two-volume work, *Mainly Mental*, belongs in the library of every would-be mentalist. Volume one deals with billet reading (secretly discerning the message that a spectator has written), a standard ploy in the arsenal of the mentalist. Volume two has been justifiably heralded as the authoritative exposition on book tests (in these experiments, the performer mysteriously discerns or predicts the spectator's choice of one or more words from a book). Boarde presents over seventy methods and refinements of his own. A widely recognized peer, Al Baker, has made a similarly valuable contribution to the literature of mentalism. His *Mental Magic* is a classic introduction to the secrets and subterfuges of the mentalist. In addition to the effects themselves, Baker spells out his philosophy of mentalism.

Magic of the Mind, by Lewis Ganson, has been described by Robert Gill as "the best collection of mental magic since the publication of Annemann's works." Certainly no student of mentalism can afford to overlook this anthology of more than fifty effects by Ganson and other experts in the field. Ormond McGill's *Psychic Magic* is a one-volume, revised edition of six booklets by the same name that were published at mid-century. These writings and others by McGill have found their niche in the literature of mentalism. Areas covered, sometimes in a skeletal way, include telepathy, clairvoyance, crystal gazing, psychometry, X-ray vision, animal magnetism, psychic phenomena, automatic writing, trance phenomena, astral projection, spirit manifestations, ectoplasm, table tipping, East Indian mysteries, and levitation. *Twenty-One Gems of Magic*, by Ormond McGill, contains material for the mentalist or spiritualist; topics include telepathy, a book test, and the spirit seance.

Life and Mysteries of the Celebrated Dr. Q, by C. Alexander and published in the first quarter of this century, is a penetrating investigation of favorite stratagems in the arsenal of the magician who purports to be a mind-reader. *Practical Mental Effects*, with more than three hundred pages, stands as Theodore Annemann's major contribution to the literature of mentalism. This superb compilation of nearly two hundred feats earned him the prestigious "Genii Award" which was conferred by Bill Larsen, editor of *Genii* magazine. Among Annemann's writings, which have inspired myriad would-be mentalists, are *Incorporated Strange Secrets*, *Mental Bargain Effects: Eleven Miracles of Mentalism*, *Mental Club Act: A Completely Routined and Fully Described Thirty-Minute Act for One Person*, and *No Code Telepathy: A Completely Routined Act Demonstrating Pseudo Telepathy between Two People*. James Auer's monograph, *The Spirit Is Willing*, adds spiritualistic themes to standard material on mentalism. Contents also include patter, an opening lecture, and a bibliography. Quite often the mentalists' opening remarks and subsequent patter are calculated to suggest that he or she actually possesses extraordinary mental powers. Fellow magicians, who know that sheer trickery is at work, sometimes question the morality of leaving such an impression with an audience, for it may render spectators more vulnerable to fraudulent mediums and other practitioners of fakery. Ironically, those mentalists who explicitly deny any abnormal powers, by virtue of reverse psychology, manage to convince the audience that they do, indeed, possess such powers. Some fellow magicians dislike mentalists, because they dub themselves "psychics" or "psychic entertainers," as if to imply disdain toward magic and magicians.

One generation after Annemann, Robert Nelson held sway as the mentalist's tutor. Nelson's *Sensational Mentalism* is the first work in which the author explains closely guarded secrets from his own act and from other noted mentalists. *Sensational Mentalism: Part Two* is the sequel to the above monograph, and *Still More Miracles in Mentalism* is one of Nelson's longer compilations of mental effects. In his *Super Prediction Tricks*, Nelson features nearly two dozen dramatic predictions by which the mentalist can gain publicity. Tips on presentation accompany the secrets themselves.

Nelson's booklet, *TV Mentalism*, provides apt suggestions for the mentalist who aspires to perform on television. Numerous appearances on network television by Kreskin, a contemporary American mentalist, demonstrate that TV is a viable medium for the mentalist of today, just as it was for Joseph Dunninger in the past. *Comedy Mentalism*, also by Robert A. Nelson, consists of three monographs for the performer who wishes to inject humor into his act. Given that some mentalists take themselves too seriously and adopt a pompous posture, Nelson's work can restore entertainment value to such performers' routines. David Hoy's *Bold and Subtle Miracles of Dr. Faust* contains the attention-getting brand of mental magic that has earned the author bookings on TV, nightclub circuits, and at universities throughout the country. This sort of material is just what is needed as an antidote for many mentalism acts in which the pace is tedious and the patter is pretentious and garrulous. For whatever reason, mentalists are prone to confuse what is prolix with what is profound. Hoy's "Tossed Out Deck" mystery, in which a pack of cards is tossed into the audience for the spectator's choice of a card, is indeed both bold and baffling.

Mentalistrix, by the Edward Maurice (pseudonym for Morris Cohen), contains twenty-five feats which have been hailed as practical, uncomplicated, and stunning. Burling Hull, a celebrated figure in mental magic, pays tribute to Maurice in the introduction. Maurice's sequel to this monograph, *Mentalistrix Encore*, explains twenty-five more mental effects with ordinary objects in the author's commendable, streamlined style.

"Mind" Your Magic, by Charles W. Cameron, emphasizes straightforward mentalism in which subtlety substitutes for skill. Practical, tested material prevails, with some attention to occult themes. *Mentalism à la Mode*, by Paul Siegal, features a fresh assortment of mysteries for the psychic entertainer. The author is interested in how to establish oneself as a mentalist rather than simply as a magician, for credibility attaches itself to the former alone. *S'Komplimentary*

Mentalism, by Stephen Skomp, is a booklet of two audience-tested mental routines; among them is a prediction, a telephone test, and the author's original handling for Hen Fetsch's classic pyschic effect, "Mental Epic." The latter, a dealer item, is a triple prediction that has been widely adopted by mentalists. *Patterns for Psychics*, by Peter Warlock, contains the sort of clever, effective material that makes other mentalists indebted to its author.

Micro-Mental Mysteries, by Joseph White, details twenty-one complete routines for the mentalist who wishes to avoid the need for great skill or elaborate equipment. *5 Micro-Mental Programs* is a sequel in which White carefully explains practical material for five half-hour acts. *Between Two Minds*, by James G. Thompson and Ned Rutledge, presents telepathic and supersensory demonstrations for the magician as well as the mentalist. An impressive newspaper prediction is one of the highlights in this collection of entertaining mysteries.

Representative specialized studies include Frank Chapman's *Twenty Stunners with a Nail Writer*, which explores the amazing prediction and telepathy feats that are made possible by a small, secret writing device that attaches to the performer's thumbnail. Teral Garrett's *Twenty-Six Living and Dead Tests* explains and analyzes various versions of a standard feat in which the mentalist demonstrates a puzzling ability to distinguish between the names of strangers who are living and those who are dead. *Sealed Vision*, by Will Dexter, is a specialized monograph that explains what are sometimes called feats of sightless vision. In these dramatic stunts, the performer, after having been carefully and elaborately blindfolded, unequivocally demonstrates his ability to see; this may, for example, take the form of driving a car through an obstacle course. Dexter's discussion of the various techniques is both literally and figuratively insightful. *Intuitional Sight*, by Eddie Joseph, fully explains the sort of sensational "sightless vision" act by which one performer received space in the Ripley's "Believe It or Not" newspaper column. Moist dough is placed over the performer's eyes; this is followed by cotton patches, a surgical bandage and, finally, two handkerchiefs. Despite his elaborate blindfold, the "seer" demonstrates his ability to read messages, describe objects, separate colored objects, and so on. It is difficult to imagine other feats in which such a minimum of means can have such a maximum of effect.

En Rapport, by Theodore Annemann, has become a classic text, as have virtually all of this ingenious author's writings. This booklet reveals the code for a two person mentalism act. Within a code, the mere expression of a question can secretly convey the desired answers. *The Master Code*, by Robert Nelson, is the author's preferred code for a two-person team of mentalist and assistant. Ken De Courcy's *Meshed Minds* presents one of the most unobtrusive codes for a two-person mind-reading routine. While such an act is uncommon today, it does have the potential for great amusement as well as amazement; the author's thorough treatment leaves nothing to be desired. *Minds in Duplicate: Easy-to-Do Mental Mysteries for Two People*, by Jack Yates, reveals the secrets for a two-person mind-reading act. Simplicity is the keynote in the author's approach to this potentially commercial form of magic. Finally, *How to Develop Mental Magic*, by Paul R. Hadley, is a veritable course in all aspects of the two-person mental act. In addition to his sophisticated verbal code, the author presents suggestions on presentation and on how to obtain bookings. Drawing upon many years of experience as a professional mentalist, the author discusses all the elements of a proven act that can be presented impromptu and without special apparatus.

One-Man Mental Magic, by Milbourne Christopher, details an entire act for the mentalist who prefers to work without any assistant. *More One-Man Mental Magic*, Milbourne Christopher's sequel to *One-Man Mental Magic*, presents another complete act for the mentalist who works alone. This booklet, like its predecessor, is marked by good practical material. *The Art of Cold Reading*, by Robert A. Nelson, instructs the would-be mentalist in the art of discerning and revealing information about the life of a complete stranger whom one has just met. Cold reading consists in making intelligent guesses about a stranger and then tracing out the implications in his responses to these guesses in order to make further remarks about his life, experiences, background, and so on. A talented cold reader, who appeals to universal wants and needs, can create the impression that he is genuinely psychic. *A Sequel to the Art of Cold Reading* gives Nelson's further thoughts on this popular stratagem of the pseudo-psychic. Similarly, *Psychotechnics* (two cassettes) by Myriam Ruthchild offers instruction by audio-tape in the techniques by which the mentalist can discern facts about a complete stranger. *Contact Mind-Reading Expanded*, by Dariel Fitzkee, analyzes the technique and the bewildering effects made possible by muscle-reading. This technique allows one to perform feats of divination through tactile clues. A related work, *Practical Contact Mind-Reading*, by Edward R. Schatz, delves into such topics as psychological mind-reading and emphasizes muscle-reading. With the latter skill, one can literally find a needle that others have hidden in a large auditorium. Obviously, this sort of stunt can result in great publicity for the mentalist. In the booklet *Sound Mentalism*, Sam Dalal reveals his favorite substitute for muscle-reading.

The Best Tricks with Slates, by Peter Warlock, is required reading for all who wish to practice or simply understand mentalism. With commendable thoroughness the author surveys effects with ordinary slates (these require manipulation), the use of the flap (a black rectangle that is used to cover and conceal writing on the surface of a slate), mechanical slates and accessories, chemical writing, and other subtleties. An exposé of the subterfuges used by phony mediums and a bibliography round out this valuable monograph. *Mini-Slate Magic*, by Lewis Ganson, is a booklet that explores novel possibilities for the pocket-sized version of the well-known effect in which writing inexplicably appears on the surface of a pair of slates that have been previously shown to be blank. *Fifty Sealed Message Reading Methods*, by Burling Hull, instructs one in the basic techniques by which he or she can ascertain secret messages that have been sealed in an opaque container such as an envelope. Such readings are a part of the stock-in-trade of mentalists and bogus mediums. Robert Nelson's booklet *How to Read Sealed Messages* also reveals various methods for discovering the contents of such messages. Jean Hugard's *Mental Magic with Cards* is a helpful booklet for the cardician who wishes to incorporate mentalism in his act. Simplicity and effectiveness are the hallmarks of Hugard's effects. Card workers will again find practical effects by cardicians like Gerald Kosky in William W. Larsen's anthology, *Mental Mysteries with Cards*. All of the over twenty feats can be performed with a borrowed deck; this fact will help dispel the spectator's suspicion that any specially prepared cards or trickery is at work. Warren Wiersbe's *Mental Cases with Cards* presents solid mental effects and routines for the card magician who appreciates brisk, direct material. *Paul Curry Presents*, by Curry, contains several versions of the author's classic ESP effect, ''Out of This World.'' In this mental mystery, the spectator himself or herself separates the red cards from the black ones—without looking at the faces of the cards. Surely any mentalist would include this gem in his top ten feats with playing cards. *Magic with an E.S.P. Deck*, by Sam Dalal, details several impressive but easy mental effects that are designed for use with a special deck of cards that has E.S.P. symbols rather than the usual face values. In a typical effect, the author relies upon a set-up of the cards as opposed to skill. Nick Trost's *E.S.P. Session with Nick Trost* is another booklet devoted to simple but effective feats of mentalism using cards with the five E.S.P. symbols instead of conventional faces. *Stage Mentalism*, by North Bigbee, concentrates upon large-scale, flashy feats for the stage performer. No playing cards are employed in the author's wide-ranging collection of mental effects. Some mentalists believe that it is wise to avoid cards, for they are associated with sleight of hand and chicanery. John D. Pomeroy's monograph, *Mentology*, will also appeal to those who seek to avoid apparatus that arouses suspicion because it appears unnatural.

In the following books, spiritualism or the occult is thematic. Reginald Scot's *The Discoverie of Witchcraft*, published in 1584, is recognized as the first book in English to expose the secrets of conjuring. Motivated by a desire to end the cruelties of witchcraft trials, Scot revealed that legerdemain was accomplished by natural means rather than any diabolical intervention. For interesting comments on the significance of Scot's exposé, see Edwin A. Dawes' *The Great Illusionists*. King James regarded the book as so heretical that he commanded that all copies be burned. Scot's work was so informative on the subject of witches and witch trials that it survived as a much-consulted manual during the seventeenth and eighteenth centuries. Contemporary students of witchcraft will find Scot's book to be among the relatively few primary sources for the study of the black arts. *Cagliostro: A Sorcerer of the Eighteenth Century*, by Henry Ridgely Evans, is a revealing study of the Italian charlatan who seemed to possess supernatural powers. Such deceivers have always had much to fear from the professional magician who has the knowledge to expose them. *Modern Spiritualism*, by John Nevil Maskelyne, was written by a magician whose expertise in exposing frauds was recognized by the Crown of England, for just after the publication of this book, Maskelyne was summoned to testify against the bogus medium, Henry Slade. On the strength of Maskelyne's revealing testimony, Slade was sentenced to jail; but, alas, he escaped his fate because of a technicality.

Readers may wish to compare Frank Podmore's *Modern Spiritualism* with Maskelyne's book of the same title. Both works were published in London, but the latter preceded the former by a quarter of a century. A related study, Rev. C. M. Davies' *Mystic London; or, Phases of Occult Life in the Metropolis*, will appeal to those interested in a nineteenth-century account of spiritualism in London.

Stanley Collins' *Confessions of a Medium*, which was originally published in 1882, preceded Houdini's exposé of fraudulent psychics by over three decades. *Houdini's Spirit Exposes: From Houdini's Own Manuscripts, Records, and Photographs, and Dunninger's Pyschical Investigations*, by Joseph Dunninger, presents the findings of two prominent American magicians in their battle against spurious mediums. In 1924, two years before his untimely death, Harry Houdini's *A Magician among the Spirits* was published in New York. This exposé of fraudulent mediums reflects the author's obsession with debunking the many tricksters who masqueraded as genuine psychics. As a world famous magician and premier escape artist, Houdini had impeccable credentials for his campaign against such cheats. That these charlatans still abound today is no criticism of Houdini and other crusaders who have presented their findings to the public; instead, it is a criticism of the general public, which has ignored any such data and has been driven by wishful thinking. *Miracle Mongers and Their Methods*, also by Houdini, is a study that is related to the above book and is an equally enlightening exposé. In *Spirit Mediums Exposed*, by Samri Frikell (pseudonym for Fulton Oursler), the author reveals the techniques of bogus mediums; not surprisingly, he draws upon material from Houdini's own investigations. *Behind the Scenes with the Mediums*, by David P. Abbott, explains the techniques of the fradulent medium as practiced in the early part of this century. Today practitioners still employ many of the methods or principles that are explained in fascinating detail by the author.

Beware Familiar Spirits, by the distinguished magician and historian of magic, John Mulholland, is an illuminating discussion of psychic phenomena as presented by sham mediums and magicians. Originally published in the first half of this century, a recent edition carries a sage introduction by Martin Gardner. This volume could hardly be more topical, for the annual crop of suckers shows no signs of diminishing. Of course, few potential victims ever bother to read such literature, but Mulholland, at least, has made it available. Mulholland's critical survey begins with the infamous Fox sisters in whose presence inexplicable rapping sounds were produced. Eventually it was discovered that a kind of toe-snapping was responsible for the exotic noises. On the topic of skeptics and believers, Mulholland comments wisely, "Both these groups always come with their minds made up beforehand and no matter what occurs take it as proof backing their own opinions." His account of the Davenport brothers (there is nothing chauvinistic about the history of fraudulent mediums) reveals that they used the secrets of the escape artist to free themselves from restraints and played musical instruments during their pseudo-seances. If there is one recurring motif or moral in this study, it is that despite the frequency with which mediums have been detected in acts of fraud, there remains an illustrious list of sympathizers. Among such believers were Elizabeth Barrett Browning (Robert Browning was, however, a skeptic, proving that being a romantic is not tantamount to surrendering one's critical faculties), Alexander Dumas, John Ruskin, Sir Arthur Conan Doyle (whose character "Sherlock" demonstrated such exemplary logical thinking), and Alfred Russel Wallace (who, together with Darwin, advanced the theory of evolution). Some contemporary scientists at Stanford University, who were conned by Uri Geller, can be added to this list. Of course, there have always been equally eminent figures who took a dim view of mediums and openly denounced them. Mulholland cites Charles Dickens as one example. That the latter was a vocal critic of psychics is not surprising, for Dickens was an accomplished amateur magician and thereby in an excellent position to detect the tricks of the bogus spiritualist. Other topics treated in Mulholland's absorbing investigation include slate-writing mysteries, supply houses for apparatus used by pseudo-psychics, and courtroom battles. Mulholland concludes his book with a disclaimer; he emphasizes that he is not denying the existence of real psychic phenomena; in fact, he actually recites a number of cases that he labels "unanswered and perhaps genuine." But his overall thesis is clear. It is only prudent for one to be wary of purported mediums; after all, Harry Houdini once remarked that he never failed to find fraud in the over five thousand seances that he attended. We can only add the sobering observation that supposed psychics and mediums tend to become bashful in the presence of professional magicians.

Howard P. Albright's *Forbidden Wisdom* sets forth pseudo-demonstrations of palmistry, graphology, astrology, fortune-telling, and numerology. Stephen Minch's *The Book of Thoth*, a first-of-its-kind monograph, contains twenty-two effective feats with a Tarot pack of cards. Anyone with a basic knowledge of card magic will readily be able to perform Minch's effects. Those interested in an informed account of psychics can hardly do better than to consult *ESP, Seers, and Psychics* by Milbourne Christopher, a past president of the Society of American Magicians and biographer of Houdini. Uriah Fuller's *Confessions of a Psychic* exposes the actual techniques of contemporary pseudo-psychics, such as Uri Geller, who have convinced some learned members of the scientific community that they have witnessed genuine demonstrations of psychokinesis. The author's name is perhaps a pseudonym, punning on the name of the sham psychic Uri Geller. In a similar vein, *Flim-Flam*, written by the famous magician and escape artist James Randi, has been praised by Isaac Asimov as a powerful expression of rational thought. Randi, like Houdini, is devoting the last part of his active career to debunking pseudo-feats of the supernormal. In the present work, his targets include supposed cases of E.S.P., levitation, dowsing, psychic detectives, psychic surgery, psychokinesis and the like. Randi's intelligence, perceptiveness, and integrity are all evident in this enthralling exposé. *The Truth about Uri Geller*, also by Randi, is a refreshing and trenchant critique of Geller's pseudo-stunts such as bending a spoon through mental power alone. The celebrity-scientist, Carl Sagan, has described this book as "A healthy antidote to charlatanism on all levels." For a true exercise in gullibility, one may read Dr. J. B. Rhine's article "An Investigation of a 'Mind-Reading' Horse," which he coauthored with his wife for the *Journal of Abnormal and Social Psychology* in 1929. The Rhines actually concluded that telepathy was at work between the horse and its female owner, when any magician would have pointed out that simple, but secret signals were conveyed to the horse by its owner. In *What's on Your Mind?* Dunninger gives the impression of being a genuine mind-reader—even including detailed E.S.P. tests for those who want to discover their own abilities. Of course, Dunninger was simply using the tricks of the magician to simulate psychic feats.

Eccentric ideas or emphases are hallmarks of the following studies. Arthur Setterington's *Off Beat Mentalism* contains thirteen weird and psychic feats with the author's original plots and twists. In one effect, the spectator is taken along on a déjà vu experiment; in another, tissue paper somehow supports several pounds of books, tearing and giving way only after the performer stops "concentrating" on this fragile paper. With proper presentation, the performer should be able to get good publicity through Setterington's material, which is marked by a flair for the sensational. "Weird," "bizarre," and "uncanny," are the relevant key words for the sort of magic treated in the periodical *Invocation*, which is edited by Tony Audruzzi. This editor distinguishes between bizarre magic and psychic magic, for in the case of the latter, if an inanimate object inexplicably moves, the effect is attributed to telekinesis on the part of the psychic, but in the context of bizarre magic, the same motion would be attributed to some cosmic force. Those fascinated by the macabre will enjoy Charles W. Cameron's *Handbook of Horror*, a monograph devoted to conjuring in a ghostly vein. Some performers earn a living by presenting "spook shows" to enthusiastic teenage audiences.

Witches' Brew is Cameron's sequel to *Handbook of Horror* for those who seek more sensational mysteries with a gothic flavor. At just over a hundred pages, Robert Nelson's *The Encyclopedia of Mentalism and Allied Arts* is hardly an exhaustive survey. Instead it is a compilation of material for the pseudo-psychic magician who wants to put on a ghost show and the medium who wishes to conduct a seance. Nelson is certainly one of the most prolific authors in his field, and the would-be mentalist or medium will want to be familiar with all of Nelson's writings. A more specialized work, Nelson's *The Ghost Book of Dark Secrets*, divulges techniques for producing a ghost show on stage or conjuring up spirits at an intimate seance. *Startling Effects*, by Janel (pseudonym for James M. Nelson), contains such ghost-show illusions as the "Floating Dragon." Each feat is especially designed to satisfy an audience's hunger for thrills and the sensational.

Micro-Magic Ghost Show, by Arthur Setterington, details a complete ghost-show act that has been designed especially for the close-up worker. This monograph is profusely illustrated by Ken De Courcey. In *The Celestial Agent*, Charles Maly weaves such feats as table lifting and mind-reading into an entire act for the magician who is disposed toward the occult. *Thirteen!!!* is Tony Shiels' first collection of bizarre, attention-grabbing items. This author has since become famous for his magic routines, which fuse the fantastic and the psychic. *Something Strange*, also by Shiels, presents more magic in the Dracula-type vein. *Daemons, Darklings, and Doppelgangers*, also by Shiels, features such eerie themes as conjuring up the stench of brimstone. Those with a decided preference for occult material will not be disappointed by this unusual monograph.

Exclusive Weird and Psychic Effects is the first work in a four-part series by Clettis V. Musson. Items run the gamut from a prediction to an ectoplasm effect. *More Weird and Psychic Effects* is Musson's second contribution on his announced topics. With effects like his "Flash Frog Vanish," he lives up to the promise for strange stunts. *Additional Weird and Psychic Effects* is the third work by Musson; each study focuses upon feats of spiritualism and mentalism. Whether a magician wants to put on a ghost show or masquerade as a medium, he will find practical, effective material in the author's series. This installment includes such items as a "Blood from Your Fingers" effect. *Further Weird and Psychic Effects* is the fourth and final release in Musson's series on mentalism and bizarre feats. The diverse contents include a telepathy mystery and how to conjure up a "cute" ghost.

BIBLIOGRAPHIES

By far the most monumental bibliographical contribution comes in the form of *The Master Index to Magic in Print*, by Jack Potter. His three decades of research have resulted in a fourteen-volume opus that indexes some 2,700 entries. But undoubtedly the single most useful bibliographic tool is Robert Gill's *Magic as a Performing Art: A Bibliography of Conjuring*. This work judiciously surveys writings published during the exceptionally fertile period between 1935 and 1975. Gill, who possesses the unusual qualifications of being a librarian and a magician, has listed over a thousand publications, briefly describes them, and provides evaluations. Further enhancing the value of his text, Gill discusses "General Bibliographies on Magic," from the earliest offerings to contemporary studies. The author's intelligent, succinct appraisals and his encyclopedic interests make this book the most informative single-volume bibliographical compendium that has ever been published. Scrupulous scholarship has earned Trevor H. Hall's *A Bibliography of Books on Conjuring in English from 1580 to 1850* the status of a standard reference work. The 323 carefully detailed entries of this book can be effectively supplemented by Edgar Heyl's work.

In *Conjuring Books, 1580 to 1850*, Edgar Heyl maintains the high bibliographical standards set by his predecessor. *Cues for Collectors*, also by Edgar Heyl, is an authoritative treatment of such topics as American magic books, mythical magic books, peripheral bibliographies, and odd and unusual books. Of related interest, Frances Marshall's *The Magic Bookman* is an engaging and all-too-short compilation of statements by famous bibliophiles in the world of magic. Among the topics are collecting magic books, classifying them (neither the Dewey Decimal System nor the Library of Congress Classification is quite adequate), specialized collections, reviewing magic books, and rarities in the field. Interspersed throughout this anthology are succinct observations such as the fact that Walter B. Gibson has written more magic books than any other author. Contributors to this monograph include J. B. Findlay, Edwin A. Dawes, John Mulholland, Robert Lund, and Edgar Heyl. James B. Findlay's *How's Your Library?* is a valuable booklet by an outstanding collector of magic books. The author discusses books themselves in the course of his remarks on handling, organizing, and developing one's personal library. Bibliophiles will be delighted with Findlay's knowledgeable observations.

A Checklist of Magic Lecture Notes, by J. Gary Bontjes, will acquaint the reader with the wide variety of lecture notes that have recently and significantly expanded the literature of magic. Many magicians, who specialize in lecturing before other members of the magic fraternity, now sell notes that summarize the material that they have demonstrated in their lectures. Because some of the secrets divulged in such notes appear in no other publications, Bontjes' survey of over one hundred sets of notes will be of interest to anyone who wishes to know what is available in this popular, relatively new format. F. William Kuethe, Jr.'s *Checklist of Magical Periodical History in Print* is also of bibliographical interest. *A Conjuring Bibliography of "Forcing" Items* is a second work by Kuethe. *Bibliography of Memory*, by Morris N. Young, will appeal to those magicians and mentalists who seek information on the kind of memory demonstrations by which figures such as Harry Lorayne have earned national reputations. Because bibliographic data is scant, the book lists and book catalogs of magic dealers are important resources. See the Appendix for information on representative magic dealers.

BIBLIOGRAPHY

Abbott, David P. *Behind the Scenes with the Mediums*. Chicago: Open Court, 1907.
Ackerman, Alan. *The Esoterist*. Fort Lauderdale: Paul Diamond, 1974.
Adair, Ian H. *A la Zombie—Plus*. Bideford, England: Supreme Magic, 1970.
———. *Conjuring as a Craft*. London: David & Charles, Newton Abbot, 1970.
———. *Encyclopedia of Dove Magic*. 3 vols. Bideford, England: Supreme Magic, 1968–1973.
———. *Magical Menu*. 2d. ed. Bideford, England: Supreme Magic, 1973.
———. *Oceans of Notions*. Bideford, England: Supreme Magic, 1973.
———. *Paddle-Antics*. Bideford, England: Supreme Magic, 1971.
Alan, Don. *Close-Up Time with Don Alan*. Chicago: Magic Inc., 1951.

———. *Pretty Sneaky*. Chicago: Magic Inc., 1956.
Albenice. *Reel Magic*. New York: Louis Tannen Inc., 1950.
Albright, Howard P. *Advanced Card Magic*. London: Gem Pub., 1948.
———. *Forbidden Wisdom*. London: Gem Pub., 1948.
Aldini, Al. *New Concepts In Magic*. Seattle: Micky Hades Intl., 1970.
———. *Novel Concepts with Cards*. Seattle: Micky Hades Intl., 1970.
———. *Roughingly Yours*. Seattle: Micky Hades Intl., 1969.
Alexander, C. *Life and Mysteries of the Celebrated Dr. Q*. Los Angeles: Author, 1921.
Allerton, Bert. *The Close-Up Magician*. Chicago: Magic Inc., 1958.
Allin, David. *Magic for the Master*. Colon, Mich.: Abbott's Magic, 1977.
Ammar, Michael. *The Topit Book*. Bluefield, W. Va.: Secret Service Press, 1983.
Anderson, Gene. *Topper's Mad, Mad Magic*. Chicago: Magic Inc., 1974.
Anderson, Gene and Frances I. Marshall. *Newspaper Magic*. Chicago: Magic Inc., 1968.
Anderson, George B. *It Must Be Mindreading!* Chicago: Magic Inc., 1949.
———. *Magic Digest: Fun Magic for Everyone*. Northfield, Ill.: Digest Books, 1972.
———. *You, Too, Can Read Minds!* Chicago: Magic Inc., 1968.
Andrews, Max. *Sixteen Card Index Gems*. N.p.: Author, 1943.
Andrews, Val. *Gags in Close-Up*. London: Inzani-Henley, 1963.
Andrus, Jerry. *Andrus Deals You In: Advanced Card Magic*. Portland, Oreg.: Star Magic, 1957.
———. *Safety-Pin Trix*. Portland, Oreg.: Star Magic, 1955.
———. *Sleeving from the Deck (At the Table)*. Albany, Oreg.: J. A. Enterprises, 1961.
———. *Sleightly Miraculous: A Treatise on the Panoramic Shift*. Albany, Oreg.: J. A. Enterprises, 1961.
———. *Steals and Palms*. Albany, Oreg.: J. A. Enterprises, 1961.
Annemann, Theodore. *The Book without a Name*. New York: Max Holden, 1931.
———. *Card Miracles and Mental Mysteries*. London: Davenport, 1935.
———. *En Rapport*. New York: Max Holden, 1937.
———. *Full Deck of Impromptu Card Tricks*. New York: Max Holden, 1943.
———. *Incorporated Strange Secrets*. New York: Max Holden, 1939.
———. *Mental Bargain Effects: Eleven Miracles of Mentalism*. New York: Max Holden, 1935.
———. *Mental Club Act: A Completely Routined and Fully Described Thirty-Minute Act for One Person*. London: Magic Wand, 1956.
———. *Miracles of Card Magic*. New York: Max Holden, 1948.
———. *No Code Telepathy: A Completely Routined Act Demonstrating Pseudo Telepathy between Two People*. London: Magic Wand, 1956.
———. *Practical Mental Effects*. New York: Max Holden, 1944.
———. *Sh-h-h! It's a Secret*. London: Davenport, 1934.
———. *Two Hundred and Two Methods of Forcing*. New York: Max Holden, 1933.
Armstrong, George. *Tricks of the Trade*. London: Magic Wand, 1946.
Arthur, R. E. *New Look for the Magic Show*. Chicago: Magic Inc., 1951.
Auer, James. *The Spirit Is Willing*. Chicago: Magic Inc., 1961.
Ayling, Will. *Genie Presentations*. Bideford, England: Supreme Magic, 1972.
Baker, Al. *Magical Ways and Means*. Minneapolis: Carl Waring Jones, 1941.
———. *Mental Magic*. Minneapolis: Carl Waring Jones, 1949.
———. *Pet Secrets*. Minneapolis: Carl Waring Jones, 1951.
Bamberg, Theodore, and Robert Parrish. *Okito on Magic*. Chicago: E. O. Drane, 1952.

Barnhart, Russell T. *Two Second Deals*. Chicago: Magic Inc., 1975.
Baron, Harry. *Card Tricks for Beginners*. London: Kaye & Ward, 1960.
———. *Close-Up Magic for Beginners*. London: Kaye & Ward, 1972.
———. *Magic for Beginners*. New York: Funk & Wagnall, 1967.
———. *My Best Card Trick*. London: Ridgemont, 1953.
Batchelor, Tom. *Canadian Card Control*. Chicago: Magic Inc., 1971.
Beam, Steve. *Steve Beam on Coins*. Vol. 1. N.p.: Author, 1981.
Behnke, Leo. *Entertaining Close-Up*. Alhambra, Calif.: Owen Magic Supreme, 1962.
———. *Entertaining with Cards*. Alhambra, Calif.: Owen Magic Supreme, 1962.
Bennett, Horace. *Alternative Handlings*. Greenville, S.C.: Magic Methods, 1983.
———. *Bennett's Best*. Greenville, S.C.: Magic Methods, 1975.
———. *Bennett's Fourth Book*. Greenville, S.C.: Magic Methods, 1981.
———. *Downs' Palm Technique*. Greenville, S.C.: Jerry Mentzer, 1981.
———. *Horace Bennett's Prize-Winning Magic*. Bideford, England: Supreme Magic Co., 1972.
———. *On Your Feet*. Greenville, S.C.: Jerry Mentzer, 1978.
Benzais, John. *The Best of Benzais*. Kansas City: John King and David Walker, 1967.
Berg, Joe, and Al Aldini. *Rough Stuff*. Chicago: Magic Inc., 1956.
Berland, Samuel. *Berland 1970: Tricks for Today and Tomorrow*. Chicago: Author, 1970.
———. *Berland's Portfolio of More Exclusive Tricks*. Chicago: Author, 1971.
———. *Berland's Tricks and Routines, Mark III*. Chicago: Author, 1971.
Bertram, Ross. *Magic and Methods of Ross Bertram*. Oakland, Calif.: Magic Ltd./Lloyd E. Jones, 1978.
Bey, Mohammed [Leo Horowitz]. *Mohammed Bey's Routines for the Jardine Ellis Ring on Stick*. New York: Louis Tannen Inc., 1952.
———. *Mohammed Bey's Routines with the Okito Coin Box, and More Mohammed Bey Routines*. New York: Louis Tannen Inc., 1963.
Bigbee, North. *Stage Mentalism*. Chicago: Magic Inc., 1969.
Blackstone, Harry [Harry Bouton]. *Blackstone's Modern Card Tricks*. New York: Sully, 1932.
———. *Blackstone's Secrets of Magic*. New York: Garden City Pub., 1958.
Blackstone, Jr., Harry, Charles Reynolds, and Regina Reynolds. *The Blackstone Book of Magic and Illusion*. New York: Newmarket Press, 1985.
Blake, George. *Major Magic*. Leeds, England: Author, 1968.
Boarde, C. L. *Mainly Mental*. 2 vols. New York: Author, Vol. 1, 1947; Vol. 2, 1950.
Bobo, J. B. *The New Modern Coin Magic*. 2d ed. Chicago: Magic Inc., 1966.
———. *Watch This One!: A Collection of Choice Magical Effects with Small Objects*. Oakland, Calif.: Lloyd Jones, 1947.
Bohlen, Henry. *Bohleno's Five Original Performance-Proven Mysteries*. London: George Armstrong, 1947.
Bongo, Ali [William Wallace]. *The Bongo Book*. Chicago: Magic Inc., 1966.
Bontjes, J. Gary. *A Checklist of Magic Lecture Notes*. Glen Burnie, Md.: F. Wm. Kuethe, Jr., 1962.
Bonura, Aldo. *The Electric Company Make Your Own Magic Show!* New York: Grosset & Dunlap, 1979.
Booth, John N. *Marvels of Mystery*. Philadelphia: Kanter's Magic Shop, 1941.

Brent, Lu [Boleslaw Lubrant]. *Best Magic Tricks*. 3 vols. Seattle: Micky Hades Intl., 1969–1982.
———. *Fifteen Star Card Effects*. Philadelphia: Kanter's Magic Shop, 1956.
———. *Novel Magic*. New York: Steen Pub., 1932.
———. *Totally Refreshing Ideas & Carefully Kept Secrets*. Seattle: Micky Hades Intl., 1966.
Brooke, Ken. *Ken Brooke's Magic: The Unique Years*. Bideford, England: Supreme Magic, 1981.
Buckingham, Geoffrey. *It's Easier Than You Think*. London: Harry Clarke, 1952.
Buckley, Arthur. *Card Control*. Chicago: Author, 1946.
———. *Principles and Deceptions*. Chicago: Author, 1948.
Buckley, Arthur, and John Brown Cook. *Gems of Mental Magic*. Chicago: Authors, 1947.
Cameron, Charles W. *Handbook of Horror*. Bideford, England: Supreme Magic, 1969.
———. *"Mind" Your Magic*. Bideford, England: Supreme Magic, 1972.
———. *Witches Brew*. Bideford, England: Supreme Magic, 1967.
Campbell, Loring. *Magic That Is Magic*. Colon, Mich.: Abbott's Magic, 1946.
———. *This Is Magic!* Colon, Mich.: Abbott's Magic, 1945.
Cecil, Harry E. *Magic That Perks*. Colon, Mich.: Abbott's Magic, 1937.
Chanin, Jack. *Cigar Magic*. Philadelphia: Author, 1937.
———. *The Encyclopedia of Sleeving*. Philadelphia: Author, 1948.
———. *Hello, Sucker!* Philadelphia: Author, 1934.
Chapman, Frank M. *Twenty Stunners with a Nail Writer*. Philadelphia: Kanter's Magic Shop, 1944.
Charles, Kirk. *Tips on Table-Hopping*. Seattle: Author, 1981.
Christopher, Milbourne. *Conjuring with Christopher*. New York: Max Holden, 1949.
———. *ESP, Seers, and Psychics*. New York: Thomas Y. Crowell, 1970.
———. *Fifty Tricks with a Thumb Tip: A Manual of Thumb Tip Magic*. New York: D. Robbins, 1948.
———. *Magic from M-U-M*. Forestville, Conn.: Society of American Magicians, 1954.
———. *Milbourne Christopher's Magic Book*. New York: Thomas Y. Crowell, 1977.
———. *More One-Man Mental Magic*. New York: Louis Tannen Inc., 1954.
———. *One-Man Mental Magic*. New York: Louis Tannen Inc., 1952.
———. *The Sphinx Golden Jubilee Book of Magic*. New York: The Sphinx Pub. Corp., 1951.
———. *Stretching a Rope*. Philadelphia: Kanter's Magic Shop, 1971.
———. *Tips on Tricks*. Chicago: Berland Magical Creations Co., 1942.
———. *Varied Deceptions*. London: Harry Stanley's Unique Magic Studio, 1953.
Christopher, Milbourne, and Hen Fetsch. *Magic at Your Fingertips*. N.p.: Maryland Magic Studio, 1947.
Clark, Keith. *Encyclopedia of Cigarette Tricks*. New York: Louis Tannen Inc., 1937.
———. *Rope Royale*. Cincinnati: Silk King Studios, 1942.
———. *Silks Supreme*. Cincinnati: Silk King Studios, 1942.
Clarke, Harry. *Magic*. London: Burke Pub., 1962.
Clive, Paul. *Card Tricks without Skill*. Blackpool, England: Author, 1947.
Collins, Stanley. *Confessions of a Medium*. 2d ed. Columbus, Ohio: Nelson Enterprises, 1959.
———. *A Conjuring Melange*. Fleming, N.J.: Fleming Book Co., 1947.

Corinda, Tony. *Thirteen Steps to Mentalism: A Step-by-Step Course on Mental Magic and Allied Arts*. N.p.: Author, 1958–1960.

Craggs, Douglas, ed. *Masterpieces of Magic Number 1: Advanced Conjuring for Practical Performers*. London: Academy of Recorded Crafts, Arts, and Sciences, 1946.

Crandall, "Senator" Clarke. *How to Stack Dice*. Hollywood: Author, 1974.

Curry, Paul (introd. by Martin Gardner). *Magician's Magic*. New York: Whiting & Wheaton, 1965.

———. *Paul Curry Presents*. New York: Author, 1974.

Dalal, Sam. *Magic with a Marked Deck*. Calcutta: Ramdev, 1972.

———. *Magic with an E.S.P. Deck*. Calcutta: Author, 1973.

———. *Sound Mentalism*. Bideford, England: Supreme Magic, 1971.

Davies, Rev. C. M. *Mystic London; or, Phases of Occult Life in the Metropolis*. London: Tinsley, 1875.

Dawes, Edwin A. *The Great Illusionists*. Secaucus, N.J.: Chartwell Books, 1979.

De Barros, Jules. *The Coins of Ishtar*. N.p.: Author, 1971.

De Courcy, Ken. *Meshed Minds*. Bideford, England: Supreme Magic, 1971.

De La Torre, Jose. *Ascanio's World of Knives*. Edited by Marc Tessler. Belleville, N.J.: Author, 1975.

———. *Magicana of Havana*. Belleville, N.J.: Author, 1975.

Denhard, Harold. *How to Do Rope Tricks*. Chicago: Magic Inc., 1957.

Devant, David [David Wighton]. *Lessons in Conjuring*. London: Routledge, 1922.

———. *Secrets of My Magic*. London: Hutchinson, 1936.

Deveen, Devil. *Cigarette Magic and Manipulation*. London: E. Bagshawe, 1931.

———. *Expert Cigarette Magic: An Original Treatise on the Art and Practice of Cigarette Necromancy*. London: E. Bagshawe, 1932.

Dexter, Will [William Thomas Pritchard]. *Everybody's Book of Magic*. London: Arco, 1956.

———. *Magic Circle Magic: A Tribute to the Memory of George Davenport and Lewis Davenport, Instituted by the Council of the Magic Circle*. London: Harry Clarke, 1963.

———. *101 Magic Secrets*. London, Arco, 1957.

———. *The Riddle of Chung Ling Soo*. Bideford, England: Supreme Magic, 1973.

———. *Sealed Vision*. London: Magic Wand, 1956.

Dhotel, Jules. *Magic with Small Apparatus*. Translated by Paul Fleming. Fleming, N.J.: Fleming Book Co., 1947.

Dodson, Goodlette. *Exhibition Card Fans*. Atlanta: H. R. Hulse, 1935.

Doerflinger, William. *The Magic Catalogue*. New York: Dutton, 1977.

Dornfield, Werner C. *Dorny on Trix*. Chicago: Magic Inc., 1954.

Downs, Thomas Nelson. *The Art of Magic*. Buffalo, N.Y.: Downs-Edwards Co., 1909. Reprint. New York: Dover, 1980.

———. *Modern Coin Manipulation*. London: T. Nelson Downs Magical Co., 1900.

Dunninger, Joseph. *Dunninger's Complete Encyclopedia of Magic*. New York: L. Stewart, 1967.

———. *Houdini's Spirit Exposes: From Houdini's Own Manuscripts, Records, and Photographs, and Dunninger's Psychical Investigations*. New York: Experimenter Pub., 1928.

———. *What's on Your Mind?* Cleveland: World Pub., 1944.

Duval, Ade. *A Rhapsody in Silk*. Chicago: Magic Inc., 1962.

Easley, Bert, and Eric P. Wilson. *Doing Magic for Youngsters, Including the Art of Conjuring to Children*. New York: Louis Tannen Inc., 1972.
Elliott, Bruce, ed. *The Best in Magic*. New York: Harper's, 1956.
———. *Classic Secrets of Magic*. New York: Harper's, 1952.
———. *Magic as a Hobby: New Tricks for Amateur Performers*. New York: Harper's, 1948.
———. *Phoenix*. 6 vols. Fleming, N.J.: Fleming Book Co., 1952–1954.
———. *Professional Magic Made Easy*. New York: Harper's, 1958.
Enochs, Edward Loyd. *Loyd's Master Manipulation of Thimbles*. New York: Author, 1931.
———. *Producing Lighted Cigarettes*. Philadelphia: Kanter's Magic Shop, 1943.
Erdnase, S. W. [E.S. Andrews]. *The Expert at the Card Table*. Chicago: Charles T. Powner, 1953.
Ervin, E. G. *Club Deceptions*. Philadelphia: Kanter's Magic Shop, 1949.
Evans, Henry Ridgely. *Cagliostro: A Sorcerer of the Eighteenth Century*. New York: Masonic Bibliophiles, 1931.
Farelli, Victor. *Card Magic*. London: Edward Bagshawe, 1933.
———. *Convincing Coin Magic*. London: Magic Wand, 1946.
———. *"Lend Me Your Pack."* London: Edward Bagshawe, 1936.
———. *Thanks to Leipzig: The Cleanest Method of Passing Three Freely Selected Cards from One Packet to Another . . . and a Convincing Mental Effect*. London: Magic Land, 1948.
Feinman, Jeffrey. *The Catalogue of Magic*. New York: Simon & Schuster, 1978.
Findlay, James B. *How's Your Library?* Chicago: Magic Inc., 1958.
Fischer, Ottokar. *Hofzinser's Card Magic*. Teaneck, N.J.: Gutenberg Press, 1974.
———. *Illustrated Magic*. Translated and edited by Fulton Oursler and J. B. Mussey. New York: Macmillan, 1931.
Fitzkee, Dariel. *The Card Expert Entertains*. San Rafael, Calif.: St. Raphael House, 1948.
———. *Contact Mind-Reading*. San Rafael, Calif.: St. Raphael House, 1935.
———. *Rings on Your Fingers*. San Rafael, Calif.: St. Raphael House, 1946.
———. *Rope Eternal, Or The Only Six Ways to Restore a Rope*. New York: Louis Tannen Inc., 1957.
———. *The Trick Brain*. San Rafael, Calif.: St. Raphael House, 1944.
Fleischman, Sidney. *Between Cocktails—with a Packet of Matches*. Colon, Mich.: Abbott's Magic, 1962.
Florek, Bruce. *The Tahoe File: Card Magic by Terry Lagerould*. Lake Tahoe: Author, 1982.
Foster, Neil, ed. *Tops Treasury of Cigarette Magic*. Colon, Mich.: Abbott's Magic, 1965.
———. *Tops Treasury of Illusions*. Colon, Mich.: Abbott's Magic, 1965.
Fox, Karrell. *Comedy a la Card*. Chicago: Magic Inc., 1960.
———. *Kornfidentially Yours!* Chicago: Magic Inc., 1954.
Francis, Douglas. *Right under Your Nose*. London: Harry Stanley's Unique Magic Studio, 1947.
Frikell, Samri [Fulton Oursler]. *Spirit Mediums Exposed*. New York: New Metropolitan Fiction, 1930.
Fromer, Roy. *Floating Ball Magic*. New York: D. Robbins, 1972.
Fuller, Uriah. *Confessions of a Psychic*. Teaneck, N.J.: Gutenberg Press, 1975.
Fulves, Karl. *The Book of Numbers*. Teaneck, N.J.: Gutenberg Press, 1971.

———. *Faro & Riffle Technique*. Teaneck, N.J.: Gutenberg Press, 1969.
———. *Close-Up Mental Magic*. Teaneck, N.J.: Gutenberg Press, 1974.
———. *Gene Finnell's Card Magic*. Teaneck, N.J.: Gutenberg Press, 1973.
———. *The Magical World of Slydini*. 2 vols. New York: Louis Tannen Inc., 1979.
———. *Methods with Cards*. 3 vols. Teaneck, N.J.: Gutenberg Press, 1975.
———. *Mexican Monte & Other Tricks*. Teaneck, N.J.: Gutenberg Press, 1972.
———. *More Self-Working Card Tricks*. New York: Dover, 1984.
———. *Notes from Underground*. Teaneck, N.J.: Gutenberg Press, 1973.
———. *Packet Switches* (Part One). Teaneck, N.J.: Gutenberg Press, 1974.
———. *Riffle Shuffle Set-Ups*. Teaneck, N.J.: Gutenberg Press, 1974.
———. *Riffle Shuffle Technique*. Teaneck, N.J.: Gutenberg Press, 1974.
———. *Self-Working Card Tricks*. New York: Dover, 1976.
———. *Self-Working Mental Magic*. New York: Dover 1979.
———. *Self-Working Table Magic: 97 Foolproof Tricks with Everyday Objects*. New York: Dover, 1981.
———. *Transpo Trix*. Teaneck, N.J.: Gutenberg Press, 1978.
Futagawa, Shigeo. *Introduction to Coin Magic*. Oakland, Calif.: Lloyd E. Jones, 1978.
Galloway, Andrew. *Diverting Card Magic*. Ayr, Scotland: Author, n.d.
———. *The Ramsay Classics*. Ayr, Scotland: Author, 1977.
———. *The Ramsay Legend*. Birmingham, England: Goodliffe Publications, 1969.
Ganson, Lewis. *The Art of Close-Up Magic*. 2 vols. London: Harry Stanley's Unique Magic Studio, 1966.
———. *Cy Enfield's Entertaining Card Magic*. 3 parts. London: Harry Stanley's Unique Magic Studio, 1955–1958.
———. *The Dai Vernon Book of Magic*. London: Harry Stanley's Unique Magic Studio, 1957.
———. *Dai Vernon's Cups and Balls Routine*. London: Harry Stanley's Unique Magic Studio, 1958.
———. *Dai Vernon's Further Inner Secrets of Card Magic*. London: Harry Stanley's Unique Magic Studio, 1961.
———. *Dai Vernon's Inner Secrets of Card Magic*. London: Harry Stanley's Unique Magic Studio, 1959.
———. *Dai Vernon's More Inner Secrets of Card Magic*. London: Harry Stanley's Unique Magic Studio, 1960.
———. *Dai Vernon's Symphony of the Rings*. London: Harry Stanley's Unique Magic Studio, 1958.
———. *Dai Vernon's Tribute to Nate Leipzig*. London: Harry Stanley's Unique Magic Studio, 1963.
———. *Dai Vernon's Ultimate Card Secrets*. London: Harry Stanley's Unique Magic Studio, 1967.
———. *Expert Manipulation of Playing Cards*. London: Academy of Recorded Crafts, Arts, and Sciences, 1946.
———. *Give a Magician Enough Rope—and He'll Do a Trick!* London: Harry Stanley's Unique Magic Studio, 1966.
———. *Magic of the Mind*. London: Harry Stanley's Unique Magic Studio, 1960.
———. *The Magic of Slydini*. London: Harry Stanley's Unique Magic Studio, 1960.
———. *Magic with Faucett Ross*. Bideford, England: Supreme Magic, 1975.
———. *Malini & His Magic*. London: Harry Stanley's Unique Magic Studio, 1963.

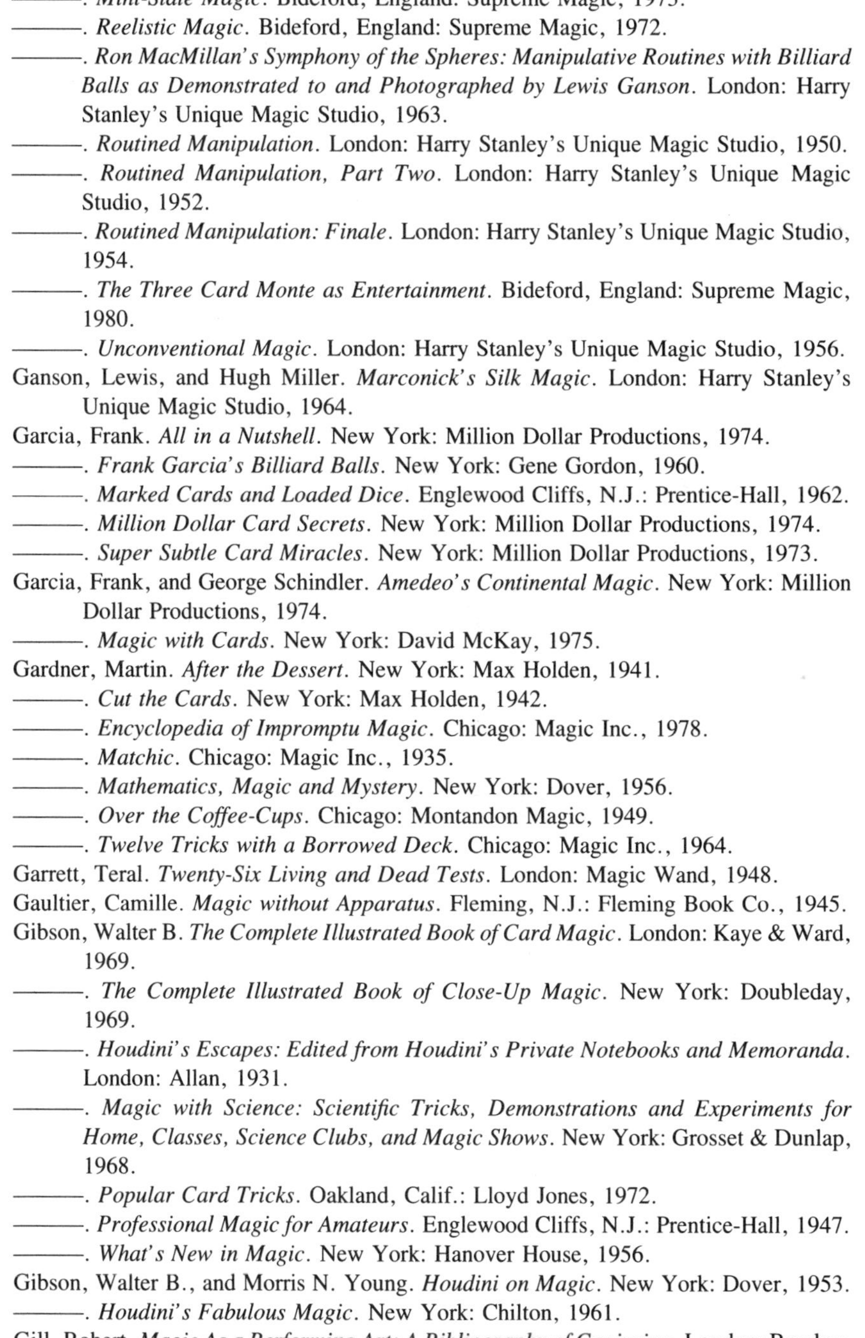

———. *Mini-Slate Magic*. Bideford, England: Supreme Magic, 1973.
———. *Reelistic Magic*. Bideford, England: Supreme Magic, 1972.
———. *Ron MacMillan's Symphony of the Spheres: Manipulative Routines with Billiard Balls as Demonstrated to and Photographed by Lewis Ganson*. London: Harry Stanley's Unique Magic Studio, 1963.
———. *Routined Manipulation*. London: Harry Stanley's Unique Magic Studio, 1950.
———. *Routined Manipulation, Part Two*. London: Harry Stanley's Unique Magic Studio, 1952.
———. *Routined Manipulation: Finale*. London: Harry Stanley's Unique Magic Studio, 1954.
———. *The Three Card Monte as Entertainment*. Bideford, England: Supreme Magic, 1980.
———. *Unconventional Magic*. London: Harry Stanley's Unique Magic Studio, 1956.
Ganson, Lewis, and Hugh Miller. *Marconick's Silk Magic*. London: Harry Stanley's Unique Magic Studio, 1964.
Garcia, Frank. *All in a Nutshell*. New York: Million Dollar Productions, 1974.
———. *Frank Garcia's Billiard Balls*. New York: Gene Gordon, 1960.
———. *Marked Cards and Loaded Dice*. Englewood Cliffs, N.J.: Prentice-Hall, 1962.
———. *Million Dollar Card Secrets*. New York: Million Dollar Productions, 1974.
———. *Super Subtle Card Miracles*. New York: Million Dollar Productions, 1973.
Garcia, Frank, and George Schindler. *Amedeo's Continental Magic*. New York: Million Dollar Productions, 1974.
———. *Magic with Cards*. New York: David McKay, 1975.
Gardner, Martin. *After the Dessert*. New York: Max Holden, 1941.
———. *Cut the Cards*. New York: Max Holden, 1942.
———. *Encyclopedia of Impromptu Magic*. Chicago: Magic Inc., 1978.
———. *Matchic*. Chicago: Magic Inc., 1935.
———. *Mathematics, Magic and Mystery*. New York: Dover, 1956.
———. *Over the Coffee-Cups*. Chicago: Montandon Magic, 1949.
———. *Twelve Tricks with a Borrowed Deck*. Chicago: Magic Inc., 1964.
Garrett, Teral. *Twenty-Six Living and Dead Tests*. London: Magic Wand, 1948.
Gaultier, Camille. *Magic without Apparatus*. Fleming, N.J.: Fleming Book Co., 1945.
Gibson, Walter B. *The Complete Illustrated Book of Card Magic*. London: Kaye & Ward, 1969.
———. *The Complete Illustrated Book of Close-Up Magic*. New York: Doubleday, 1969.
———. *Houdini's Escapes: Edited from Houdini's Private Notebooks and Memoranda*. London: Allan, 1931.
———. *Magic with Science: Scientific Tricks, Demonstrations and Experiments for Home, Classes, Science Clubs, and Magic Shows*. New York: Grosset & Dunlap, 1968.
———. *Popular Card Tricks*. Oakland, Calif.: Lloyd Jones, 1972.
———. *Professional Magic for Amateurs*. Englewood Cliffs, N.J.: Prentice-Hall, 1947.
———. *What's New in Magic*. New York: Hanover House, 1956.
Gibson, Walter B., and Morris N. Young. *Houdini on Magic*. New York: Dover, 1953.
———. *Houdini's Fabulous Magic*. New York: Chilton, 1961.
Gill, Robert. *Magic As a Performing Art: A Bibliography of Conjuring*. London: Bowker, 1976.

Ginn, David. *Children Laugh Louder*. Norcross, Ga.: Author, 1978.
———. *Close-Up-A-Ginn*. Atlanta: Scarlett Green Pub., 1974.
———. *David Ginn's Comedy Linking Rings*. Norcross, Ga.: Author, 1974.
———. *Kidbiz*. Atlanta: Scarlett Green Pub., 1982.
———. *Matchbox Delights*. Atlanta: Scarlett Green Pub., 1977.
———. *Professional Magic for Children*. Atlanta: Scarlett Green Pub., 1976.
Gordon, Gene. *Gene Gordon's Magical Legacy*. Norcross, Ga.: A Snowflake Publication, 1980.
Gore, George. *The Linking Rings of Jack Miller*. N.J.: Author, 1973.
Grant, Ulysses F. *Clever Little Ideas Presented by U. F. Grant*. Oakland, Calif.: Lloyd Jones, 1947.
———. *Twenty-Five Rising Card Tricks*. Chicago: Magic Inc., 1970.
Gravatt, Glenn G. *Collected Writings of Glenn Gravatt*. Oakland, Calif.: Lloyd Jones, 1974.
———. *50 Modern Card Tricks You Can Do!* Oakland, Calif.: Lloyd Jones, 1974.
———. *Glenn Gravatt's Treasure Trove of Tricks*. Oakland, Calif.: Lloyd Jones, 1971.
Green, Cliff. *Professional Card Magic*. New York: Louis Tannen Inc., 1961.
Griffin, Al. *"Step Right Up, Folks!"* Chicago: Henry Regnery, 1934.
Griffin, Ken, and Roberta Griffin. *Illusion Show Know-How*. Colon, Mich.: Abbott's Magic, 1972.
Griffith, Tony. *Griff on Cards*. Bideford, England: Supreme Magic, 1963.
———. *Griff on Close-Up*. Bideford, England: Supreme Magic Co., 1967.
———. *An Invitation to Mystery*. Bideford, England: Supreme Magic, 1969.
Hades, Micky, ed. *The Conjuror's Book of Stage Illusions: Selected from The Conjuror's Magazine, And Released by Edward W. Dart*. Seattle: Micky Hades Intl., 1974.
Hadley, Paul R. *How to Develop Mental Magic*. Minneapolis: Denison, 1961.
Hall, Trevor H. *A Bibliography of Books on Conjuring in English from 1580 to 1850*. Minneapolis: Carl Waring Jones, 1957.
———. *The Card Magic of Edward G. Brown*. London: Magic Circle, 1973.
———. *Nothing Is Impossible*. London: Academy of Recorded Crafts, Arts, and Sciences, 1946.
———. *Reading Is Believing*. Alcester, England: Goodliffe, 1947.
———. *The Testament of Ralph W. Hull*. London: Academy of Recorded Crafts, Arts, and Sciences, 1945.
Harbin, Robert [Ned Williams]. *How to Be a Wizard*. London: Oldbourne, 1957.
———. *Magic of Robert Harbin*. London: Author, 1970.
Harris, Paul. *Close-Up Entertainer*. San Diego: Chuck Martinez Productions, 1979.
———. *Close-Up Fantasies: Book I*. San Diego: Chuck Martinez Productions. 1980.
———. *Close-Up Fantasies: Book II*. San Diego: Chuck Martinez Productions, 1980.
———. *Close-Up Fantasies: Finale*. San Diego: Chuck Martinez Productions, 1981.
———. *Las Vegas Close-Up*. San Diego: Chuck Martinez Productions, 1978.
———. *Paul Harris Reveals Some of His Most Intimate Secrets*. N.p.: Rainbow Magic Machine, 1976.
Hay, Henry. *The Amateur Magician's Handbook*. 4th ed. New York: Harper & Row, 1982.
———. *Cyclopedia of Magic*. New York: David McKay, 1949.
Heinemann, Richard. *Original Magic*. Toledo: Carlo's Magic Shop, 1945.
Heyl, Edgar. *Conjuring Books, 1580 to 1850*. Baltimore: Author, 1963.

———. *Cues for Collectors*. Chicago: Magic Inc., 1964.

Hilliard, John Northern. *Card Magic*. Minneapolis: Carl Waring Jones, 1944.

———. *Greater Magic*. Minneapolis: Carl Waring Jones, 1938.

Hiraiwa, Hakufu. *Stage Magic Highlights*. Tokyo; Arakai, 1961.

Hodson, A. S., and S.A.S. McMillan, ed. *Fifty Years Later: Produced by the Scottish Conjurors Association to Celebrate Their Half Century*. Glasgow: S.C.A., 1974.

Hoffmann, Professor [Angelo John Lewis]. *Later Magic*. London: Routledge, 1904.

———. *Modern Magic: A Practical Treatise on the Art of Conjuring*. London: Routledge, 1876. Reprinted as *Hoffman's Modern Magic*. New York: Dover, 1969.

———. *More Magic*. London: Routledge, 1890.

Hollingsworth, Scott. *Cashing in with Close-Up Restaurant Magic: A Personal Portfolio*. Houston: Author, n.d.

Holmes, Donald [Donald H. Aladorf]. *The Magic Art*. Kansas City: Author, 1920.

Hopkins, Albert A. *Magic: Stage Illusions and Scientific Diversions, Including Trick Photography*. New York: Benjamin Blom, 1897.

Hopkins, Charles H. *''Outs,'' Precautions, and Challenges: For Ambitious Card Workers*. Philadelphia: Author, 1940.

Houdini, Harry. *Handcuff Secrets*. London: George Routledge & Son, 1910.

———. *Magical Rope Ties and Escapes*. London: Will Goldston, 1921.

———. *A Magician among the Spirits*. New York: Harper & Bros., 1924.

———. *Miracle Mongers and Their Methods*. New York: E. P. Dutton, 1920.

———. *The Right Way to Do Wrong: An Expose of Successful Criminals*. Las Vegas: Gamblers Book Club, 1906.

Houdini, Harry, and Clinton Burgess, eds. *Elliott's Last Legacy: Secrets of the King of All Kard Kings*. New York: Adams Press Print, 1923.

Howarth, David. *''Winners All.''* London: W. H. Stephenson, 1962.

Howatt, Gordon. *Let's Make Magic*. Chicago: Magic Inc., 1966.

Howie, John. *Routines with the Jardine Ellis Ring*. London: Magic Wand, 1955.

Hoy, David. *Bold and Subtle Miracles of Dr. Faust*. Chicago: Magic Inc., 1963.

Hugard, Jean [John Gerard Rodney Boyce]. *Card Manipulations Series 1–5*. New York: Max Holden, 1934–1936.

———. *Close-Up Magic for the Night Club Magician*. 2d ed. New York: Max Holden, 1938.

———. *Coin Magic*. New York: Max Holden, 1935.

———. *Hugard's Magic Monthly: Book Editions*. 9 vols. Fleming, N.J.: Fleming Book Co., 1945–1953.

———. *Mental Magic with Cards*. New York: Max Holden, 1935.

———. *Modern Magic Manual*. New York: Max Holden, 1939.

———. *More Card Manipulations, Series 1–4*. New York: Max Holden, 1938–1941.

———. *Silken Sorcery*. New York: Max Holden, 1937.

———. *Thimble Magic*. New York: Max Holden, 1936.

———, ed. *The Encyclopedia of Card Tricks*. New York: Dover, 1975.

Hugard, Jean, and Frederick Braue. *Expert Card Technique*. Brooklyn: Authors, 1944.

———. *The Invisible Pass*. Brooklyn: Authors, 1946.

———. *Miracle Methods: Casting New Light on the Stripper Deck. A Treatise on the Science and Art of Manipulating Biseaute Cards*. New York: Authors, 1941.

———. *Miracle Methods: Miracle Shuffles and Tricks. A Treatise on the Science and Art of Stock, Cull, Odd-number and Cull-Stock Shuffles*. Calif.: Authors, 1942.

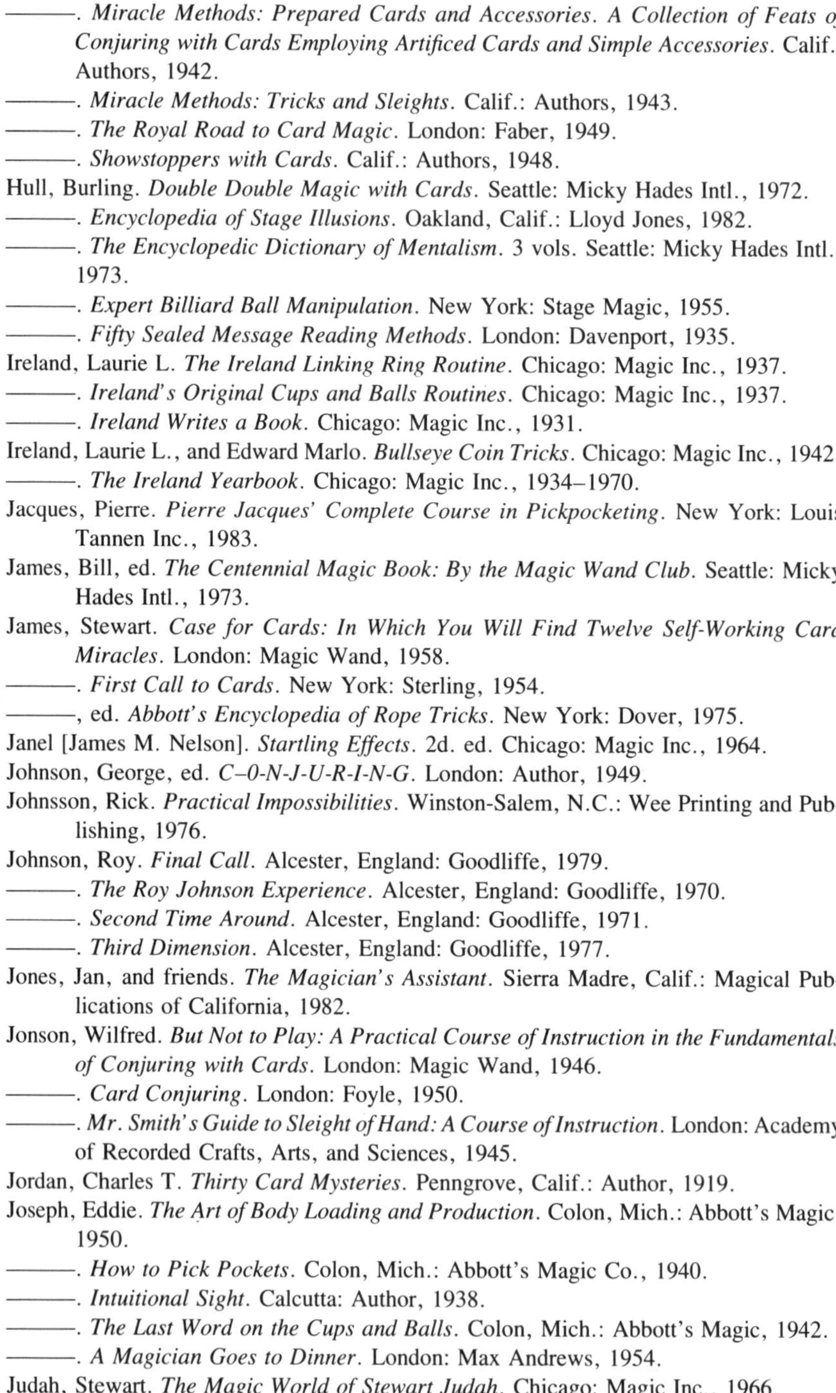

———. *Miracle Methods: Prepared Cards and Accessories. A Collection of Feats of Conjuring with Cards Employing Artificed Cards and Simple Accessories*. Calif.: Authors, 1942.

———. *Miracle Methods: Tricks and Sleights*. Calif.: Authors, 1943.

———. *The Royal Road to Card Magic*. London: Faber, 1949.

———. *Showstoppers with Cards*. Calif.: Authors, 1948.

Hull, Burling. *Double Double Magic with Cards*. Seattle: Micky Hades Intl., 1972.

———. *Encyclopedia of Stage Illusions*. Oakland, Calif.: Lloyd Jones, 1982.

———. *The Encyclopedic Dictionary of Mentalism*. 3 vols. Seattle: Micky Hades Intl., 1973.

———. *Expert Billiard Ball Manipulation*. New York: Stage Magic, 1955.

———. *Fifty Sealed Message Reading Methods*. London: Davenport, 1935.

Ireland, Laurie L. *The Ireland Linking Ring Routine*. Chicago: Magic Inc., 1937.

———. *Ireland's Original Cups and Balls Routines*. Chicago: Magic Inc., 1937.

———. *Ireland Writes a Book*. Chicago: Magic Inc., 1931.

Ireland, Laurie L., and Edward Marlo. *Bullseye Coin Tricks*. Chicago: Magic Inc., 1942.

———. *The Ireland Yearbook*. Chicago: Magic Inc., 1934–1970.

Jacques, Pierre. *Pierre Jacques' Complete Course in Pickpocketing*. New York: Louis Tannen Inc., 1983.

James, Bill, ed. *The Centennial Magic Book: By the Magic Wand Club*. Seattle: Micky Hades Intl., 1973.

James, Stewart. *Case for Cards: In Which You Will Find Twelve Self-Working Card Miracles*. London: Magic Wand, 1958.

———. *First Call to Cards*. New York: Sterling, 1954.

———, ed. *Abbott's Encyclopedia of Rope Tricks*. New York: Dover, 1975.

Janel [James M. Nelson]. *Startling Effects*. 2d. ed. Chicago: Magic Inc., 1964.

Johnson, George, ed. *C–0-N-J-U-R-I-N-G*. London: Author, 1949.

Johnsson, Rick. *Practical Impossibilities*. Winston-Salem, N.C.: Wee Printing and Publishing, 1976.

Johnson, Roy. *Final Call*. Alcester, England: Goodliffe, 1979.

———. *The Roy Johnson Experience*. Alcester, England: Goodliffe, 1970.

———. *Second Time Around*. Alcester, England: Goodliffe, 1971.

———. *Third Dimension*. Alcester, England: Goodliffe, 1977.

Jones, Jan, and friends. *The Magician's Assistant*. Sierra Madre, Calif.: Magical Publications of California, 1982.

Jonson, Wilfred. *But Not to Play: A Practical Course of Instruction in the Fundamentals of Conjuring with Cards*. London: Magic Wand, 1946.

———. *Card Conjuring*. London: Foyle, 1950.

———. *Mr. Smith's Guide to Sleight of Hand: A Course of Instruction*. London: Academy of Recorded Crafts, Arts, and Sciences, 1945.

Jordan, Charles T. *Thirty Card Mysteries*. Penngrove, Calif.: Author, 1919.

Joseph, Eddie. *The Art of Body Loading and Production*. Colon, Mich.: Abbott's Magic, 1950.

———. *How to Pick Pockets*. Colon, Mich.: Abbott's Magic Co., 1940.

———. *Intuitional Sight*. Calcutta: Author, 1938.

———. *The Last Word on the Cups and Balls*. Colon, Mich.: Abbott's Magic, 1942.

———. *A Magician Goes to Dinner*. London: Max Andrews, 1954.

Judah, Stewart. *The Magic World of Stewart Judah*. Chicago: Magic Inc., 1966.

Kane, Peter. *A Card Session with Peter Kane*. Manchester, England: Author, 1967.

———. *Another Card Session with Peter Kane*. Manchester, England: Author, n.d.

Kaplan, George G. *The Fine Art of Magic*. Fleming, N.J.: Fleming Book Co., 1948.

Kattner, Wilbur [Howard Holden]. *Off the Beaten Path*. Minneapolis: Lloyd Jones, 1947.

Kaufman, Richard. *Balls! Lessons in Side-Arm Snookery*. New York: Author, 1977.

———. *Card Magic*. Boulder: Richard Kaufman and Alan Greenberg, 1979.

———. *Cardworks*. Boulder: Author, 1981.

———. *Coin Magic*. New York: Richard Kaufman and Alan Greenberg, 1981.

———. *The Complete Works of Derek Dingle*. Boulder: Richard Kaufman and Alan Greenberg, 1982.

———. *The Interlocked Production of Coins*. New York: Author, 1977.

Kaye, Marvin. *Catalog of Magic*. New York: Doubleday, 1977.

———. *The Complete Magician*. New York: Macmillan, 1974.

———. *The Handbook of Mental Magic*. New York: Stein & Day, 1975.

Kenyon, John. *Thumbs Up!* Alcester, England: Goodliffe, 1946.

Kerns, Ernie. *How to Be a Magic Clown*. Chicago: Magic Inc., 1960.

Kerns, Ernie, Fred Olsen, and G. Elmer Jones. *How to Be a Magic Clown, Volume 2*. Chicago: Magic Inc., 1968.

Kort, Milton. *Kort Is Now in Session*. Chicago: Magic Inc., 1962.

———. *Off-Color Card Tricks*. Chicago: Magic Inc., 1970.

Kosky, Gerald. *The Magic of Gerald Kosky*. Oakland, Calif.: Lloyd Jones., 1975.

Kosky, Gerald, and Arnold Furst. *The Magic of Tenkai*. Oakland, Calif.: Lloyd Jones, 1974.

Kuethe, F. William. *Checklist of Magical Periodical History in Print*. Glen Burnie, Md.: Author, 1963.

———. *A Conjuring Bibliography of "Forcing" Items*. Glen Burnie, Md.: Author, 1962.

Kumar, S.K.V. *Illusionsesame*. Seattle: Micky Hades Intl., 1971.

Lamb, Geoffrey Frederick. *Illustrated Magic Dictionary*. New York: Elsevier/Nelson Books, 1979.

Lamonte, Jack. *Stunts with Stage Money*. London: Magic Wand, 1948.

Langham, Jack. *Magic!* Edinburgh: Nelson, 1961.

Larsen, William W. *Conjuring for Children*. 2d ed. Seattle: Micky Hades Intl., 1973.

———. *Mental Mysteries with Cards*. 2d ed. Seattle: Micky Hades Intl., 1974.

Lawton, Don. *Lots of Lawton*. Chicago: Magic Inc., 1971.

Leamon, Earl. *Handbook of Chemical Magic*. Chicago: Magic Inc., 1939.

Lee, Wallace. *Math Miracles*. Durham, N.C.: Author, 1960.

Leech, Al. *Cardmanship*. Chicago: Magic Inc., 1959.

———. *Card Man Stuff*. Chicago: Magic Inc., 1953.

———. *For Card Men Only*. Chicago: Magic Inc., 1949.

———. *Handbook of Card Sleights*. Chicago: Magic Inc., 1954.

———. *Super Card Man Stuff*. Chicago: Magic Inc., 1965.

Lees, Walt. *Ron MacMillan's Modern Art of Coin Manipulation*. London: Ron MacMillan's Intl. Magic, 1982.

LePaul, Paul. *The Card Magic of LePaul*. Danville, Ill.: Interstate, 1949.

———. *LePaul Presents the Card Magic of Bro. John Hamman, S.M.* St. Louis: Don Lawton, 1958.

Lewis, Eric C., and Wilfred Tyler. *Open Sesame*. Alcester, England: Goodliffe, 1947.

Lewis, Shari and Abraham B. Hurwitz. *Magic for Non-Magicians*. Los Angeles: J. P. Tarcher, 1975.
Liebertz, Arnold. *Marvellous Mysteries of Marvillo*. Seattle: Micky Hades Intl., 1975.
Lorayne, Harry. *Afterthoughts*. New York: Author, 1975.
———. *Best of Friends*. New York: Author, 1982.
———. *The Card Classics of Ken Krenzel*. New York: Author, 1975.
———. *Close-Up Card Magic*. New York: Louis Tannen Inc., 1962.
———. *Deck-Sterity*. New York: Louis Tannen Inc., 1967.
———. *My Favorite Card Tricks*. New York: Louis Tannen Inc., 1965.
———. *Personal Secrets*. New York: Louis Tannen Inc., 1964.
———. *Quantum Leaps*. New York: Author, 1979.
———. *Reputation Makers*. New York: Author, 1971.
———. *Richard Himber's Ideas in the $100.00 Book*. New York: Gimmicks Unlimited, 1963.
———. *Rim Shots*. New York: Author, 1973.
Lorraine, Sid. *The Early Stuff*. Chicago: Magic Inc., 1973.
MacCarthy, E. Brian. *Impromptu*. London: Magic Wand, 1939.
MacDonald, Gordon, ed. *Tips on "Soft Soap."* Colon, Mich.: Abbott's Magic, 1947.
MacDougall, Michael. *Card Mastery: With Which Is Combined the Expert at the Card Table*. New York: Circle Magic Shop, 1944.
McCarron, B. W. *The Gambling Magician*. New York: D. Robbins, 1976.
McGill, Ormond. *Psychic Magic*. Colon, Mich.: Abott's Magic, 1984.
———. *Twenty-One Gems of Mental Magic*. Colon, Mich.: Abbott's Magic, 1946.
McGuire, Eddie. *The Phantom of the Card Table: The Real Secrets of . . . Walter Scott*. Nevada: Gambler's Book Club, 1959.
Majax, Gerard. *The Secrets of the Card Sharps*. New York: Sterling Pub., 1977.
Majikans [Leo Burns]. *Magic Feats: A Miscellany of Practical Magic*. Alcester, England: Goodliffe, 1948.
Maly, Charles J. *Celestial Agent*. Chicago: Magic Inc., 1944.
Mardo, Senor. *The Act*. Chicago: Magic Inc., 1967.
———. *The Cups and Balls*. Oakland: Lloyd Jones, 1955.
———. *Magic for Bartenders*. Hollywood: Hollywood Magic Shop, 1950.
———. *Routined Magic*. New York: Max Holden, 1945.
Marlo, Edward [Edward Malkowski]. *Advanced Fingertip Control*. Chicago: Author, 1970.
———. *Amazing Isn't It?* Chicago: Magic Inc., 1941.
———. *Card Control*. Chicago: Author, 1952.
———. *Card Fan Productions*. Chicago: Magic Inc., 1941.
———. *The Cardician*. Chicago: Magic Inc., 1953.
———. *Coining Magic*. Chicago: Ireland Magic, 1957.
———. *Discoveries*. Chicago: Magic Inc., 1946.
———. *Future Reverse*. Chicago: Magic Inc., 1952.
———. *Let's See the Deck*. Chicago: Magic Inc., 1942.
———. *The Magic Seven*. Chicago: Magic Inc., 1954.
———. *Marlo in Spades*. Chicago: Magic Inc., 1947.
———. *Marlo Meets His Match*. Chicago: Magic Inc., 1959.
———. *Marlo's Objectives*. Chicago: Magic Inc., 1973.
———. *Off the Top*. Chicago: Magic Inc., 1945.

———. *Pasteboard Presto*. Chicago: Magic Inc., 1938.
———. *Peek and Shuffle Controls*. Chicago: Author, 1958.
———. *Revolutionary Card Technique: Chapter One: Miracle Card Changes*. Chicago: Magic Inc., 1954.
———. *Revolutionary Card Technique: Chapter Two: The Action Palm*. Chicago: Magic Inc., 1956.
———. *Revolutionary Card Technique: Chapter Three: Fingertip Control*. Chicago: Magic Inc., 1956.
———. *Revolutionary Card Technique: Chapter Four: The Side Steal*. Chicago: Magic Inc., 1956.
———. *Revolutionary Card Technique: Chapter Five: The Tabled Palm*. Chicago: Magic Inc., 1957.
———. *Revolutionary Card Technique: Chapter Six: Faro Shuffle*. Chicago: Magic Inc., 1958.
———. *Revolutionary Card Technique: Chapter Seven: Faro Notes*. Chicago: Magic Inc., 1959.
———. *Revolutionary Card Technique: Chapters Eight, Nine, and Ten: Seconds, Centers & Bottoms*. Chicago: Magic Inc., 1960.
———. *Revolutionary Card Technique: Chapter Eleven: The Multiple Shift*. Chicago: Magic Inc., 1961.
———. *Revolutionary Card Technique: Chapter Twelve: Card Switches*. Chicago: Magic Inc., 1962.
———. *Revolutionary Card Technique: Chapters Thirteen and Fourteen: Estimation*. Chicago: Magic Inc., 1963.
———. *Riffle Shuffle Systems*. 2 vols. Chicago: Author, 1959.
———. *Shoot the Works*. Chicago: Magic Inc., 1943.
Marshall, Frances Ireland. *Kid Stuff*. 6 vols. Chicago: Magic Inc., 1954–1974.
———. *The Magic Bookman*. Chicago: Magic Inc., 1974.
———, ed. *The Sponge Book*. Chicago: Magic Inc., 1960.
Marshall, Jay. *How to Perform Instant Magic*. Folkstone, Kent Ct., England: Bailey Bros. & Swinfed, 1980.
Martineau, Francis B. *Victory Bouquet*. Cincinnati: Silk King Studios, 1944.
———. *Walsh Cane Routines*. Tuscaloosa, Ala.: Silk King Studios, 1945.
Maskelyne, John Nevil. *Modern Spiritualism*. London: Frederick Warne, 1876.
———. *Sharps and Flats*. London: Longman's Green, 1894.
Maurice, Edward [Morris Cohen]. *Mentalistrix*. Seattle: Micky Hades Intl., 1964.
———. *Mentalistrix Encore*. Seattle: Micky Hades Intl., 1969.
Mayer, Ralph. *Short Changed*. Seattle: Micky Hades Intl., 1977.
Mayoh, William. *The Magic of Ho-Yam*. South Bend, Ind.: Peterson, 1949.
Mendoza, John. *The Book of John*. N.p.: Author, 1978.
———. *John: Verse Two*. N.p.: Viking Enterprises, 1980.
Mentzer, Jerry. *Another Close-Up Cavalcade*. Greenville, S.C.: Author, 1975.
———. *Card Cavalcade*. Parma, Ohio: Author, 1972.
———. *Card Cavalcade 2*. Parma, Ohio: Author, 1974.
———. *Card Cavalcade 3*. Greenville, S.C.: Author, 1975.
———. *Card Cavalcade 4*. Greenville, S.C.: Author, 1977.
———. *Card Cavalcade—Finale*. Greenville, S.C.: Author, 1979.
———. *Close-Up Cavalcade*. Greenville, S.C.: Author, 1973.

———. *Close-Up Cavalcade—Finale*. Greenville, S.C.: Author, 1977.

———. *Counts, Cuts, Moves and Subtlety*. Greenville, S.C.: Author, 1977.

———. *Magician Nitely: The Magic of Eddie Fechter*. Greenville, S.C.: Author, 1974.

———. *Multiple Push-Through Control*. Greenville, S.C.: Author, 1973.

Merlin, Jack. "*. . . And a Pack of Cards*." Edited by Jean Hugard. New York: Max Holden, 1940.

Merrill, R. D. *Merrill's Knife Book*. Pomeroy, Ohio: Lee Jacob's Productions, 1981.

Meyer, Orville. *Magic in the Modern Manner: A Unique Collection of Magical Gems*. Oakland, Calif.: Lloyd Jones, 1949.

Miesel, William P. *The Creative Card Magic of William P. Miesel*. Beverly, Mass.: Unicorn Magik, 1978.

Miller, Charles E. *Black Art Well Tricks*. Chicago: Magic Inc., 1969.

Miller, Gordon, ed. *Abbott's Anthology of Card Magic*. 3 vols. Colon, Mich.: Abbott's Magic, 1968.

Miller, Hugh. *Al Koran's Legacy*. London: Repro 71, 1973.

———. *Al Koran's Professional Presentations*. London: Harry Stanley's Unique Magic Studio, 1967.

———. *The Art of Eddie Joseph*. London: Harry Stanley's Unique Magic Studio, 1969.

———. *Rink's Original Rope Mysteries*. Bideford, England: Supreme Magic, 1972.

Miller, Leonard H. *Thrilling Magic*. Colon, Mich.: Abbott's Magic, 1946.

Minch, Stephen. *Any Second Now: Part Two of the Professional Card Technique of Martin A. Nash*. Seattle: Micky Hades Intl., 1977.

———. *The Book of Thoth*. Seattle: Micky Hades Intl., 1974.

———. *Ever So Sleightly: The Professional Card Technique of Martin A. Nash*. Seattle: Micky Hades Intl., 1975.

———. *Sleight Unseen: The Professional Card Technique of Martin A. Nash*. Seattle: Micky Hades Intl., 1979.

Mishell, Ed. *Hold-Out Miracles*. New York: Louis Tannen Inc., 1969.

Morris, Bud. *Magic with Electronics*. Calif.: Author, 1966.

Moss, Floyd. *Card Cheats—How They Operate*. New York: William-Frederick Press, 1950.

Mulholland, John. Beware Familiar Spirits. New York: Charles Scribner's Sons, 1938. Reprint. New York: Dover, 1975.

———. *John Mulholland's Book of Magic*. New York: Charles Scribner's Sons, 1963.

Musson, Clettis V. *Additional Weird and Psychic Effects*. Seattle: Micky Hades Intl., 1983.

———. *Exclusive Weird and Psychic Effects*. Seattle: Micky Hades Intl., 1983.

———. *Fire Magic*. Chicago: Magic Inc., 1952.

———. *Further Weird and Psychic Effects*. Seattle: Micky Hades Intl., 1983.

———. *Minute Magic*. Chicago: Magic Inc., 1953.

———. *More Weird and Psychic Effects*. Seattle: Micky Hades Intl., 1983.

Nathanson, Leon. *Slydini Encores*. New York: Slydini Studio, 1966.

Neil, C. Lang. *The Modern Conjuror and Drawing-Room Entertainer*. Hackensack, N.J.: Wehmen Bros., 1937.

Nelson, Earl. *Variations*. N.p.: Magic Corner, 1978.

Nelson, Robert A. *The Art of Cold Reading*. Seattle: Micky Hades Intl., 1971.

———. *Comedy Mentalism*. 3 vols. Columbus, Ohio: Author, 1962–1964.

———. *The Encyclopedia of Mentalism and Allied Arts*. Columbus, Ohio: Nelson Enterprises, 1944.
———. *The Ghost Book of Dark Secrets*. Columbus, Ohio: Author, n.d.
———. *How to Read Sealed Messages*. Columbus, Ohio: Nelson Enterprises, 1961.
———. *The Master Code*. Columbus, Ohio: Nelson Enterprises, 1959.
———. *Sensational Mentalism*. Columbus, Ohio: Nelson Enterprises, 1966.
———. *Sensational Mentalism: Part Two*. Columbus, Ohio: Nelson Enterprises, 1968.
———. *A Sequel to the Art of Cold Reading*. Seattle: Micky Hades Intl., 1971.
———. *Still More Miracles in Mentalism*. Columbus, Ohio: Nelson Enterprises, 1961.
———. *Super Prediction Tricks*. Columbus, Ohio: Nelson Enterprises, 1947.
———. *TV Mentalism*. Columbus, Ohio: Nelson Enterprises, 1966.
Nemoto, Takeshi. *Tokyo Trickery*. Chicago: Magic Inc., 1967.
Norman, Anthony [Norman Binns]. *Basic Card Technique: A Textbook for the Student of Card Magic*. London: Max Andrews, 1948.
Novak, Bob. *Jack Miller's Linking Ring Routine*. New York: Louis Tannen Inc., 1945.
Osborne, Tom. *Coin Tricks*. Pennsylvania: Author, 1945.
———. *Cups and Balls Magic*. Philadelphia: Lee Grey, 1973.
———. *Three Shell Games*. Pennsylvania: Author, 1938.
Ostin, Bob. *Fingertip Fantasies*. Alcester, England: Goodliffe, 1968.
Our Mysteries. New York: Sphinx Pub., 1941.
Ovette, Joseph. *Tricks and Illusionettes*. Chicago: Samuel Berland, 1944.
Page, Patrick, magical adviser. *Bell's Magic Book*. N.p.: Bell Pub., 1973.
Palmer, Tom. *Cagey Doves*. Chicago: Magic Inc., 1962.
———. *Modern Illusions*. Chicago: Magic Inc., 1959.
Parrish, Robert. *An Evening with Charlie Miller*. Chicago: Magic Inc., 1961.
———. *For Magicians Only: A Guide to the Art of Mystifying*. New York: Bernard Ackerman, 1944.
———. *New Ways to Mystify: A Guide to the Art of Magic*. New York: Bernard Ackerman, 1945.
Parrish, Robert, and John Goodrum. *"You'd Be Surprised."* New York: Max Holden, 1938.
Parrish, Robert, and Oscar Weigle. *Do That Again!* New York: Max Holden, 1939.
Pecor, Charles J. *The Craft of Magic: Easy-to-Learn Illusions for Spectacular Performances*. Englewood Cliffs, N.J. : Prentice-Hall, 1979.
Permin, Ib. *Hocus Pocus: Rope and Scarf Tricks*. New York: Sterling Pub., 1977.
Podmore, Frank. *Modern Spiritualism*. London: Methuen, 1902.
Poland, Ellison. *The First Addendum to Wonderful Routines of Magic*. Boston: Winston-Salem, 1973.
———. *Wonderful Routines of Magic*. Boston: Author, 1969.
Pomeroy, John D. *Mentology*. Seattle: Micky Hades Intl., 1973.
Postgate, Bruce. *Dove Pan-Orama*. Montreal: Herb Morrisey Products, 1972.
———. *Table Hopping*. Cincinnati: Haines House of Cards, 1975.
Potter, Jack. *The Master Index to Magic in Print*. 14 vols. Seattle: Micky Hades Intl., 1967–1975.
Racherbaumer, Jon. *The Lost Pages of the Kabbala*. N.p.: Danny Korem, 1981.
Raffles, Mark. *The Pickpocket Secrets of Mark Raffles*. Isle of Wight, England: The Magic Box, 1983.
Randi, James. *Flim-Flam*. Buffalo: Prometheus Books, 1982.

———. *The Truth about Uri Geller*. Buffalo: Prometheus Books, 1982.
Ravelle and Andree. *Tips Galore*. Cambridge, England: Premier Magic, 1961.
Read, Bob. *Thanks to Pepys*. Kenton, England: Author, 1974.
Read, Ralph W. *The Three Shell Game*. Philadelphia: Kanter's Magic Shop, 1938.
Rhine, J. B., and L. E. Rhine. "An Investigation of a 'Mind-Reading' Horse." *Journal of Abnormal and Social Psychology* 23 (1929): 449–466; 24 (1929): 287–292.
Rice, Harold R. *Encyclopedia of Silk Magic*. 3 vols. Pennsylvania: Author, 1948–1962.
Robert-Houdin, Jean Eugene. *The Secrets of Conjuring and Magic*. London: Routledge, 1878.
Robertson, Robin. *Handle with Care*. Seattle: Micky Hades Intl., 1964.
Rogers, Mike. *The Complete Mike Rogers*. Chicago: Magic Inc., 1975.
Ross, Richard. *The Ring Routine*. Herrenberg, West Germany: The Magic Hands, 1982.
Roterberg, A. *New Era Card Tricks*. London: Hamley's, 1897.
Roth, David. *Expert Coin Magic*. New York: Richard Kaufman and Alan Greenberg, 1985.
Ruthchild, Myriam. *Psychotechnics*. Two cassettes (audio-tapes). Pomeroy, Ohio: Lee Jacobs Productions, 1982.
Rutledge, Ned, and J. G. Thompson, Jr. *Card Party: A Sparkling Assortment of Card Chicanery*. Beaver Springs, Pa.: Bo-Print, 1965.
Rydell, Wendy, and George Gilbert. *The Great Book of Magic*. New York: Abrams, 1976.
Sachs, Edwin T. *Sleight of Hand*. N.p.: Bazaar Office, 1877. Fifth edition. Fleming, N.J.: Fleming Book Co., 1953.
Sands, George. *Sands' Improved Ropesational*. N.p.: Author, 1962.
Sankey, Jan. "Concerning Magic as an Art Form." *Magic Manuscript* August/September (1983): 14–15.
Sardina, Maurice. *The Magic of Rezvani*. San Rafael, Calif.: St. Raphael House, 1949.
Scarne, John. *Scarne on Card Tricks*. New York: Crown, 1950.
———. *Scarne's Magic Tricks*. New York: Crown, 1951.
Scarne, John, and Clayton Rawson. *Scarne on Dice*. Harrisburg, Pa.: Military Service Pub., 1945.
Schatz, Edward R. *Practical Contact Mind-Reading*. Seattle: Micky Hades Intl., 1974.
Scot, Reginald. *The Discoverie of Witchcraft*. London: William Brome, 1584. Reprinted as *The Discovery of Witchcraft*. New York: Dover, 1975.
Searles, Lynn. *The Card Expert*. Colon, Mich.: Abbott's Magic, 1938.
Setterington, Arthur. *Micro-Magic Ghost Show*. Bideford, England: Supreme Magic, 1970.
———. *Off Beat Mentalism*. Seattle: Micky Hades Intl., 1975.
———. *Straight Line Mysteries*. Seattle: Micky Hades Intl., 1972.
Severn, Bill. *Bill Severn's Big Book of Magic*. New York: David McKay, 1973.
———. *Bill Severn's Impromptu Magic*. New York: Charles Scribner's Sons, 1982.
———. *Bill Severn's Magic Workshop*. New York: Henry Z. Walck, 1976.
———. *Magic across the Table*. New York: Cassell, 1972.
———. *Magic from Your Pocket*. New York: Faber, 1965.
Sharpe, Alton C. *Expert Card Conjuring*. Chicago: Author, 1968.
———. *Expert Hocus-Pocus*. Chicago: Author, 1961.
Sharpe, S. H., and Will Ayling. *Oriental Conjuring and Magic*. Bideford, England: Supreme Magic, 1981.

Shiels, Tony. *Daemons, Darklings, and Doppelgangers*. Bideford, England: Supreme Magic Co., 1969.

———. *Something Strange*. Bideford, England: Supreme Magic Co., 1968.

———. *Thirteen!!!: A Devil's Dozen of Macabre Miracles*. Bideford, England: Supreme Magic Co., 1968.

Siegal, Paul J., *Mentalism à La Mode*. N.p.: Author, 1975.

Simon, Bill. *Controlled Miracles*. Chicago: Magic Inc., 1949.

———. *Effective Card Magic*. Edited by Jean Hugard. New York: Louis Tannen Inc., 1952.

———. *Mathematical Magic*. London: Allen & Unwin, 1965.

———. *Sleightly Sensational*. New York: Louis Tannen Inc., 1954.

Skomp, Stephen. *S'Komplimentary Mentalism*. Seattle: Micky Hades Intl., 1975.

Smith, J. Stewart. *The Collected Works of J. Stewart Smith*. Seattle: Micky Hades Intl., 1983.

Sorcar, P. C. *Sorcar on Magic: Reminiscences and Selected Tricks*. Calcutta, Indrajel Pub., 1960.

Spooner, William E. *Here's "Hoo" with Coins: The Hook-coin Book*. Raleigh, N.C.: Author, 1974.

Stanley, Harry. *"I Wouldn't Like to Play Cards with You!"* Bideford, England: Supreme Magic, 1974.

Stanyon, Ellis. *Card Tricks for Everyone*. New York: Emerson Books, 1968.

Starke, George, ed. *Stars of Magic*. New York: Louis Tannen Inc., 1961.

Steele, W. F. Rufus. *52 Amazing Card Tricks: Professional Tricks Anyone Can Do*. Chicago: Author, 1949.

———. *The Last Word on Cards*. Chicago: Author, 1952.

———. *Paul Rosini's Magical Gems: A Memorial*. Chicago: Author, 1950.

Steranko, John. *Steranko on Cards*. Chicago: Magic Inc., 1960.

Strong, David. *Magic Tricks*. New York: Platt & Munk Pub., 1977.

Swinford, Paul. *Faro Fantasy*. Connersville, Ind.: Halet Press, 1968.

———. *More Faro Fantasy*. Connersville, Ind.: Halet Press, 1971.

Tan, Choon Tee. *Variations on 2 Card Classics*. Seattle: Micky Hades Intl., 1965.

Tan, Hock Chuan. *Rough and Smooth Possibilities*. London: Academy of Recorded Crafts, Arts, and Sciences, 1948.

Tanner, Don. *How to do Cigarette Tricks*. Chicago: Magic Inc., 1957.

———, ed. *Fifty Ways to Use a Card Box*. Chicago: Magic Inc., 1969.

Tarbell, Harlan, ed. *The Tarbell Course in Magic*. 7 vols. New York: Louis Tannen Inc., 1941–1972.

Tarr, Bill, and Barry Ross. *Now You See It, Now You Don't!: Lessons in Sleight of Hand*. New York: Random House, 1976.

Taylor, Gerald. *The Classical Technique of Fire Eating*. Seattle: Micky Hades Intl., 1980.

Thompson, James G. *The Living End: Over 200 Impromptu Take-a-Card Endings*. Norwood, Ohio: Haines House of Cards, 1972.

———. *Magic to Delight: Pleasing Tricks in Abundant Variety*. New York: Louis Tannen Inc., 1970.

———. *The Miracle Makers*. Oakland, Calif.: Lloyd Jones, 1975.

———. *My Best: A Collection of the Best Originations Conceived by Eminent Creators*. Philadelphia: C. H. Hopkins, 1945.

———. *Sleight Intended: Expressway to Playing-Card Expertise.* Omaha, Nebraska: Modern Litho, 1973.

———. *Top Secrets of Magic: Routined Mystification with Small Objects.* 3 vols. Vol. 1: New York: Gene Gordon, 1956; Vol. 2: Hanover, Pa.: Messenger, 1967; Vol. 3: N.p.: Bojalad, 1968.

Thompson, James G., and Ned Rutledge. *Between Two Minds.* Hanover, Pa.: Messenger, 1967.

Tong, Dan. *Dan Tong's Close-Up Magic.* N.p.: Magic Art Book Co., 1982.

Torino, Senor [Tony Kardyro]. *Kardyro's Kard Konjuring.* N.p.: Author, 1955.

Tricks with a Folding Coin. 2d ed. Chicago: Magic Inc., 1971.

Trixer, Hans E. *Conjuring Trix and Jardine Ellis Ring Effects.* London: Magic Wand, 1955.

Trost, Nick. *E.S.P. Session with Nick Trost.* 2d ed. Seattle: Micky Hades Intl., 1971.

———. *Gambling Tricks with Dice: This is a Fifty-Dollar Book.* Columbus, Ohio: Author, 1974.

———. *Nick's Routine with the Cups and Balls.* Seattle: Micky Hades Intl., 1971.

Tucker, W. M. *The Short Change Artist: Bullshit.* Greenville, S.C.: Author, n.d.

Tuffs, J. Elsden. *Teach Yourself Conjuring.* N.p.: E. U. P., 1954.

Turner, Bill. *The Card Wizard: An Easy Course of Tricks.* Philadelphia: David McKay, 1949.

Vermes, Hal G. *The Collier Quick and Easy Guide to Magic.* New York: Collier/Macmillan, 1963.

Vernon, Dai. *Early Vernon: The Magic of Dai Vernon in 1932.* Chicago: Magic Inc., 1962.

———. *Select Secrets.* New York: Max Holden, 1941.

Victor, Edward. *Billiard Ball Manipulations in Seven Easy Lessons.* Croydon, England: Willane, 1953.

———. *Card Manipulation in Six Easy Lessons.* Croydon, England: Willane, 1954.

———. *Coin Manipulation in Six Easy Lessons.* Croydon, England: Willane, 1954.

———. *Further Magic of the Hands.* London: Author, 1945.

———. *Magic of the Hands.* London: Waddilove, 1937.

———. *More Magic of the Hands.* London: Davenport, 1942.

———. *Thimble Manipulation in Six Easy Lessons.* Croydon, England: Willane, 1954.

Volkmann, Kurt. *The Oldest Deception (Das Becherspiel): Cups and Balls in the Art of the 15th and 16th Centuries.* Minneapolis: Carl Waring Jones, 1956.

Walsh, Audley V. *John Scarne Explains Why "You Can't Win!"* New York: Author, 1935.

———. *Sponge Ball Manipulation.* New York: Louis Tannen Inc., 1947.

Walsh, Audley V., and Ed Mishell. *Dice Deceptions.* New York: Louis Tannen Inc., 1953.

Walton, Roy. *The Complete Walton.* London: Lewis Davenport, 1981.

Warlock, Peter [Alec Bell]. *The Best Tricks with Slates.* New York: Louis Tannen Inc., 1942.

———. *Come a Little Closer . . .* Billericay, Essex, England: Penshaw Press, 1953.

———. *Designs for Magic.* London: Magic Wand, 1941.

———. *The Magic of Pavel.* Bideford, England: Supreme Magic, 1971.

———. *Patterns for Psychics.* London: Academy of Recorded Crafts, Arts, and Sciences, 1947.

———. *Peter Warlock's Book of Magic*. London: Arco, 1956.
Wass, Verrall. *Magically Yours*. London: Magic Wand, 1953.
Wels, Byron G. *The Great Illusions of Magic*. New York: Louis Tannen Inc., 1977.
White, Joseph. *5 Micro-Mental Programs*. Seattle: Micky Hades Intl., 1966.
———. *Micro-Mental Mysteries*. Seattle: Micky Hades Intl., 1965.
Wiersbe, Warren. *Action with Cards*. Chicago: Magic Inc., 1944.
———. *Mental Cases with Cards*. Chicago: Magic Inc., 1946.
———. *Tantalizing Thimbles*. Chicago: Magic Inc., 1948.
Willmarth, Philip R. *Jim Ryan Close-Up: (1) Sensational Stunners*. N.p.: James P. Ryan and Philip R. Willmarth, 1981.
———. *Jim Ryan Close-Up: (2) Entertaining Card Quickies*. N.p.: James P. Ryan and Philip R. Willmarth, 1981.
———. *Jim Ryan Close-Up: (3) Classic Card Routines*. N.p.: James P. Ryan and Philip R. Willmarth, 1981.
———. *Jim Ryan Close-Up:(4) The Famous Cups and Balls Routine*. N.p.: James P. Ryan and Philip R. Willmarth, 1981.
———. *The Magic of Matt Schulien*. Chicago: Magic Inc., 1959.
———. *The Ring and Rope Book*. N.p.: Author, 1975.
———. "Starting in Mentalism—An Unorthodox View." *The Linking Ring* 63, no. 10 (1983): 65–66.
Wilson, Mark. *The Chop Cup Book*. Los Angeles, Calif.: Mark Wilson Publications, 1979.
———. *The Mark Wilson Course in Magic*. Hollywood: Author, 1975.
Yates, Jack. *Minds in Close-Up: A Collection of Mental Mysteries Using Small Accessories*. Alcester, England: Goodliffe, 1954.
———. *Minds in Duplicate: Easy-to-Do Mental Mysteries for Two People*. Alcester, England: Goodliffe, 1956.
Young, Morris N. *Bibliography of Memory*. Philadelphia: Chilton, 1961.
Zavis, William. *Diverse Deceits*. Alcester, England: Goodliffe, 1973.

4

MAGIC IN RELATION TO OTHER ARTS

Magic clearly does not enjoy the high esteem that is accorded to other performing arts such as dance, music, and drama. Indeed, magicians themselves sometimes shrink from calling their activity art; thus, we have magic books entitled *The Craft of Magic*. Professional philosophers of art, such as R. G. Collingwood, have reinforced the general bias against craft as opposed to art, according to which the former is associated with the mechanical and the routine, but the latter is linked with creativity. Undoubtedly there are numerous factors that militate against classifying magic as an art form, but this seems like an appropriate place to consider, at least, some of them. Etymology reveals that the concept "art" most often means the representation of life, the communication of emotion, or the production of significant form. But in a less-distinguished, derivative, and somewhat trivial sense, the term refers to a stratagem, trick, subterfuge, ruse, or cunning ploy. If one regards magic as an art in this restrictive, morally dubious sense, then he or she will surely relegate magic beneath the traditional fine arts. However, it will shortly be argued that the magician does far more than simply exemplify such a limited sense of art.

Often magic is regarded as a form of entertainment that is best suited for children. This particular prejudice seems to rest upon a confusion between that which is childish (puerile, immature, or silly) and that which is childlike (innocent or open). Magic, at its best, caters to the latter sort of spirit, a spirit of openness, receptivity, and wonder, a spirit that has not been extinguished except in the most unfortunate of adults.

There is ample evidence that the status of magic as art is threatened due to what may be called "guilt by association." Consider the observation of the prominent psychologist Joseph Jastrow, "To gain the confidence of the person to be deceived is the first step alike in sleight of hand and in criminal fraud"

(See Richard Weibel's *Conjuring Psychology*, p. 6). All too often the magician is unfairly linked with the pickpocket, swindler, crooked gambler, phony psychic, con man, or medical quack. Admittedly, some magicians have engaged in such chicanery, but the vast majority of magicians are not guilty of such practices. It is one thing for the magician to have a professional interest in the conceits of the counterfeiter (who, for example, bleaches a one dollar bill to get the correct paper for printing counterfeit bills of a larger denomination) and the shoplifter (who sometimes uses a false "third mit" or arm so that one of his two real arms can be at work even though both supposed arms are engaged in innocent activity), but it is quite another thing to conclude that the magician will use such information for anything other than the purposes of entertainment. The bromide "crime does not pay" is given some credence by the fact that the magician who performs a stage pickpocket act, strictly for amusement, can sometimes earn more than an unscrupulous pickpocket.

Magic has been further degraded by the fact that magic feats are traditionally featured in that paradigm of vulgarity, the side show with its biological freaks and bizarre specialists like fire-eaters and sword-swallowers. Incidentally, the sword-swallower is not practicing magic as such; instead of presenting an illusion, he actually does shove the sword blade down his throat, through the esophagus, and toward the stomach. For that matter, the fire-eater also actually does what he purports and appears to do. As has been noted, those who view magic as an intellectual challenge rather than as an art form that is uniquely suited to resurrect one's childlike sense of wonder, are prone to denigrate magic, for they perceive it as a threat to their cognitive powers. In antiquity, Plato deprecated magic on cognitive grounds, since not only is magic noninformative, but still worse, it misinforms or deceives. A novel may change one's world view; a poem may capture an important truth; a play may give us insights into the human condition. By contrast magic may seem frivolous, for it does not appear to illume life or to intersect with what is most significant in human experience. Recognizing this last sort of deficiency, Sam Sharpe has spoken of the need to reinvest magic with its power to elicit awe:

> When presented so that a deep feeling of wonder is evoked, an illusion can be lifted onto a different plane from that of mere demonstration and puzzlement. . . . Isolating an illusion from the myth, so as to present it apart from its natural environment has resulted in the magic departing, so that only element of wonder left is the wondering how. . . . We no longer have the truly artistic spirit which, by permeating an activity, makes it fine art. This truly artistic spirit only springs from the awareness of a spiritual element, secretly working in nature; however dimly sensed or expressed. The magician represents this hidden spiritual cause. . . . Magic Art in the Grand Style should make men aware of something beyond mere natural appearances, by throwing a rainbow bridge across the abyss separating natural and spiritual consciousness; which is why magic, of all the arts, has been given the task of arousing Wonder; which so said the ancients, is the beginning of wisdom. . . . The Magic Art is descended from The Mystery Religion. . . . And only

> to the extent that modern magic reflects this long tradition . . . can it really be called magic. (*The Magic Play*, p. 33)

In 1983, in the July issue of *M-U-M* magazine, David Goodsell's column "Nothing Up My Sleeve" is also interested in underlining the religious dimension of magic when he quotes Cathy Gibbons on the topic of celebration:

> One of the most important qualities of celebration is its power to help us "forget ourselves," take up beyond our private/personal self-involvement, and lift us into another time frame where we live out the promise that life is "good," where "we" become one and whole, and death is "overcome.". . . As we free ourselves and enter into different levels of our being, a "higher" world perhaps (which some will call the living God and others the living bonds of humanity), celebration and its components are transformers that serve to "re-create," renew and refresh us. (9)

Religion, love, art, philosophy, science, and anything else of profound value speak to a primordial emotion, our sense of wonder; magic at its best can quicken this numinous sense, which is universal in humankind. Speaking of religion, some spectators may be put off by the magician because, like the scientist, he seeks to control the universe. Both can be perceived as usurping power that has sacrilegiously been wrested from God; or, at a minimum, both can be viewed as encroaching upon the domain of the Deity by affecting an omnipotent posture. One final fact may shed light on why magic is assigned such low status among the arts. Frequently, magic is not presented as a dramatic expression, for drama exists, if and only if, a story is presented; a narrative of some sort must unfold. Many magicians fail to capitalize on the fact that we are story-telling, story-loving creatures. Like the second-rate comedian with his string of disconnected one-liners, the inferior magician may present nothing more than a chain of heterogeneous effects. But comedians who excel deliver more than unrelated jokes; such comedians weave their humor into the larger pattern of a narrative. Witness the films of W. C. Fields or Chaplin, the pantomime routines of Red Skelton, or the sketches of television figures like Ernie Kovacs. Similarly, some of the most successful magicians have mounted their magic in the context of stories or vignettes. Doug Henning integrated his magic into the musical plot of *The Magic Show*, a play that ran for four and a half years on Broadway in the 1970s. Of course the narrative element can appear in the act of a silent magician who, for example, produces lit cigarettes to the accompaniment of background music. As the Great Cardini illustrated, the audience can be treated to far more than feats of magic; it can enjoy the emergence of a distinct personality, the development of a character sketch. In a more general sense, the magician fails as a dramatist if, to use Aristotelian categories, there is no beginning, middle, and end to his presentation. Mediocre magicians are especially guilty of neglecting the first phase in their routines; they do not clearly set the stage for what is to follow, but instead they rush to a premature and understandably unappreciated climax. The magician who shows a set of discrete effects, which lack any unifying narrative thread, has much to learn from a theater artist like Marcel Marceau. This great mime presents more than isolated stunts; his graceful, illusory movements are suffused with anecdotal and allegorical import.

Nevil Maskelyne's *Maskelyne on the Performance of Magic* is an unabridged reprint of Part 1, "The Art of Magic," from the classic *Our Magic* by Maskelyne and David Devant. Published in 1911, this material on the aesthetics of magic remains unsurpassed to this day. Maskelyne, a member of the most illustrious dynasty of British magicians, appeals to Aristotelian principles in order to apply a philosophy of art to conjuring. Agreeing with a famous predecessor, Robert-Houdin, Maskelyne conceives of magic as a theater art and of the magician as an actor who plays the role of a being endowed with supernatural abilities. According to Maskelyne, the "magical performer should imitate, and, thus convey to the spectators, the impression of effects produced by super-normal powers." By viewing the magician as a thespian, the author seeks to justify the status of magic as an art. Perceiving a hierarchy among magical types, he distinguishes between magic as false art, normal art, and high art. Creativity becomes the capstone for the magician as practitioner of high art. Thus, the author advocates a philosophy of idealism that places a premium upon magic as an intellectual pursuit, not as mere manipulative skill. Citing Aristotle's *Poetics* in which the criterion of unity is paramount, Maskelyne observes, "As in other arts, so in magic, unity is a first essential to success; since, without it, artistic results are impossible." A bit later he adds, "in order to obtain a perfect effect, the only possible course is to rivet the attention of the audience upon one continuous chain of events, which will lead up to one definite and impressive result" (26–27). Some two dozen canons are explicated and defended; for example, "Avoid complexity of procedure." The axiom of simplicity that is thematic in Occam's razor or the principle of parsimony becomes nothing less than a golden rule for the performance of magic. Throughout the book, actual feats of magic are interspersed to illustrate the principles that are explained theoretically. Concerning unity, it should be pointed out that the recurring motifs of a magic act (some magicians specialize in silk magic, others emphasize doves, and the contemporary magician Marvin Roy features light bulbs—including one large enough to hold a female assistant) find their synthesizing counterpart in the reappearing themes of a musical composition.

Maskelyne's remarks lend credence to the aesthetic attitude theory (according to this doctrine, one must take up a distinctive frame of mind, if he is to have an aesthetic experience), "The spectators . . . have to set aside their critical faculties in order to enter into the spirit of the thing" (42). In a chapter entitled "Justification," the author quotes Aristotle to support his contention that the end cannot justify the means in magical performances. During a chapter on the elements of surprise and repetition, Maskelyne proposes a definition by which magic can be distinguished from other arts, "Somebody or something is caused to pass mysteriously from one place or condition to another" (60). This might be abridged to read, "Something undergoes a mysterious change in its condition.'' In the same chapter, the author asserts that the magician should not declare his intentions in advance—unless there are extenuating circumstances. This procedure insures the desired effect of surprise and diminishes the likelihood that the magician's method will be detected. The aesthetician Monroe Beardsley, who is famous for his critique of appeals to intentions, would add that it is fallacious to judge a work of art by the intentions of the artist; after all, noble intentions are often unfulfilled and modest intentions are sometimes transcended; thus, it is wisest to evaluate the art work on its own merit as a public object rather than turn to extrinsic matters like the artist's psychological states or intentions. In the final paragraph of the same chapter, Maskelyne offers a definition of art: ''Art is work which stimulates imagination'' (69). Aestheticians such as Dewitt Parker would agree, but add that the definition must be expanded if we are to mark art off from, say, science.

In a chapter devoted to the concept of ''Climax,'' the author makes the following distinction between plays and magic performances: ''In magic, the climax is also the completion'' (79). Appealing to the aesthetic mandate of artistic unity, Maskelyne holds that ''A magical item presented in the course of a play should, therefore, form an essential part of that play. It should be an episode without which the plot would be incomplete'' (85). As we have noted earlier, the impact of magic is heightened by its fusion with the narrative mode. During the course of a discussion of rehearsals, Maskelyne quotes Tolstoy at length and presents a counterpart to the auteur theory of film-making and criticism. This theory holds that there must be one guiding artist, usually the director, if a film is to succeed. For without this singular power, the work is left in the hands of a committee or an assembly line. In Maskelyne's words, ''The first essential in any production is the avoidance of divided authority. There can be only one 'producer,' who must be in supreme command'' (107). Aristotle's *Poetics* is appealed to in an exposition on patter (the speech that accompanies the performance of magic). Agreeing again with aesthetic attitude theorists, Maskelyne states, ''The people in front of the footlights must, if possible, be taken out of themselves—must be led to forget their own concerns, and made to think only of the performance they are witnessing'' (132). But, of course, it is not enough that the audience be appropriately predisposed or have the proper mental set in order to have the maximum aesthetic experience. Thus, Maskelyne comments upon the correlative responsibility of the magician:

> The man is an actor; as every magician should be. He does not appear to the audience clothed in his own personality. He assumes, for the time, a personality not his own, but that of the magician he wishes to represent. . . . Spectators . . . are not allowed to see the man himself, but only the man he intends them to see. Therein we have the highest art, of acting and magic alike (19).

Maskelyne's remarks on the spectators' need to take up an aesthetic perspective call to mind Jean-Paul Sartre's observations in *The Psychology of the Imagi-*

nation. He speaks of the person who is having an aesthetic experience as performing "an intentional act of an imaginative consciousness" (246). In Sartre's words, "the spectator assumes the imaginative attitude" (247). According to Sartre, the spectator denies real objects in order to posit imaginative substitutes. Hence, a spectator who sees the actor Sir Laurence Olivier perform as Hamlet must deny the real person Olivier in order to dwell in the unreal domain of Hamlet and thereby aesthetically experience the drama. Maskelyne concludes his admirably theoretical discussion with a plea that magicians approach their discipline with a grasp of the artistic principles that are at work.

Before continuing the present chapter on magic in relation to other arts, some additional remarks on the aesthetics of magic are germane. Like motion pictures that take as their raw materials the actual objects of the material world, magic turns to the real physical world of humans and all sorts of other entities. But unlike film, which—except for the novelty of 3-D movies—renders three dimensional objects in two dimensional terms, a magic performance preserves the three dimensional character of such objects. In this regard, magic is closer to the live drama or play than it is to the motion picture. But if we consider the capacity to radically transform the character of ordinary objects and experiences, then magic is closer to the special effects of the movies. Of the three arts—drama, film, and magic—only the last combines the use of real persons and objects (not mere images) with the production of supernatural illusions.

As with any performing art, magic, by definition, is a dynamic expression, for, as in the case of, say, music or dance, magic exists only when and where it is being presented. We have repeatedly noted that the magician is an actor; from this, it follows that magic is a type of acting. By contrast, when we turn to plastic arts, we can readily identify the spatial-temporal location of paradigm cases; the painting of the Mona Lisa is in the Louvre Museum in Paris, Rodin's sculpture, "The Thinker," may be found in the same city, and the Empire State Building is visible in Manhattan. But philosophers have argued that some works of art are not to be identified with any such fixed, spatial-temporal objects. Magic, like other performing arts and literature, belongs in this latter category. Consider the novel *Moby Dick*; surely it cannot be identical with any one copy or edition of the text, not even the original manuscript by Herman Melville, for if this novel is identified with any one copy or edition, then it follows that to destroy the copy is to destroy the work of art. Returning to the performing arts, just as Beethoven's Fifth Symphony continues to exist after Beethoven's physical body and the original written composition have perished, the levitation illusion continues to exist long after Harry Kellar, who popularized the feat, and the original apparatus have decayed. Also, just as the recipe cannot be identified with the entree, the composer's score cannot be equated with the music, for the latter is *something written* and the former is *something heard*. Similarly, the levitation illusion cannot be identified with any printed secret and set of instructions, for the latter is *something written* and the former is *something seen*. Even if the instructions include illustrations, such pictures are necessarily static, but a levitation is a dynamic, visible phenomenon. For that matter, braille can make the former accessible to a blind person, but braille cannot convey the act of levitation.

What then is the existential or ontological status of the levitation illusion? Conceptually, it is a generic category (a type) as contrasted with any particular version (token). As a general notion, the "levitation illusion" is a catch-all label that can accommodate all the highly diverse, specific presentations that have ever been performed as well as those that have yet to be devised. One's answer to the above question will depend upon her or his metaphysical assumptions. Philosophical nominalists would regard the levitation illusion as a collective name for all of the various individual versions and nothing more. If the nominalist is correct, the "levitation illusion" is just a classificatory expression that embraces all past, present, and future instances of the floating-woman motif. From this it would follow that the levitation illusion exists only when it is being performed. In short, this and all other feats of magic would have intermittent existence. They would be more like the sporadic rain that falls on a mountain than like the relatively stable mountain itself. Cases of intermittent existence do, of course, raise the philosophical problem of identity. Is the rain at 9:30 this morning the same rain that began at 9:00 a.m., continued unabated until 9:29 a.m., but ceased for the minute between 9:29 and 9:30? Is Harry Blackstone's levitation the same as the one featured by his father? With music, we are in a better position to answer such questions as: "Is the same piece being performed in two or more presentations?" For we can often refer to the original score or composition in order to decide if a given performance is so deviant as to be a different piece altogether. With dance, the matter is more problematic, because, as Adina Armelagos and Mary Sirridge have persuasively argued in "The Identity Crisis in Dance," deciding what is to be included in the notation of a choreographic text is surely controversial. As they observe, so-called incidental or nonessential elements may include costumes and lighting. But obviously some dances would lose their identity were such ingredients altered. This leads Armelagos and Sirridge to discuss the following distinction: "Let us speak of a work of art as autographic . . . if and only if even the most exact duplication of it does not thereby count as genuine. . . . Thus painting is autographic, music non-autographic, or allographic" (132). The authors point out that independent choreographers, who invent and perform their own works, can make significant changes in a work from one performance to the next without jeopardizing the identity of the work. Thus, despite problems of notation, "Dance clearly tends toward being an allographic art" (138). By the above criteria, it could be argued that magic is more allographic than dance, for conjuring lacks anything like the sort of notation systems that exist for music and, to a lesser extent, for dance. With magic, there are no well-defined parameters such as one finds for classical ballet. Instead, the conjurer has such simple imperatives as: "Conceal your methods and be entertaining." In fine, magic is devoid of any formal notation that furnishes standards of action to guide the magician in how to best stage a levitation illusion. The remarks of Armelagos and Sirridge on particular artists are also germane to conjuring: "individual performers are of more than incidental importance. It is plausible to claim that we have 'Frontier' by Martha Graham only if it is performed by Graham or by some surrogate explicitly designated by her" (130). Similarly, certain feats of magic may be said to belong to one magician alone. Because, for example, Neil Foster brought such freshness and distinctive style to his presentation of the "Zombie" (a floating ball routine), it has become inseparably associated with his persona; there is a sense in which no one else can do it. Were a protégé of Foster to replicate all phases of his distinctive yet quintessential routine, he or she would surely be on the verge of reducing artistry to mechanical activity or mere copying.

If, however, one is a Platonist as opposed to a nominalist, the levitation illusion has an altogether different ontological status, for Plato was a dualist who recognized two distinct realms. By the world of becoming, he meant the ever-changing domain of sense perceptions, the physical, empirical world. Plato considered this sphere to be less real or less enduring than the second sphere, the transcendental realm of eternal, unchanging forms. For every imperfect particular in the realm of becoming, Plato postulated the existence of a perfect, immaterial, but actual paradigm in the realm of being. Thus, this latter world is populated by countless ideals, archetypes, or forms toward which all the inferior particulars aspire. All particulars were reduced to the status of faint copies of exemplary universals. While our senses preoccupy us with the realm of becoming, our intellect, at least in some cases, is capable of knowing the forms that inhabit the realm of reality or being. A Platonist might reason as follows in support of Plato:

> We have never perceived a perfect circle, for under sufficient magnification, we will discover that any drawn or printed circle is less than perfect. Yet we do have the notion of a perfect circle, i.e., a geometric shape in which all points are equidistant from the center. Therefore, this concept must have been arrived at by an act of intellect in which we grasped the perfect form "circle" in the realm of being. It is important to realize that, for Plato, such forms or concept-objects do exist independently of us, they have an abiding existence quite apart from our consciousness of them.

Hence, for Plato, it would be false to say, with the nominalists, that the levitation illusion exists only when some particular version of it is being presented. On the contrary, the ideal levitation, the perfect levitation is an enduring form and all particular approximations are both fleeting and inferior. This timeless and flawless form can only be emulated and never realized in the domain of becoming. Consider an example from the field of card magic. The "pass" is a sleight by which one tries to secretly and indetectably cut a deck of cards. The ideal is an invisible pass, one that cannot be seen from any angle. But this as such is impossible; the multifarious particular versions of the pass necessarily fall short, to one degree or another, of the archetypal pass.

Whether one conceives of magic as a Platonist or a nominalist, the fact remains that it must be recognized as a type of process-art. Related to this is the relational character of magic by which the magician can be distinguished from, at least, some painters, sculptors, architects, musicians, and authors, for these sorts of artists can often serve as the audience as well as the creators of their art. But, in one sense, this is not possible in the case of the tri-part, relational nature of magic, in which there must be a performer, an effect, and a spectator. The magician himself cannot play this last role of spectator because the element of deception—a crucial aspect in the aesthetic experience of a magic performance—would be absent.

Magic Artistry, by S. H. Sharpe, is an insightful monograph on the author's philosophy of magic. In 1983, he was awarded a ''Literary Fellowship'' by the Academy of Magical Arts and Sciences in Hollywood, California, in recognition of his scholarly contributions to the theory and history of conjuring. S. H. Sharpe's *Neo Magic: The Art of the Conjuror* has become a standard work on the philosophy and aesthetics of magic. Magicians with a theoretical turn of mind will appreciate this thoughtful book. One can only hope that other talented writers will turn their attention to this neglected area of investigation. Robert Parrish's *For Magicians Only: A Guide to the Art of Mystifying* combines the author's philosophy of magic as a performing art with instruction in basic effects. In *A Manual of Magic Psychology: A Search for Pure Magic*, Michael Ammar correctly points out that if a magician practices his sleights in isolation from each other, then his complete routine is apt to be spasmodic rather than a continuous flow of action. Such pointers can greatly enhance the aesthetic value of one's presentation. Treating related matters, Alan Kronzek's *The Secrets of Alkazar* contains sound advice on routining one's act or show; open with a strong effect, change the pace to keep the audience's attention, and vary the effects are among his suggestions.

For an informative look at the status of the magician as a variety artist, the reader may turn to a contemporary sociologist. In a recent issue of *The Journal of Popular Culture*, Robert A. Stebbins, professor and head of the Department of Sociology, at the University of Calgary in Alberta, contributed an article entitled, ''Making Magic: Production of a Variety Art.'' This essay analyzes the magician's preparation into five categories: learning, acquiring equipment, routining, rehearsing and practicing, and promotion and bookings. The author discusses an interesting distinction between the magician conceived of as a service worker and the magician conceived of as an entertainer; in the former and less prestigious case, the audience that has assembled does not know that a magician will be performing; in the latter case, the magician is an entertainment attraction whose performance has been advertised. Among other worthwhile points is the author's psychological observation that magicians are poor audiences for other magicians, since fellow magicians are prone to become preoccupied with technical considerations rather than entertainment value. Relating magic to other arts, Stebbins notes, ''The excitement centering on a new trick is similar to that which grips a thespian or musician who meets for the first time a new play or selection of music'' (120). The author's fascinating study is based upon dozens of interviews with both amateurs and professionals and upon attendance at magicians' conventions.

Edwin A. Dawes' *The Great Illusionists* has already been cited for its contribution to the history of conjuring, but it should be noted that, in addition to the author's recurrent motif of magic in relation to science, there is a parallel treatment of magic in relation to art. Informative illustrations abound; for example, Hieronymus Bosch's ''The Juggler'' is reproduced and discussed. This lucid and witty oil painting portrays a magician who is performing the cups and balls for a small group of spectators. At the rear of the group is the magician's secret accomplice who is engaged in picking the pocket of a rapt spectator. In chapter eleven, Dawes discusses Charles Dickens' involvement with magic and his daughter's enthusiastic recollection of her father's routines. Another literary figure, Oliver Goldsmith, is also cited for his skillful sleight of hand. Dawes reproduces two of William Hogarth's engravings, ''Masquerades and Operas'' and ''Southwick Fair,'' in which magic is thematic. On the art of drama, Dawes notes that the celebrated magician John Henry Anderson, known to his audiences as the ''Great Wizard of the North,'' served as an inspiration for the one-act play ''The Great Gun Trick—A Magical Squib in One Act,'' which was published in 1856. For a second example of the magician's association with the theater, Dawes turns to another nineteenth-century prestidigitator, John Henry Pepper, who was responsible for producing a ghost illusion during a performance of Dickens' *Haunted Man* in 1862. From the area of popular literature, Dawes singles out the novelist Sax Rhomer (pseudonym for Arthur Henry Ward, 1883–1959), whose interest in magic and friendship with Houdini led him to create a number of short stories about a magician named Bazarada. Among Dawes' numerous references to the intersection between magic and other arts, attention is devoted to Matthew Buchinger, a dwarf who was born without normal hands or legs, but used his stunted appendages to perform the classics of magic with enviable adroitness. It was this diminutive magician, who exemplified the triumph of mind over matter, that Jonathan Swift immortalized in a lengthy punning elegy (in E.J. Wood, *Giants and Dwarfs*, London: Bentley, pp. 278–300).

Several studies relate magic to creativity, the hallmark of art. Those interested in the aesthetics of the creative process will want to be familiar with the ill-fated *The Trick Brain*, by Dariel Fitzkee, which has been cited in discussing the psychology of magic. Those concerned with the aesthetics of magic will be interested in the article, ''Concerning Magic As an Art Form,'' by Jay Sankey. This author is a talented, close-up specialist who, like Maskelyne, emphasizes creativity as a necessary condition for arthood. Sankey correctly observes, ''magic as a whole lacks a sound and universal body of philosophical, psychological, and well-defined aesthetical information'' (15). As was noted in connection with Maskelyne, once a person posits creativity as a necessary condition for magic as art, it becomes obvious that creativity is not, however, a sufficient condition. In short, any such notion is incomplete for it does not distinguish between magic and other creative endeavors. Charles J. Pecor's ironically titled *The Craft of Magic* proposes some criteria for considering the magician as an artist. These include creating one's own effects, figuring out those of others, acquiring a unique style, being able to transcend a mistake, and establishing rapport with one's audience. Demonstrating that artfully fashioned apparatus enhances the beauty of an act, Micky Hades' *The New Make-Up of Magic* offers valuable information on the making and aesthetic decoration of one's props.

One recent study focuses upon the intersection of magic and theater. *The Magic Play*, by S. H. Sharpe, is a unique publication that analyzes magic in relation to drama. This is a treasury of quotes, observations, and speculations on the art form of the magic play. On the first page of this delightful text, Sharpe draws attention to the fact that, for whatever reason, most modern magic plays are light-hearted rather than serious. Casting an eye on antiquity, he locates magical ritual dramas in ancient Greece and Egypt, notes that the transubstantiation of water into wine was a common practice, and reminds us of the magical dimension in creation myths. In his discussion of mystery and miracle plays, Sharpe points out that one of the "miracles" in such plays was the decapitation illusion which is graphically exposed in Reginald Scot's *The Discoverie of Witchcraft*. Moving at a quick, impressionistic pace, the author identifies magical elements in Euripides, Shakespeare, and many classical ballets. In somewhat more detail, Sharpe explores Christopher Marlowe's play *Doctor Faustus* and Goethe's *Faust*. Relating magic to religion, Sharpe quotes from E. M. Butler, "Faust himself, cutting the poor figure that he does, is a telling symptom of the times and of the great change for the worse Christianity has effected in the status of the magician" (16). From Marlowe's play, the author cites passages such as the following: "Faust: Come, show me some demonstrations magical, That I may conjure in some lusty grove, And have these joys in full possession" (37). From Goethe's play, Sharpe quotes, "Come! Rise to higher spheres" (39). This entreaty is directed to Faust, whose soul is about to rise from his dead body. At this point Sharpe speculates on the theological import of levitation illusions: "Here we have the true poetic function of the combined ghost and levitation illusions in their highest form: such as could be used appropriately and ceremoniously in a cathedral to symbolize the apotheosis of a human being; and for which purpose it may possibly have been employed in antiquity during initiation mysteries" (23).

After an introductory essay, the author devotes a brief chapter to magic and supernatural motifs in Shakespeare. In act 1, scene 2, of "A Comedy of Errors," for example, we find, "As nimble jugglers that deceive the eye." At this point, Sharpe reminds the reader that, in the Elizabethan era, the term *juggler* was synonymous with *conjurer*. Quoting freely from the Shakespearean plays, Sharpe demonstrates that four kinds of magic are exemplified. Near the close of this essay, he credits Nevil Maskelyne and David Devant for their convincing staging of supernatural events in *The Witches of Macbeth*, a drama that was presented at St. George's Hall, in 1908. Sharpe's citations of publications that treat Shakespeare and the mysterious are interspersed throughout the discussion. In subsequent sections of Sharpe's study, we learn that Robert-Houdin ingeniously conjured up a ''ghost'' in the melodrama *La Czarine*, which was presented at the Ambigu Theater in Paris in 1868. The magician George Melies, whom film historians recognize as a pioneer in the production of special effects, is cited for writing and performing in some thirty magical sketches at the Theater Robert-Houdin in Paris. As he proceeds further in his valuable book, Sharpe's comments tend to come in the form of an annotated bibliography; his hundreds of citations guarantee that this seminal study will be of enduring value. The complete script of *The Will, The Witch, and The Watchman*, a famous magic play by Nevil Maskelyne, is included in Sharpe's well-researched work.

Since the publication of the above book in 1976, *Merlin*, a play devoted to magic and music, was presented on Broadway in 1983. Its star, the Canadian illusionist Doug Henning, explains the genesis of this production in the souvenir program of the play,

> The idea of doing a magical musical about the life of Merlin as a young man came to me in 1976. I imagined a grand musical with the kind of magic a real magician would do, where magic would be infused into his surroundings, his life and all his adventures. ''Merlin'' grew from these seeds and, for six years, was nurtured to fulfillment thanks to the hard work and dedication of many wonderful people. Upon realizing that I could not create magic on such an enormous scale by myself, I enlisted the help of my magical consultant Charles Reynolds, magic technical supervisor Glen Priest, and, most recently, Jim Steinmeyer, a magical creative designer. Together we formed a ''magical think tank,'' in which we brainstormed magical ideas for the show.

Backed by Columbia Pictures Stage Productions, Henning had an unprecedented, multi-million dollar budget for a magic production. The over thirty illusions designed for the play match—or eclipse—in scale, splendor, and creativity the greatest of the old-time full evening extravaganzas that flourished in the first half of this century. In the opening scene, the curtains part to reveal a field of stars such as movies like *Star Wars* have made a cliché in the science-fiction film. One has to keep reminding himself, however, that this is a live performance. One of the stars, the only red one, begins to move forward, expanding visually as it does so. Eventually the enlarged star, actually a sphere, reaches a size that could contain a man. Translucent now, the star contains a human body; still mysteriously suspended, the sphere functions as a womb, for an ancient wizard oozes out of it—the first ''miracle'' has occurred. During the course of the play, a variety of innovative and truly awe-inspiring illusions are presented in the context of large-scale, musical production numbers for which Broadway is famous. But the play closed in less than a year. What went wrong? Lay critics and magic critics alike have identified the central flaw. The play failed on the level of a narrative. One lay critic—magic critics were understandably more sympathetic—summed up matters with brutal candor by asserting that there were three things that Henning was incapable of doing—singing, dancing, and, perhaps worst of all, acting. Other critics drew attention to the threadbare plot and the eminently forgettable music. One magical reviewer singled out a lack of integration between the music and the magic.

Judged by the canons of magic, the play was a triumph; judged by the criteria of drama, the play faltered pathetically. Magic critics demonstrated a greater sense of proportion in their assessment of the production, for they acknowledged the obvious problems in the play, but enjoined their readers to see the show sheerly for its stupefying array of illusions. Lay critics, who readily conceded that the magic was marvelous, dwelled upon detractions and thereby discouraged attendance. One lay reviewer, Brendan Gill of *The New Yorker* magazine, expressed what was potentially the most damaging of all critiques, namely that the gap between magic and musical comedy could not be aesthetically closed. Future magicians, who might seek to synthesize magic and musical comedy or drama, can, however, breathe a sigh of relief, for Gill's argumentation in support of his thesis is diffuse and unconvincing. In his terms, magic defies the natural order (so far so good) but musical comedy accommodates itself to the natural order (what is this claim supposed to mean? and what is Gill's evidence?). Such a priori injunctions against the fusion of magic and musical comedy smack of unmitigated dogmatism. In simple terms, Gill's assertions are ungrounded and silly. But it must be admitted that any magician who undertakes the production of a magic play will surely want to analyze the difficulties that undermined *Merlin*. One moral seems clear. If one cannot successfully wed good magic and good drama, he should revert to good magic alone. In the seventies, Henning himself proved that a magical musical, *The Magic Show*, could succeed on Broadway for nearly half a decade. At present, the magic world does have one resident magic company that has been remarkably successful, Le Grand David Show at the Cabot Street Theatre in Beverly, Massachusetts. In 1986, the cast of over five dozen performers celebrated its one thousandth performance. With appearances at the White House, nearly ten years at the Cabot Theatre, and numerous stories in newspapers and national periodicals, the triumvirate of Le Grand David, Marco the Magi, and the young Seth the Sensational plus its supporting cast did, indeed, have grounds for jubilation. As Robert Lund, curator of the American Museum of Magic in Marshall, Michigan, has noted, this talented troupe has greatly surpassed Harry Kellar's run of 320 performances in Philadelphia in 1885.

The Magician on the American Stage, 1752–1874, also by Charles Joseph Pecor, is a detailed study of magic and its relation to early American theater. The author is surely one of the most prolific contemporary historians of magic. Magicians' riveting posters, aswarm with archetypal motifs from devils to virgins, were crucial in attracting large crowds to the theater. Charles and Regina Reynolds' *100 Years of Magic Posters* reproduces over one hundred of the flamboyant posters that so many magicians have favored. Without such a collection, the distinctive, eye-catching art of the magic poster would be known only to the specialist or collector. Exhibited outside on the street, posters brought a glimpse of the magician's wonderland to the everyday world. In effect, such posters were aesthetic "windows" that were as crucial to the architecture of the theater as were its actual doors. Others who have taken steps to preserve this aspect of our magical heritage include Robert Lund, curator of the American Museum of Magic in Marshall, Michigan, who exhibits a stunning array of mint-condition posters in his museum. Lee Jacobs, the American magician and magic dealer, has also rendered a genuine service to the magic fraternity by reproducing a number of the great posters. Lee Jacobs Productions, of Pomeroy, Ohio, 45769, is the world's largest dealership for both contemporary and rare magic posters. Among the recent items available is "The Doug Henning 'Water Torture Escape' Poster." The artist, Seymour Chwast, is internationally known, having exhibited his works in such prestigious institutions as the Louvre in Paris and the Museum of Modern Art in New York. For a discussion of the play *The Honorable History of Friar Bacon and Friar Bungay*, one may read I. G. Edmonds' *The Magic Makers: Magic and the Men Who Made It*. Although a Franciscan monk, Bacon devoted attention to magic, science, and philosophy, as well as to religion.

Part artists and part scientists, magicians served as special-effects men in plays before contributing their skills to film making. For an exposition of spirit apparitions on the London stage, one can consult Henry Dircks' *The Ghost, As Produced in Spectre Drama*. With John Henry Pepper, Dircks, who was a civil engineer, patented a device in 1863. This piece of equipment was employed in the production of Charles Dickens' *Haunted Man*. Those interested in nineteenth-century England will also enjoy Henry Morley's *Journal of a London Playgoer: from 1851 to 1866* in which John Henry Anderson is discussed. For remarks on magic during the Elizabethan era, one may read L. B. Wright's article, "Juggling Tricks and Conjuring on the English Stage before 1642," which appeared in *Modern Philology*.

For a unique article on magic and narrative art, one can read "Mixing Magic with Opera," by Wil and Janii Staar. As participants in a fund-raising activity for the San Diego Opera Guild, this pair was challenged by a request to adapt their magic to operatic themes. This brief essay sketches their approach to *Hansel and Gretel*, *Madama Butterfly*, *Don Pasquale*, *La Boheme*, and *Salome*. The authors report that their numbers were "well-received by some two hundred opera enthusiasts, one of whom was the illustrious Tito Capobianco, Director of the famous San Diego Opera" (53). Wil and Janii draw from standard props in the magician's repertoire, but add appropriate patter in order to fuse magic with operatic motifs. Those interested in related theater arts will enjoy Eric Hawkesworth's *A Magic Variety Show: Novelty Acts for the Amateur Entertainer*, which discusses chapeaugraphy (making diverse hats from a single piece of cloth), Chinese paper-folding (forming animals, boats, fans, and other objects), paper-tearing (creating figures and designs), and shadowgraphy (using one's hands and props to create shadow-images). *Cards as Weapons*, by Ricky Jay, is a unique, witty book that instructs one in the virtually lost art of card-scaling. This artistic flourish enables one to throw cards from the stage to the uppermost balconies in a huge theater or auditorium. Part of Howard Thurston's great reputation was founded upon his considerable dexterity at this practice. Fascinating historical material is interspersed with Jay's wacky brand of humor; the latter being illustrated by his subtitle for this manual: *Treatise on the art of throwing, scaling, juggling, boomeranging, and manipulating playing cards, with particular emphasis upon impressing one's friends and providing a deadly yet inexpensive means of self-defense.*

The Magician and the Cinema, by Erik Barnouw, is an engaging study that pinpoints the role of the magician in the evolution of motion pictures. Drawing upon the literature of magic, a body of information with which the average film historian is unfamiliar, the author credits magicians with contributing to the prehistory of the cinema, for they produced illusions dependent upon the use of a concealed magic lantern; in fact, such projected images were part of magicians' programs for over a hundred years before the advent of the cinema as a commercial enterprise. As film historians like Arthur Night have observed, Barnouw notes that the success of early movies inspired magicians to pioneer in the creation of "trick films." Ironically enough, such films tended to undermine the status of the stage magician, for anyone adept at film editing was capable of producing spectacular marvels—feats that some found more impressive than the most stupendous illusions of the live stage show. Turning his attention to the nineteenth century, Barnouw relates that by 1849, Etienne Gaspard Robert, under the stage name "Robertson," had used rear projection technique in order to produce spirit apparitions on stage. This particular device was, of course, eventually adopted by filmmakers and it continues to be one of their standard tools. The author adds that filmmakers also profited from the stage magician's use of the combination of magic lantern, mirror, and clear glass to conjure up ghostly appearances.

Barnouw reports that for a time magicians followed an "if you can't beat them, join them" philosophy by featuring short movies as a part of their programs. Unfortunately for magicians, the films rapidly became the main attraction or drawing card. By 1899, transformation effects were being accomplished in films by making cuts between segments; it is hardly surprising to read that the professional magician Melies was one of the most adept editors. We also learn that at about this time, J. Stuart Blackston, a former magician, had incorporated the use of miniatures or models for special effects in a war film. Barnouw reminds us that the greatest escape artist and most celebrated magician of this century, Harry Houdini, made five feature films from 1919 to 1923. Thus the magician became not only the figure behind the scenes in the making of early films but also a player in motion pictures themselves. Although perhaps predictable, it was regrettable that Houdini's escape stunts, which were integrated into the melodramatic plots, lost credibility, for the reason that a growing number of spectators realized that virtually anything was possible through film editing. There is some basis for the claim that the most highly paid magicians of today are the special effects artists who are responsible for the dazzling scenes in such contemporary movies as *Jaws*, *Star Wars*, and *An American Werewolf in London*. Just as knowing magicians' secrets alters one's perception of their performances, knowing the tricks of special-effects artists changes one's reactions to their films. If one is familiar with the rear-view projection process, for example, its appearance in a film can be a distraction that subtracts from the intended realism of the filmmakers.

Though television is the prevailing medium today, little has been written on TV and magic. Señor Mardo's *White Sorcery* offers brief advice for performers who wish to entertain through the medium of television. *TV, Magic, and You*, by Jay Marshall and Frances Ireland Marshall, is a comprehensive manual for magicians who are disposed toward the medium of television. Drawing upon his own considerable experience and that of a panel of other experts, Marshall discusses obtaining bookings, tested-material, actual scripts, music, previous magic TV series, and other related topics. In the nearly thirty years since the publication of this book, magicians like Doug Henning and David Copperfield have achieved celebrity status through their television appearances. Moreover, close-up magicians have capitalized on the fact that their routines, which cannot be seen by a theater audience, can be appreciated by millions through the vehicle of television.

To study the role of magic and magicians in what the American philosopher John Dewey called a vital art, one must turn to the funny papers. In 1934, King Features Newspaper Syndicate purchased Lee Falk's comic strip "Mandrake the Magician." Phil Davis served as the illustrator of this highly popular strip, one that today would have been consigned to the oblivion of specialists were it not for the fact that Nostalgia Press has recently reprinted all the daily strips from January 31 to July 9, 1938, in *Mandrake the Magician: Mandrake in Hollywood*. In the introduction, Maurice Horn reveals that the young Falk had been fascinated with magic and magicians ever since serving as a youthful volunteer for such magic greats as Thurston and Cardini. Horn adds that the distinctive artwork, which was supplied by Davis, has been praised by filmmakers such as Federico Fellini. Mandrake sometimes acted as a neo-Houdini by exposing the methods of immoral charlatans who use trickery to bilk the public. On one occasion, Mandrake hypothesized that the famous Indian or East Indian rope trick (see the Introduction of the present work) was accomplished by a feat of mass hypnosis. Despite its consideration of such serious subjects, the strip was usually marked by a light-hearted tone and a directness of plot. It is likely that the fictional Mandrake inspired as many neophyte magicians as did the flesh and blood greats such as Thurston and Keller, again demonstrating that life imitates art. In the 1950s the converse was exhibited when the real-life Blackstone became the springboard for the comic book devoted to him.

Moving from the domain of popular culture to more prestigious literature, *The Magic of Lewis Carroll*, by the English magician/author John Fisher, is a pleasant miscellany of magic effects, logical puzzles, and mathematical stunts.

As the author points out, it is no accident that the props of the magician (a white rabbit, mirrors, and playing cards) find their way into Carroll's Alice stories, for in addition to being a lecturer in mathematics and logic, an inventor of such things as double-sided adhesive tape, a prototype of the board game "Scrabble," and an adept amateur photographer, Carroll (pseudonym of Henry Lutwidge Dodgson) dabbled in magic. Dickens was another British author who was very taken with magic. "Charles Dickens in and about Magic: A Preliminary Sketch," by Steven S. Tigner, editor of *The Journal of Magic History*, is a well-researched and engrossing account of the role magic played in the life of a great man of letters. One writer, quoted by Tigner, offers especially high praise for Dickens as a magician: "The best conjuror I every saw . . . [His magic] . . . would enable him to make a handsome subsistence let the book seller trade go as it please—!" (97–98) We also learn that Dickens pioneered in the battle against exploitive spiritualists and charlatans of the supernatural, a never-ending fight that was later taken up by the likes of Houdini, John Mulholland, and the Amazing Randi. Of course, Dickens' Scrooge was hardly intimidated by a ghost when, in response to this specter he speculates that it might just be the product of an undigested bit of beef or a blob of mustard. Tigner's article describes the impressive feats of magic that Dickens performed and also reveals his estimate of such contemporary magicians as John Henry Anderson, the self-professed "Wizard of the North." In short, Tigner's scholarly article, with it copious footnotes, can be paid the highest sort of compliment, for it makes the reader wish for a book-length study of Dickens and his magic.

BIBLIOGRAPHY

Ammar, Michael. *A Manual of Magic Psychology: A Search for Pure Magic*. Bluefield, W.Va.: Author, n.d.

Armelagos, Adina, and Mary Sirridge. "The Identity Crisis in Dance." *The Journal of Aesthetics and Art Criticism* 37 (1978): 129–139.

Barnouw, Erik. *The Magician and the Cinema*. New York: Oxford University Press, 1981.

Dawes, Edwin A. *The Great Illusionists*. Secaucus, N.J.: Chartwell Books, 1979.

Dircks, Henry. *The Ghost, As Produced in Spectre Drama*. London: Spon, 1863.

Edmonds, I. G. *The Magic Makers: Magic and the Men Who Made It*. Nashville: Thomas Nelson, 1976.

Falk, Lee, and Phil Davis. *Mandrake the Magician: Mandrake in Hollywood*. Franklin Square, N.Y.: Nostalgia Press, 1970.

Fisher, John. *The Magic of Lewis Carroll*. London: Nelson, 1973.

Fitzkee, Dariel. *The Trick Brain*. San Rafael, Calif.: St. Raphael House, 1944.

Gill, Brendan. "Ambitious Illusionist." *The New Yorker*, 28 February 1983, p. 82.

Goodsell, David. "Nothing Up My Sleeve." *M-U-M*, July 1983, p. 9.

Hades, Micky, ed. *The New Make-Up of Magic*. 2d ed. Seattle: Micky Hades Intl., 1974.

Hawkesworth, Eric. *A Magic Variety Show: Novelty Acts for the Amateur Entertainer*. London: Faber, 1973.

Henning, Doug. "The Magic of 'Merlin'." *Merlin: The Magical Musical* (the souvenir program from the play *Merlin*) (1983), p. 3 of unnumbered pages.

Jay, Ricky. *Cards as Weapons*. New York: Darien House, 1977.

Kronzek, Alan Z. *The Secrets of Alkazar*. New York: Four Winds Press, 1980.

Mardo, Senor. *White Sorcery*. Calif.: Morcom, 1951.

Marshall, Jay, and Frances Ireland Marshall. *TV, Magic, and You*. Chicago: Magic Inc., 1955.

Maskelyne, John Nevil, and David Devant. *Our Magic*. London: Routledge, 1911.

Maskelyne, Nevil. *Maskelyne on the Performance of Magic*. New York: Dover, 1976.

Morley, Henry. *Journal of a London Playgoer, from 1851 to 1866*. London: Routledge, 1891.

Parrish, Robert. *For Magicians Only: A Guide to the Art of Mystifying*. New York: Bernard Ackerman, 1944.

Pecor, Charles J. *The Craft of Magic: Easy-to-Learn Illusions for Spectacular Performances*. Englewood Cliffs, N.J.: Prentice-Hall, 1979.

———. *The Magician on the American Stage, 1752–1874*. Washington, D.C.: Emerson and West, 1977.

Reneaux, James. *The Professional Technique for Magicians*. Colon, Mich.: Abbott's Magic, 1968.

Reynolds, Charles, and Regina Reynolds. *100 Years of Magic Posters*. New York: A Darien House Book, 1976.

Sankey, Jay. "Concerning Magic As an Art Form." *Magic Manuscript* (August/September 1983): 14–15.

Sartre, Jean-Paul. *The Psychology of Imagination*. New York: Washington Square Press, 1966.

Scot, Reginald. *The Discovery of Witchcraft*. New York: Dover, 1975.

Sharpe, S. H. *Magic Artistry*. London: Author, 1938.

———. *The Magic Play*. Chicago: Magic Inc., 1976.

———. *Neo Magic: The Art of the Conjuror*. London: Magic Wand, 1932.

Staar, Wil, and Janii Staar. "Mixing Magic with Opera." *The Linking Ring* 63 (1983): 53–54.

Stebbins, Robert A. "Making Magic: Production of a Variety Art." *The Journal of Popular Culture* 16 (1982): 116–126.

Tigner, Steven S. "Charles Dickens in and about Magic: A Preliminary Sketch." *The Journal of Magic History* 1, no. 2 (1979): 88–110.

Weibel, Richard. *Conjuring Psychology*. New York: Magico Magazine Publications, 1980.

Wright, L. B. "Juggling Tricks and Conjuring on the English Stage before 1642." *Modern Philology* 24 (1927): 269–84.

5

BIOGRAPHIES AND AUTOBIOGRAPHIES

Certain works, which highlight the lives of several magicians, can readily be recommended. The first chapter of *Milbourne Christopher's Magic Book* gives an anecdotal and revealing glimpse into the lives and feats of a number of famous magicians. Harry Kellar, Max Malini, Alexander Herrmann, Howard Thurston, and Harry Houdini appear in photographs from the author's private collection. In the same vein, *The World's Greatest Magic*, by Hyla M. Clark, is a beautifully illustrated text that features biographical sketches of such contemporary greats as Houdini, Slydini, and Dai Vernon. This biographical material is followed by a well-chosen assortment of close-up and stage feats. In *Adventures in Magic*, Henry Ridgely Evans treats such twentieth-century giants as the redoubtable Okito. George B. Anderson's general book, *Magic Digest: Fun Magic for Everyone*, also features biographical sketches of prominent magicians. James G. Thompson's *My Best: A Collection of the Best Originations Conceived by Eminent Creators* again includes biographical profiles of its contributors.

Other excellent books feature a single, short profile. A brief biography of the much-esteemed Dai Vernon may be found in Lewis Ganson's *The Dai Vernon Book of Magic*. Similarly, a succinct biography of Leipzig is included in Lewis Ganson's *Dai Vernon's Tribute to Nate Leipzig*. Leipzig is best remembered for his captivating personality and his virtuoso status as a card manipulator. Again, Ganson provides biographical material in *Malini & His Magic*. Max Malini became an internationally renowned performer because of his distinctive touch with such classics of magic as the egg bag. *An Evening with Charlie Miller*, by Robert Parrish, includes biographical material on an outstanding close-up entertainer. W. F. Rufus Steele, a cardician whose books emphasize feats that require minimal skill, offers some biographical information in *Paul Rosini's Magical Gems*.

Playbills and critical reviews contribute to any well-rounded biography or autobiography. Arnold Furst's *Famous Magicians of the World* is a collection of the author's photographically illustrated reviews of such magical paragons as Dante, Sorcar, and Blackstone. Written as entries for *Genii* magazine in the 1950s, Furst's compact evaluations transport the reader to one of the golden ages in the history of conjuring. Max Holden's *Programmes of Famous Magicians* is a similar booklet that features the programs of more than a hundred great magicians; among those included are Blackstone, Houdini, Dante, Thurston, Cardini, and Dunninger. This illustrated monograph can serve as a valuable reference tool for the historian and as a compendium of ideas on routining for the active magician. Tony Taylor's *Spotlight on 101 Great Magic Acts* may be compared with similar works by Furst and Holden. Unique, but related to the above is *Melody Magic*, compiled by Harry Clapham, with a biographical sketch by Henry Ridgely Evans and reproductions of photographs, handbills, and sheet music that were used by the magician, mimic, and composer Robert Heller.

Among the myriad autobiographies and biographies, the following are highly recommended. Percy Abbott's *A Lifetime in Magic* chronicles the life of an Australian magician who established one of the largest magic dealerships in the United States. His magical tours took him to Java, Manila, Shanghai, Siberia, and ultimately to a tiny town, Colon, Michigan, where he founded his world-famous magic factory. Painted black and decorated with white skeletons, there is visual irony in the location of this building, for the surrounding countryside is populated by austerely religious Amish people. The book is as fascinating as was the man. Another visitor to America, John Henry Anderson, the self-proclaimed "Great Wizard of the North," is thematic in James B. Findlay's informative monograph *Anderson & His Theatre*. Anderson was a flamboyant figure who did not balk at including "bullet catching" in his program any more than he hesitated to exploit the advertising possibilities of this sensational feat. Anderson's "North" refers to the north of Scotland. In *Dedicated Magic*, Val Andrews, a magician and biographer of such magic greats as Dante, presents an engrossing account of his own experiences as a conjurer. *Four Seasons in the Life of Val Andrews: An Autobiography of Val Andrews*, written over a decade after the above book, traces the author's life from birth to the present and, in doing so, gives us a magician's eye view of performing in a circus, the war years, and English music halls. Eleven of his "pet" routines are also included in this compact and engaging piece of revery.

Nothing up My Sleeve! the autobiography of Douglas Beaufort, introduces the reader to an accomplished performer whose long career, travels, and performances for members of royalty parallel those of Okito. Charles Bertram's *A Magician in Many Lands* provides a turn-of-the-century autobiographical narrative of one magician's fascinating odyssey. *Around the World with a Magician and a Juggler*, by H. J. Burlingame, deals with the travels and experiences of a magician during the nineteenth century. Signor Blitz's *Fifty Years in the Magic Circle* recounts the magical exploits of the man who is credited with inspiring

Scotland's most illustrious magician, John Henry Anderson. *The John Booth Classics*, by John N. Booth, contains the reminiscences and effects of one of the best-known figures in the world of magic. A complementary work, *Booth's Fabulous Destinations*, is a magical travelogue that will captivate any magic lover. In *The Barrister in the Circle*, by Edwin A. Dawes, the lawyer is Sidney Clarke, who wrote *The Annals of Conjuring, from the Earliest Times to the Present Day*, and the "Circle" refers to England's most prestigious fraternity of conjurers, The Magic Circle. Dawes' scholarship casts considerable light on a figure who is sometimes credited with writing the first satisfactory history of conjuring. Clarke's sources, his method for obtaining previously unobtainable data, his relations with his publisher, and his letters with fellow historians of magic are all included.

In *Goodnight Mr. Dante*, Val Andrews writes the first biography of Dante (pseudonym of Harry A. Jensen), an exemplary magician whose career spanned over sixty years. Howard Thurston, who had the greatest magic show of his day, appointed Dante as his successor. Dante's compelling and somewhat demonic stage presence eventually landed him a role in the 1942 Laurel and Hardy film, *A-Haunting We Will Go*. *My Magic Life*, by David Devant, chronicles the exciting experiences of the magician who was selected for an unprecedented command performance before George V and whose career flourished after appearances at Maskelyne's Egyptian Hall in London. In *Magic As a Performing Art*, Robert Gill, a fellow Englishman, notes that "Devant is considered by most magicians in this country to have been the master performer of his time, and perhaps the greatest magician of all time." Devant's *Woes of a Wizard* is shorter and appeared three decades earlier than the above. Given the author's stature in the magic world and given his associations with other great conjurers, Devant's record of himself and his times is indispensable for a grasp of the state of magic from the last quarter of the nineteenth century to the first half of the present century. *Charles Dickens and His Magic*, by James B. Findlay, is a brief but valuable booklet that examines the role that magic played in Dickens' life.

Germain, the Wizard and his Legerdemain is Stuart Cramer's second study of the man and his magic. This book and its predecessor will insure that Germain retains his place in the history of stage magic. Four years earlier, Cramer wrote the seminal study, *Secrets of Karl Germain*. *Gene Gordon's Magical Legacy*, by Gordon himself, relates the colorful experiences of a magician who spent twenty years on the road and then went on to run a magic dealership for a quarter of a century. The author's anecdotes and rare photographs enrich his collection of superbly commercial routines. A similar background is evident in *The Magic Man*, by Herman Hanson and John Zweers, which details the intriguing life of Herman Hanson, a figure who mounted his own show, was featured in Howard Thurston's show, became a magic dealer, and organized numerous magic shows.

Magician's Handbook, by H. J. Burlingame, published originally in Chicago in 1897, contains a wealth of biographical material on the celebrated Herrmanns, Carl and Alexander, plus a discussion of their premier mysteries. Feminists would be interested in noting that Alexander's widow, Adelaide, perpetuated his show for thirty years following his death in 1896. It is even more arresting to discover that in 1897 Adelaide performed the "bullet-catching stunt," which the likes of Houdini shunned, in the Chicago Grand Opera House. In her version, she used her hand to apparently catch six bullets fired from the rifles of six militiamen. It is indeed ironic that Houdini, whose forte was escape artistry rather than magic, endures as the most famous magician of all times. *Houdini: The Untold Story*, by Milbourne Christopher, remains the finest biography of the man who could walk through walls. Complemented by five dozen photographs and illustrations, this study is essential reading for all devotees of magic. *Houdini: His Life and Art*, by James Randi and Bert Randolph Sugar, is a richly illustrated treatment of its subjects. Given that Randi is Houdini's most successful successor in the area of escapes, the book is an authoritative source for Houdini's actual methods.

Houdini on Magic, by Walter B. Gibson (a personal friend of Houdini) and Morris N. Young, is a wide-ranging study that incorporates historical and biographical material as well as an exposé of Houdini's techniques for escaping from handcuffs, ropes, and a wide variety of other restraining devices. The authors observe that by 1920 Houdini had become a household word, for in that year *Funk and Wagnalls Standard Dictionary* included the verb "houdinize," defining it as "to release or extricate oneself from confinement, bonds, or the like, as by wriggling out." Gibson and Young regard Houdini's estimate of his peers as an important contribution to the history of conjuring. While Houdini's evaluations of other magicians may have been unduly critical, such remarks balance those of historians who are excessively salubrious. Even when Houdini's opinions were unfair or mistaken, they had the virtue of encouraging the research of his detractors. One chapter is given over to the required topic of Houdini's crusade against sham mediums; a last chapter treats such unsavory types as bunco men and pickpockets. Walter B. Gibson's *The Original Houdini Scrapbook* is an outstanding, largely pictorial compilation of photographs, magic feats, posters, and letters of Houdini. Gibson has drawn from his own collection (six decades in the making); the American Museum of Magic in Marshall, Michigan; The Houdini Hall of Fame in Niagara Falls; and the Library of Congress (see the Appendix to the present work for information on these institutions).

Houdini, His Life-Story, by Harold Kellock, draws upon the observations and documents of Houdini's wife Beatrice. Since Houdini's allegiance to his wife was superseded only by his commitment to his mother, this work is an important addition to the literature. J. C. Cannell's *The Secrets of Houdini*, originally published in 1931, has become a standard treatment of the world's most famous escapologist. Personal material enriches this account of Houdini's exciting on-land and underwater escapes. For example, his campaign against fake mediums, who profess to have supernatural powers, is discussed. Ironically enough, many people attributed just such powers to Houdini himself. In the October 1983 issue of *M-U-M* magazine, Richard J. Weibel quotes Houdini's response to such suppositions:

> Many scientists and students of psychic phenomena say I have supernatural power. This is obviously absurd. No one possesses supernatural power. No supernatural power is manifested in this world. Do not, therefore, be superstitious. Don't be afraid of spirits or spooks! There are none. Don't dash by graveyards. Don't fear the dark. I have slept in haunted houses and cemeteries, and the only thing I ever caught was a cold (28).

The Great Houdini, Magician Extraordinary, by Beryl Williams and Samuel Epstein, is still of value amidst the ever-growing literature on the supreme escape artist. *Houdini—The Man who Walked through Walls*, by William Lindsay Gresham, is a photographically illustrated work which has earned its status as a standard biography. *Houdini: His Legend and His Magic*, by Doug Henning and Charles Reynolds, is marked by its reproduction of a wide variety of Houdini memorabilia including photographs, letters, newspaper accounts, and posters. Henning himself has presented a version of Houdini's Chinese water torture escape on network television.

Houdini and Conan Doyle: The Story of a Strange Friendship was coauthored by Bernard Ernst, who served as President of the Society of American Magicians, and Hereward Carrington, a member of the Society for Psychical Research; both authors' interests coincided in the remarkable friendship of Houdini and Doyle. Houdini, fully conversant with the tricks of every breed of charlatan, delighted in exposing the subterfuges of purported psychics and mediums. Doyle was deeply committed to the "truths" of spiritualism. To Houdini, Doyle was "a victim of the foolery of darkened rooms." To Doyle, Houdini was "one of the greatest mediums of all time." Until his death, Doyle held that Houdini's feats of escape were achieved by dematerialization of his body. Houdini always insisted that his apparent "miracles" were accomplished through sheer natural trickery. Letters exchanged between Houdini and Doyle form the fascinating connective tissue of this engrossing narrative. From the foreword to the conclusion, each figure is relentlessly committed to converting the other to his position. On the side of Houdini is the fact that Doyle was largely ignorant of the ruses, devices, and gimmicks with which all informed magicians are familiar. On the side of Doyle is the fact that Houdini refused to explain some of his most inexplicable feats. The authors do permit the reader to feel the pull, the attractiveness, of each man's posture, but given the data presented, Houdini's case becomes more persuasive. The more knowing a reader is in the wiles of the magician (some of Houdini's secrets are divulged by the writers), the more gullible Doyle appears and the more jolting is the realization that his fictional character Sherlock Holmes, the very personification of rational thinking, is still cited in logic textbooks.

Bernard C. Meyer, M.D., authored *Houdini: A Mind in Chains: A Psychoan-*

alytic Portrait, a unique study that seeks to uncover the psyche of the larger-than-life escape artist. Sharing Houdini's Jewish heritage, Meyer is particularly interested in demonstrating the religious aspects of Houdini's character. *Death and the Magician*, by Raymund Fitzsimons, is a recent and worthwhile biography of Houdini which suggests that he will forever remain a somewhat opaque character in whom each generation will invest its sense of wonder. Joseph Dunninger's *100 Houdini Tricks You Can Do* contains anecdotal material on both Houdini and Dunninger himself. *Murray*, by Val Andrews, details the life and magic of an Australian counterpart to Houdini, for both performers emphasized sensational escape stunts.

Houdini was both the namesake and the defamer of Jean Eugenė Robert-Houdin, one of the most distinguished of all showmen. *King of Conjurors: Memoirs of Robert-Houdin* relates the adventures and magical creations of the most illustrious French magician of all time. Given his flair for sensational magic, it is not surprising that he served as an inspiration for the supreme sensationalist, Harry Houdini. *The Unmasking of Robert-Houdin* is Houdini's famous, some would say infamous, assault on the magical competency of his French predecessor. Henry Ridgely Evans has also authored a standard biography of Robert-Houdin, *A Master of Modern Magic: The Life and Adventures of Robert-Houdin*. This thoughtful monograph is just one of the publications one should read in order to draw his or her own conclusions on Houdini's critique of Robert-Houdin. *Where Houdini Was Wrong: A Reply to the Unmasking of Robert-Houdin*, by Maurice Sardina (translated by Victor Farelli), seeks to rebut the charges that Houdini leveled against Robert-Houdin. I. G. Edmond's *The Magic Makers: Magic and the Men Who Made It* is noteworthy for its spirited defense of Robert-Houdin against the accusations of Houdini. Samuel Sharpe's *Salutations to Robert-Houdin* is a painstakingly researched volume that stands as the definitive study of the father of modern magic. As in the case of Maurice Sardina, Sharpe concerns himself with setting the historical record straight on the matter of Robert-Houdin's actual accomplishments.

For the magical itinerary of a nineteenth-century conjurer, one may read J. W. Holden's *A Wizard's Wanderings from China to Peru*. Another traveler wins the award for prolixity of titles among magicians' autobiographies with *A Magician's Tour Up and Down and Round the Earth: Being the Life of an American Nostradamus, Harry Kellar*. That an undisputed master of conjuring could remain gullible is evidenced in the following observation by Kellar: "Fifteen years spent in India and the Far East have convinced me that the high-caste fakirs, or magicians, of Northern India have probably discerned natural laws of which we in the West are ignorant. They succeed in overcoming forces of nature which seem insurmountable, my observation satisfies me beyond doubt"(216).

Jarrett, by Guy Jarrett, is available in a new edition that has been enlarged by Jim Steinmeyer; the original 1936 text is now a rare item. Jarrett's credentials rest on his services as illusion designer for such greats as Thurston and Kellar. In addition to the more than fifty impressive mysteries that are explained, the text contains Jarrett's unexpurgated observations on a number of famous magicians. The publisher at once cautions and entices the reader, "Jarrett's text is sprinkled with profanities and he played rough with many legends of magic. We have not deleted any of it, so don't say we didn't warn you!" One of Jarrett's publishers is herself responsible for three autobiographical additions to the literature of conjuring. *My First Fifty Years*, by Frances Ireland Marshall, commemorates her half-century involvement with magic as performer, author, editor, teacher, and magic dealer. Covering the period from 1931 to 1981, this is a lively, anecdotal account of one extraordinary woman's experiences in a predominantly male-oriented world. *With Frances in Magicland*, by the above author, combines sketches of leading magicians with her own fascinating experiences. This is magic history at its delectable best. *You Don't Have to Be Crazy*, also by Ms. Marshall, contains autobiographical recollections, biographical anecdotes, and an analysis of the ethics of conjuring.

For British paragons of prestidigitation, one turns inevitably to the Maskelynes. *White Magic: The Story of the Maskelynes*, the autobiography of Jasper Maskelyne, also recounts the experiences of Jasper's father, grandfather, and a number of sterling magicians who were employed by the Maskelynes. George A. Jenness' *Maskelyne and Cooke: Egyptian Hall, London, 1873–1904* enlightens the reader on a British institution that showcased the talents of such greats as Adalbert Frikell. Jasper Maskelyne's *Magic—Top Secret* is an autobiographical account in which the author explains how he drew upon the principles of stage magic while serving as a soldier.

The War Magician, by David Fisher, is a novel that remains true to the real-life adventures of Jasper Maskelyne, the great British conjurer who put his expertise in conjuring to good use on the battlefields of World War II. While some of the characters are composites, the phenomenal accomplishments attributed to this outstanding magician are genuine. Drawing upon the principles of stage magic, Maskelyne worked to thwart the advance of Hitler. He disguised tanks so that they would appear to be innocent trucks when seen from the air, made the Suez Canal "disappear" from the perspective of enemy air craft on night missions (through the use of bright, disorienting ground lights), and created armies of scarecrow soldiers to intimidate enemy planes. L. H. Branson's *A Lifetime of Deception*, like Jasper Maskelyne's *Magic—Top Secret*, focuses upon a magician who incorporated magic in his military service. *Those Entertaining Years*, by H. C. Mole, offers entertaining recollections and anecdotes in the format of a monograph.

Magic for Magicians, F. B. Nightingale's detailed autobiography, is punctuated by instruction in some of the author's favorite close-up and platform effects. Among the greatest of recent stage performers was Okito. *Okito on Magic*, by Theodore Bamberg, who masqueraded as an Oriental magician, combines autobiographical material with explanations for some of the timeless effects that the author popularized. Touring the world, and often performing for members of royalty, he established himself as a model for the presentation of eye-appealing magic in the Oriental manner. In later life, Okito lived in Chicago; it was during this period that I was fortunate enough to study sleight of hand under his expert instruction. *The Piddingtons*, by Russell Braddon, focuses upon two of the most famous, sometimes infamous, mentalists. Their posturing as true psychics is repeated in the acts of some contemporary mentalists. As Harry Blackstone, Jr., has noted, mind-reading tends to be less visual than magic per se. Dunninger, after all, did mentalism on radio. Deficient in the visual appeal of magic, mentalism must speak to conceptual interests. The contract between Okito and the Piddingtons underlines this distinction.

The Life and Times of Augustus Rapp, the Small-Town Showman is an octogenarian's autobiography that plunges the reader into a world of magicians, ventriloquists, mentalists, carnival workers, and other assorted entertainers. Photographs, programs, and drawings illumine this utterly absorbing account of one Midwesterner's seventy-five-year career as a magician. If Rapp was a magician for the hinterlands, Rosini exemplified the urbane professional. *Carl Rosini—His Life and His Magic*, by Robert E. Olson and Edward Dart, features the biography of a superb magician and includes some of his pet secrets. From his struggling days to his South American tour, Rosini's story rivets the reader's attention. Among the magical offerings is Rosini's construction plan for an automaton that performs the cups and balls routine. *The Amazing World of John Scarne: A Personal History* is arguably one of the most engrossing of all magical autobiographies. A self-instructed expert on gambling and cheating techniques, Scarne was unmatched in both shrewdness and skill. On the one hand, the federal government courted him, because of his ability to lecture on the artifices of the cheat. On the other hand, members of the underworld threatened his life if he would not divulge the secret of his ability to cut to each of the four aces in a shuffled deck. According to Scarne, this last practice was effected by visual estimation, for he glimpsed the position of each ace during the course of one or more riffle shuffles. His account is mesmerizing and essential reading for all lovers of magic. Comparing Scarne to Joshua Medley, one might conclude that truth is stranger than fiction. Frances L. Shine's *Conjuror's Journal, Excerpts from the Journal of Joshua Medley, Conjuror, Juggler, Ventriloquist, and Sometime Balloonist: A Novel* is a fictionalized but informative story of one character's exploits in the last decade of the eighteenth century.

Devotees of Oriental magic will be interested in the following three biographies and in Tenkai's autobiography. *A Gift from the Gods—the Story of Ching Ling Soo, Marvelous Chinese Conjurer*, by Val Andrews, is a sumptuous tribute to a deserving master magician, William E. Robinson, who masqueraded as an Oriental and adopted the mysteriously elegant costume of the Chinese magician. Over fifty of his ethereal posters have been reproduced in full color for this volume. Andrews collaborated with Robinson's son, Hector, in order to detail the life of one of the greatest showmen in the history of conjuring. Robinson not only acquired an international reputation, but he also worked with such magical luminaries as Kellar, Devant, and Horace Goldin. Andrews' study is itself a treasure that stands as the definitive narrative of Robinson, a man who literally gave his life for magic by failing at the "bullet-catching trick" in 1918. This stunt involved apparently catching a bullet between one's teeth; it was sufficiently dangerous that the Great Houdini, despite his customary bravado and braggadocio, refused to perform it. Will Goldston's *Sensational Tales of Mystery Men* includes an account of Ching Ling Soo that has itself been criticized by Will Dexter. *The Riddle of Ching Ling Soo*, by Will Dexter (pseudonym of William T. Pritchard), is an absorbing account of a truly great magician whose career ended in tragedy. The author is an adept magician, a prolific writer of magic texts, and an accomplished historian of magic.

For an account of a genuine Oriental rather than an imposter, *The Magic of Tenkai*, compiled and edited by Gerald Kosky and Arnold Furst, contains Tenkai's autobiography "My Fifty Years in Magic" as well as nearly fifty of his striking effects. *The Travels of Testot*, another valuable study by J. B. Findlay, treats the touring and performances of a French illusionist in the first half of the present century. His American counterpart was found in the figure of Howard Thurston. Robert E. Olson's *The World's Greatest Magician: A Tribute to Howard Thurston* began as a series of articles in *The New Tops* magazine. Called "the Master" by no less a magician than Ted Annemann, Thurston was one of the most charismatic performers in modern magic. His acclaim rivaled that of such giants as Blackstone and Houdini. For over a decade, Olson gathered news clippings, rare photographs, posters, letters, articles, interviews, and personal statements; the result is a definitive portrait of an American institution, a figure who entertained the president of the United States and sixteen other world rulers. For Howard Thurston's own story, one may read *My Life of Magic*; Olson's study will enhance one's appreciation of Thurston's accomplishments. It is regrettable that his fellow greats, Blackstone and Houdini, never wrote autobiographies.

BIBLIOGRAPHY

Abbott, Percy. *A Lifetime in Magic*. Colon, Mich.: Abbott's Magic Co., 1960.

Anderson, George B. *Magic Digest: Fun Magic for Everyone*. Northfield, Ill.: Digest Books, 1972.

Andrews, Val. *Dedicated Magic*. London: Harry Stanley's Unique Magic Studio, 1971.

———. *Four Seasons in the Life of Val Andrews: An Autobiography of Val Andrews*. Seattle: Micky Hades Intl., 1984.

———. *A Gift from the Gods—the Story of Ching Ling Soo, Marvelous Chinese Conjurer*. Alcester, England: Goodliffe, 1981.

———. *Goodnight Mr. Dante*. Alcester, England: Goodliffe, 1978.

———. *Murray*. Alcester, England: Goodliffe, 1974.

Bamberg, Theodore, and Robert Parrish. *Okito on Magic*. Chicago: E. O. Drane, 1952.

Beaufort, Douglas. *Nothing up My Sleeve!* London: Stanley Paul, 1938.

Bertram, Charles. *A Magician in Many Lands*. London: Routledge, 1911.

Blitz, Signor. *Fifty Years in the Magic Circle*. Hartford: Belknap & Bliss, 1871.

Booth, John N. *Booth's Fabulous Destinations*. New York: Macmillan, 1950.

———. *The John Booth Classics*. Bideford, England: Supreme Magic Co., 1975.

Braddon, Russell. *The Piddingtons*. London: Werner Laurie, 1950.

Branson, L. H. *A Lifetime of Deception: Reminiscences of a Magician*. London: Robert Hale, 1953.

Burlingame, H. J. *Around the World with a Magician and a Juggler*. Chicago: Clyde, 1891.

———. *Magician's Handbook*. Chicago: Wilcox & Follet, 1942.

Cannell, J. C. *The Secrets of Houdini*. New York: Dover, 1973.

Christopher, Milbourne. *Houdini: The Untold Story*. New York: Thomas Y. Crowell, 1969.

———. *Milbourne Christopher's Magic Book*. New York: Thomas Y. Crowell, 1977.

Clapham, Harry. *Melody Magic*. Washington, D.C.: Author, 1932.

Clark, Hyla M. *The World's Greatest Magic*. New York: Crown, 1976.

Cramer, Stuart. *Germain, the Wizard and his Legerdemain*. Calif.: Buffum, 1966.

———. *Secrets of Karl Germain*. Ohio: Mr. Merriweather, 1962.

Dawes, Edwin A. *The Barrister in the Circle*. London: The Magic Circle, 1984.

Devant, David. *My Magic Life*. London: Hutchinson, 1931.

———. *Woes of a Wizard*. London: Bousfield, 1903.

Dexter, Will [William T. Pritchard]. *The Riddle of Ching Ling Soo*. Bideford, England: Supreme Magic Co., 1973.

Dunninger, Joseph. *100 Houdini Tricks You Can Do*. Conn.: Faucett Books, 1954.

Edmonds, I. G. *The Magic Makers: Magic and the Men Who Made It*. Nashville: Thomas Nelson, 1976.

Ernst, Bernard M. L., and Hereward Carrington. *Houdini & Conan Doyle: The Story of a Strange Friendship*. 2d ed. New York: Benjamin Blom, 1972.

Evans, Henry Ridgely. *Adventures in Magic*. New York: Leo Rullman, 1927.

———. *A Master of Modern Magic: The Life and Adventures of Robert-Houdin*. New York: MaCoy Press, 1932.

Findlay, James B. *Anderson & His Theatre*. Shanklin, Isle of Wight: Author, 1967.

———. *Charles Dickens and His Magic*. Shanklin, Isle of Wight: Author, 1962.

———. *The Travels of Testot: The Story of the Wanderings of a Necromantic Nomad*. Shanklin, Isle of Wight: Author, 1965.

Fisher, David. *The War Magician*. New York: Berkeley Books, 1983.

Fitzsimons, Raymund. *Death and the Magician*. New York: Atheneum, 1980.

Furst, Arnold. *Famous Magicians of the World*. Los Angeles: Genii, 1957.

Ganson, Lewis. *The Dai Vernon Book of Magic*. London: Harry Stanley's Unique Magic Studio, 1957.

———. *Dai Vernon's Tribute to Nate Leipzig*. London: Harry Stanley's Unique Magic Studio, 1963.

———. *Malini & His Magic*. London: Harry Stanley's Unique Magic Studio, 1963.

Gibson, Walter B. *The Original Houdini Scrapbook*. New York: Sterling, 1976.

Gibson, Walter B., and Morris N. Young. *Houdini on Magic*. New York: Dover, 1953.

Goldston, Will. *Sensational Tales of Mystery Men*. London: Will Goldston, 1929.

Gordon, Gene. *Gene Gordon's Magical Legacy*. Norcross, Ga.: A Snowflake Publication, 1980.

Gresham, William Lindsay. *Houdini—The Man Who Walked through Walls*. New York: Henry Holt, 1959.

Hanson, Herman, and John U. Zweers. *The Magic Man*. Cincinnati: Haines House of Cards, 1974.

Henning, Doug, and Charles Reynolds. *Houdini: His Legend and His Magic*. New York: Times Books, 1977.

Holden, J. W. *A Wizard's Wanderings from China to Peru*. London: Dean, 1886.

Holden, Max. *Programmes of Famous Magicians*. New York: Author, 1937.

Houdini, Harry. *The Unmasking of Robert-Houdin*. New York: Publishers Printing, 1908.

Jarrett, G. *Jarrett*. Chicago: Magic Inc., 1981.

Jenness, George A. *Maskelyne and Cooke: Egyptian Hall, London, 1873–1904*. Enfield, England: Author, 1967.

Kellar, Harry. *A Magician's Tour Up and Down and Round the Earth: Being the Life of an American Nostradamus, Harry Kellar*. Chicago: R. R. Donnelly & Sons, 1896.

Kellock, Harold. *Houdini, His Life-Story. By Harold Kellock from the Recollections and Documents of Beatrice Houdini*. New York: Harcourt Brace, 1928.

Kosky, Gerald, and Arnold Furst. *The Magic of Tenkai*. Oakland, Calif.: Lloyd Jones, 1974.

Marshall, Frances Ireland. *My First Fifty Years*. Chicago: Magic Inc., 1981.

———. *With Frances in Magicland*. Chicago: Magic Inc., 1952.

———. *You Don't Have to Be Crazy*. Chicago: Magic Inc., 1946.

Maskelyne, Jasper. *Magic—Top Secret*. London: Stanley Paul, 1948.

———. *White Magic: The Story of the Maskelynes*. London: Stanley Paul, 1936.

Meyer, Bernard C. *Houdini: A Mind in Chains: A Psychoanalytic Portrait*. New York: E. P. Dutton, 1976.

Mole, H. C. *Those Entertaining Years*. Sidmouth, England: Author, 1949.

Nightingale, F. B. *Magic for Magicians*. Calif.: Knight Pub., 1964.

Olson, Robert E. *The World's Greatest Magician: A Tribute to Howard Thurston*. Seattle: Micky Hades Intl., 1981.

Olson, Robert E., and Edward Dart. *Carl Rosini—His Life and His Magic*. Chicago: Magic Inc., 1966.

Parrish, Robert. *An Evening with Charlie Miller*. Chicago: Magic Inc., 1961.

Randi, James, and Bert Randolph Sugar. *Houdini: His Life and Art*. New York: Grosset & Dunlap, 1977.

Rapp, Augustus. *The Life and Times of Augustus Rapp, the Small-Town Showman*. Chicago: Magic Inc., 1959.

Robert-Houdin, Jean Eugene. *King of Conjurors: Memoirs of Robert-Houdin*. Translated by Lascelles Wraxall. New York: Dover, 1973.

Sardina, Maurice. *Where Houdini Was Wrong: A Reply to the Unmasking of Robert-Houdin* [Les Erreurs de Robert-Houdin]. Translated by Victor Farelli. London: Magic Wand, 1950.

Scarne, John. *The Amazing World of John Scarne: A Personal History*. New York: Crown, 1956.

Sharpe, S. H. *Salutations to Robert-Houdin*. Seattle: Micky Hades Intl., 1983.

Shine, Francis L. *Conjuror's Journal: Excerpts from the Journal of Joshua Medley, Conjuror, Juggler, Ventriloquist, and Sometime Balloonist: A Novel*. New York: Dodd Mead, 1978.

Steele, W. F. Rufus. *Paul Rosini's Magical Gems: A Memorial*. Chicago: Author, 1950.

Taylor, Tony. *Spotlight on 101 Great Magic Acts*. Seattle: Micky Hades Intl., 1964.

Thompson, James G. *My Best: A Collection of the Best Originations Conceived by Eminent Creators*. Philadelphia: C. H. Hopkins, 1945.
Thurston, Howard. *My Life of Magic*. Philadelphia: Dorrance, 1929.
Williams, Beryl, and Samuel Epstein. *The Great Houdini, Magician Extraordinary*. New York: Julian Messner, 1950.

APPENDIX

SELECTED DATES IN THE HISTORY OF CONJURING

1550 Publication in Milan (?) of Francesco di Milano's . . . *Quale Potrai Facilmente Imparare Molti Giochi Di Mano* . . . [How You Can Easily Learn Card Tricks]. The booklet, which emphasized card magic, is believed to be the first conjuring manual.

1584 Publication in London of Reginald Scot's *The Discoverie of Witchcraft*, the first exposé of the conjurer's secrets in the English language.

1612 Publication in London of Sa Rid's *The Art of Conjuring or Legerdemaine*, the first book devoted entirely to conjuring.

1731 Death of Isaac Fawkes, a famous British sleight-of-hand artist who performed in the open air at Bartholomew Fair. Birth date unknown.

1734 Birth of "Philadelphia" (pseudonym for Jacob Meyer), the first American conjurer to appear in Europe. Death date unknown.

1750 Birth of Giuseppe Pinetti, a Tuscany-born magician whom some consider the greatest conjurer of the late eighteenth century. Died 1800.

1760 Birth of Eliaser Bamberg, the original member of a great dynasty of Dutch magicians. Died 1833.

1774 Publication in Vienna of Philadelphia's (Jacob Meyer's) *Kleines Tractalein seltsamer und approbierter Kunststucke* [*A Small Tract on Mysterious, Clever Tricks*], the first magic book by an American-born magician.

1783 Birth of Richard Potter, a mulatto who was the first American magician to flourish in his own country. Died 1835.

1786 Birth of David L. Bamberg, a Dutch magician who was appointed Court Conjurer by King William II of Holland in 1843. Died 1869.

1789 Thomas Denton, an itinerant magician, was hanged in England. His is the first recorded case of a magician being executed in that country.

1790 Birth of Giovanni Bartolomeo Bosco, a great Italian magician who entertained world rulers in Russia, Prussia, Sweden, and France. Died 1863.

1795 Publication in Philadelphia of Henry Dean's *The Whole Art of Legerdemain*, the first book on conjuring to be published in America.

1801 Birth of L. L. Doebler, one of Austria's greatest magicians. Died 1864.

1805 Publication in Boston of William Frederick Pinchbeck's *The Expositor: Or Many Mysteries Unravelled*, the first original book on magic to be published in America.

Birth of Jean Eugene Robert-Houdin, the father of modern magic in France, who inspired Ehrich Weiss to adopt the stage name "Houdini." Died 1871.

1806 Birth of J. N. Hofzinser, a most creative Austrian conjurer who contributed especially to the advancement of card magic. Died 1875.

1810 Birth of Signor Antonio Blitz, A London-born magician who entertained Abraham Lincoln in 1863. Died 1877.

1812 Birth of Tobias Bamberg, another member of the famous Dutch dynasty of great magicians. Died 1870.

1814 Birth of John Henry Anderson, the flamboyant and self-styled "Wizard of the North." Died 1874.

1816 Birth of Carl Herrmann, a German-born magician whose international travels made him the recipient of jewels from a number of members of royalty. Died 1887.

Birth of John Wyman, an American-born illusionist who began as a ventriloquist. Died 1881.

Birth of Wiljalba Frikell, a German-born magician who pioneered by wearing conventional evening clothes rather than a flowing robe. Died 1903.

1821 Birth of John Henry Pepper, a professor of chemistry in London, whose famous "ghost" was a reflected image on plate glass, an experiment that may have popularized the use of mirrors among magicians. Died 1900.

1839 Birth of John Nevil Maskelyne, the founder of England's most illustrious family of magicians. Died 1917.

1843 Birth of David Tobias Bamberg, a Dutch magician who continued his family's tradition of entertaining royalty by receiving an appointment as conjurer for William III of Holland. Died 1914.

Publication of the second edition of the first known English magic catalogue by the dealer W.H.M. Cambook of London.

Birth of Alexander Herrmann, justifiably known in America as "Herrmann the Great," an Austrian-born magician and successor to Carl Herrmann. Died 1896.

1847 Robert-Houdin introduced his "Ethereal Suspension," the prototype for levitation illusions.

1849 Birth of Harry Kellar, America's favorite magician during the period after Alexander Herrmann and before Howard Thurston. Died 1922.

1853 Publication in Rheims of Jean Nicholas Ponsin's *Nouvelle Magie Blanche Dévoilée*

[*New White Magic Revealed*], a text upon which Professor Hoffmann drew for his own celebrated work of 1876, *Modern Magic*.

Birth of Adelaide Scarcez, the wife of ''Herrmann the Great'' who perpetuated her husband's show for three decades after his death. Died 1932.

1854 Birth of Ching Ling Foo (pseudonym for Chee Ling Qua), a Chinese magician who introduced his elegant brand of Oriental magic to America in 1898. Died 1918.

1857 The dangerous bullet-catching stunt was performed for the first time by a female magician, the seventeen-year-old Annie Vernone, at the Theatre Royal in Hull, England.

1859 Publication in Blois, of Robert-Houdin's *Confidences d'un Prestidigitateur* [Secrets of a Magician], the memoirs of the most celebrated French magician.

1861 Birth of George Méliès, a French illusionist who is credited with creating some of the first special effects in motion pictures at the close of the nineteenth century. Died 1938.

Birth of Chung Ling Soo (pseudonym for William Ellsworth Campbell Robinson), an American magician who achieved world fame before his untimely death in 1918 while performing the bullet-catching stunt.

1863 Birth of Nevil Maskelyne, the son of John Nevil Maskelyne, coauthor of the landmark text *Our Magic* with David Devant. Died 1924.

1865 Birth of Jean Henri Servais LeRoy, an Anglo-Belgian magician who invented the ''Ashrah'' levitation, in which the floating of a woman in air is climaxed by her disappearance. Died 1953.

1867 Birth of T. Nelson Downs, an American magician whose unprecedented mastery of coin manipulation justified his title, the ''King of Coins.'' Died 1938.

1868 Publication in Paris of Robert-Houdin's *Les Secrets de la Prestidigitation et de la Magie* [*Secrets of Prestidigitation and Magic*].

Birth of David Devant (pseudonym for David Wighton), a creative genius and magical companion of another brilliant British conjurer, Nevil Maskelyne. Died 1941.

1869 Birth of Howard Franklin Thurston, an American card manipulator who enjoyed scaling playing cards from the stage to the highest reaches of the balcony. A worthy successor to Harry Kellar, Thurston soon became America's favorite illusionist. Died 1936.

1872 Birth of Jean Hugard (pseudonym for John Gerard Rodney Boyce), an Australian magician who was a prolific author and editor of high quality textbooks, especially in the area of manipulative magic with cards. Died 1959.

Birth of Lafayette (pseudonym for Siegmund Neuburger), a German-born magician who incorporated lions in his show and used his skills as a quick-change artist in an Oriental act. Died 1911.

1873 Birth of Horace Goldin, a Polish-born American magician who helped popularize ''Sawing a Lady in Half.'' Died 1939.

Birth of Nate Leipzig (pseudonym for Nathan Leipziger), a Swedish-born American magician who excelled as a creative cardician. Died 1939.

Birth of Max Malini (pseudonym for Max Katz Breit), a Polish-born American sleight-of-hand artist of the highest order. Died 1942.

1874 Birth of Al Baker, a witty American magician who was noted for his intimate magic and clever feats of mentalism. Died 1951.

Birth of Charles Joseph Carter, known as "Carter the Great," American magician who flourished in Europe while Kellar was enjoying great popularity in America. Died 1936.

Birth of Harry Houdini (pseudonym for Ehrich Weiss), the Hungarian-born American magician and master escape artist. Died 1926.

1875 Birth of Okito (pseudonym for Theodore Bamberg), a member of the famous Bamberg family, whose Oriental act was aesthetically enchanting. Died 1963.

1876 Publication in London of Thomas Frost's *The Lives of the Conjurors*, the first book-length history of magic in England.

Publication in London of *Modern Magic* by Professor Hoffmann (pseudonym for Angelo John Lewis). This seminal work is a milestone in the literature of conjuring.

1879 Birth of P. T. Selbit, the London-born magician who is credited with inventing perhaps the most famous illusion of all times, "Sawing Through a Woman." Died 1938. His actual name was Percy Thomas Tibbles.

1880 Birth of the Great Nicola (pseudonym for William Mozart Nichol), a highly successful American illusionist whose cosmopolitan experiences included entertaining maharajahs. Died 1946.

1882 Birth of Dante (pseudonym for Harry Jansen), a Danish-born American illusionist who was first associated with Thurston and then mounted his own elaborate show touring both principal and minor cities throughout the world. Died 1955.

1885 Birth of Harry Blackstone (pseudonym for Harry Bouton), a native of Chicago whose popularity placed him in the company of Houdini and Thurston. Died 1965. Harry Blackstone, Jr., is presently presenting classic mysteries from his father's full evening program.

1886 Birth of Percy Abbott, an Australian magician and the founder of one of the largest magic companies in the world. Died 1960.

Birth of George F. Reuschling, an American magician whose exciting vaudeville act drew upon his talents as a quick-change artist. This performer worked under two different names, "Rush Ling Toy" and "The Great LaFollette."

1892 Birth of Joseph Dunninger, arguably the most successful mentalist of the twentieth century. Died 1975.

1893 Birth of Kalanag (pseudonym for Helmut Schreiber), an outstanding German illusionist who enjoyed international success. Died 1963.

1894 Birth of Dai Vernon, a Canadian-born American magician whose consummate sleight of hand has earned him the nickname "The Professor."

1897 Birth of Walter B. Gibson, the world's most prolific author of magic texts. This American magician and author was chosen by Houdini, Blackstone, and Thurston as their "ghostwriter." In April of 1984, when contacted by phone, Gibson confirmed that he was the last survivor of the Houdini era. Died 1985.

Birth of John Mulholland, an outstanding magician, historian of conjuring, collector of magic books and memorabilia, and the author or editor of numerous important works. Died 1970.

1899 Birth of Cardini (pseudonym for Richard V. Pitchford), a British-born American magician whose manipulative nightclub act became a much-revered paragon. Died 1939.

1900 Publication in London of T. Nelson Downs' *Modern Coin Manipulation*, the first comprehensive exposition of coin magic.

Birth of Paul LePaul (pseudonym for Paul Braden), a superlative American cardician whose *The Card Magic of LePaul* is nothing less than a masterpiece. Died 1958.

1902 Publication of S. W. Erdnase's *The Expert at the Card Table*, perhaps the most influential work ever written on card sleights for the magician or would-be card cheat.

1903 Death of Buatier deKolta, an inventive French conjurer whose vanishing bird cage and "Vanishing a Woman" have earned him a place in the history of conjuring. His birth date has been variously cited as 1845, 1847, and 1848.

Birth of Jasper Maskelyne, a third-generation member of England's greatest dynasty of magicians. Died 1973.

1904 Birth of Fu-Manchu (pseudonym for David Tobias Bamberg), another great Dutch magician who, like his father, specialized in a graceful, Oriental wizardry.

1905 Death of Theodore Jackson, a black magician whom Houdini dubbed "the best colored magician." Birth date unknown.

1907 Birth of Theodore Annemann (pseudonym for Theodore Squires), an ingenious American magician whose writings have found their niche in the classics of conjuring literature. Died 1942.

1908 Publication in New York of Harry Houdini's *The Unmasking of Robert-Houdin*, Houdini's diatribe against his former hero.

1910 Birth of J. B. Bobo, arguably the greatest coin manipulator since T. Nelson Downs.

Birth of Frances Ireland Marshall, an eminent authority on the demanding art of performing magic for children. Her multi-volume, encyclopedic contribution, *Kid Stuff*, stands as an unprecedented classic.

Publication of J. N. Hofzinser's *Kartenkunststucke*, a profoundly influential treatise on card magic by the man who is credited with introducing such gimmicks as double-faced cards.

1911 Ionia De Vere (pseudonym for Elsei DeVere), a popular female magician, opened her act at the Hippodrome in Birmingham, England.

1912 David Devant was selected for the first Royal Command Performance before King George V at the Palace Theatre in London.

1913 Birth of Lewis Ganson, England's greatest author/editor of magic texts. Died 1980.

Birth of Edward Marlo (pseudonym for Edward Malkowski), probably the best card magician who has ever lived and surely the most prodigious author of material on card magic. One recent commentator states that Marlo has written the stunning total of over 1,500 publications.

Birth of Sorcar, a Bengali stage magician who was the most famous Indian conjurer of modern times. Died 1971.

1919 Birth of Jay Marshall (pseudonym for James Ward Marshall), a much-honored American magician whose intelligent and witty style elevates magic to the status of a genuine theatre art.

1923 Birth of Richiardi, Jr., (pseudonym for Aldo Izquierdo), a stylish, international magician whose "sawing a lady in half" is done with a buzz saw and punctuated with a fountain of blood.

1924 Publication in New York of Houdini's *A Magician among the Spirits*, a classic work on fraudulent mediums.

1928 Birth of "The Amazing Randi" (pseudonym for James Randall Zwinge), a Canadian-born performer who has duplicated some of Houdini's most exciting escapes and has emulated Houdini's attack on pseudo-mediums and psychic shams such as Uri Geller.

1941 Publication in New York of the first volume in Harlan Tarbell's seven-volume, encyclopedic *The Tarbell Course in Magic*, the definitive overview of all branches of magic.

1946 Birth of David Ginn, a highly successful professional who specializes in entertaining children and who has authored dozens of writings on the topic.

Publication in America of *Our Magic*, by Nevil Maskelyne and David Devant, an unsurpassed defense of magic as a theater art.

1947 Birth of Douglas Henning, a Canadian-born American magician whose Broadway play *The Magic Show* ran for four and a half years beginning in 1974. With this play, his numerous appearances on network television, and his recent Broadway play *Merlin*, Henning has almost single-handedly inspired a renaissance of interest in magic. David Copperfield is posing keen competition.

1951 Kalanag (pseudonym for Helmut Schreiber) presented the first postwar magical importation from Germany to England, a program of illusions that succeeded in attracting large crowds.

1956 Dell O'Dell appeared in a weekly television program for the American Broadcasting Company. She was the only female magician to achieve this distinction.

Sorcar, India's most famous prestidigitator, stunned BBC-TV audiences with a sawing-through-a-woman illusion in which he failed to revive her, thus making him the subject of numerous telephone calls to the television station, newspaper headlines, and political cartoons.

1957 Milbourne Christopher organized the first ninety-minute international television special for "Producer's Showcase" on NBC-TV.

1963 Death of Kalanag, a famous German illusionist who flourished both during and after World War II. Born 1893.

1967 Publication of *Tokyo Trickery* by Yakeshi Nemoto, the first book of Japanese magic to be published by an American firm, Magic Inc. of Chicago.

1971 Richiardi, the great South American illusionist headlined at the "World Festival of Magic and Occult" at Madison Square Garden in New York.

1974 *The Magic Show*, which showcased the talent of Doug Henning, opened on

Broadway. The long run of this play (four and a half years) and a series of television appearances soon established this Canadian performer as the best-known magician in America.

1980 *Blackstone!* starring Harry Blackstone, Jr., opened on Broadway to critical acclaim. This production enjoyed the longest run of any straight magic show in the history of Broadway, 118 performances.

1983 David Copperfield presented an unprecedentedly ambitious illusion, the disappearance of the Statue of Liberty, on network television.

1985 Fifth White House performance by members of the LeGrand David Spectacular Magic Company of Beverly, Massachusetts.

MAGIC PERIODICALS

Among the myriad magic magazines and journals that have appeared in this century are the following: *Abracadabra* (the only weekly publication), *Apocalypse*, *The Australian Magic Magazine*, *The Budget*, *The Cheat Sheet*, *Conjurer's Monthly Magazine*, *The Christian Conjurer*, *Epilogue*, *Epoptoca*, *L'Escamoteur*, *Gen*, *The Hierophant*, *Hugard's Magic Monthly*, *Ibidem*, *L'Illusionniste*, *Inside Magic*, *Invocation*, *The Jinx*, *The Journal of Magic History*, *Le Journal de la Prestidigitation*, *Legerdemain*, *The Levitator*, *Magia Moderna*, *Magic*, *The Magic Circular*, *The Magic Magazine*, *Magic Manuscript*, *The Magic Shop Newsletter*, *The Magigram*, *Magische Welt*, *Mahatma*, *Mystic Quarterly*, *Pabular*, *The Pallbearer's Review*, *The Pentacle*, *The Pentagram*, *Phoenix*, *Precursor*, *Quarterly News Sheet* (a bulletin issued by Robert Lund, curator of the American Museum of Magic, Marshall, Michigan), *Richard's Almanac*, *The Spellbinder*, *The Sphinx*, *Tricks*, *The Wizard*, *Zauberkunst*, *Der Zauberspiegel*, and *Die Zauberwelt*.

Because some of these periodicals are no longer in print and because new ones appear regularly, one should consult a magic dealer to discover which are available. Dealers can also specify the emphases of various periodicals and sometimes sell hardbound reprints of out-of-print periodicals such as *The Jinx*.

Among the more important contemporary periodicals are *The American Museum of Magic Newsletter*, published in Marshall, Michigan, since 1977. Robert Lund, proprietor of the museum, is responsible for this publication. *Apocalypse*, published in New York by Harry Lorayne since 1978, is a monthly that features advanced material for the sleight-of-hand specialist. *Genii*, published and edited in Los Angeles since 1937 by Irene and Bill Larsen, is a leading voice for magic in general and West Coast activities in particular. *The Linking Ring*, published by the International Brotherhood of Magicians, in Kenton, Ohio, since 1926, has been shaping magic and magicians since the year of Houdini's death. *M.U.M.* (*Magic, Unity, and Might*), published by the Society of American Magicians in Lynn, Massachussetts since 1910, is a monthly that corresponds to *The Linking Ring* of the International Brotherhood of Magicians. *The Magic Circular* has been published as the official organ of the International Brotherhood of Magicians in London since 1906. *Magic Manuscript*, published by Louis Tannen Inc. in New York since 1979, is one of the largest magic companies in the United States. This magazine pioneered in the use of glossy, color photographs. *The New Tops* has been published by Abbott's Magic Company, in Colon, Michigan since 1936. Abbott's Magic is another major manufacturer of magic apparatus. *The New Tops* addresses magic on a national level, but also reflects the state of the art in the cities, towns, and hinterlands of the Midwest.

DIRECTORIES

For a "Who's Who" of magicians and a "What's What" of magic apparatus, one can refer to *The 1982–83 Magic Directory*, a publication of Monson Productions of Madison, Wisconsin. This valuable compendium is a comprehensive guide to magic-related products and services in over twenty-five countries. Among the more than five dozen categories are associations, books, costumes, dealers, illusions, inventors, juggling equipment, lecturers, museums, publishers, schools, agents, and wholesalers. This well-indexed reference work includes more than 2,000 names. Although it has not been revised, this remains a very useful resource. Of related interest is *Sid Lorraine's Latest Reference File: 760 Names and Addresses Compiled for Magicians*. Lorraine (pseudonym for Sidney R. Johnson), a dean in the magic world, has long enjoyed the esteem of American as well as Canadian magicians. His list was published in Toronto, Canada in 1981 (available through Micky Hades, dealer).

In a telephone conversation, Frances Marshall, a major publisher of magic manuscripts, noted that magic directories appear only sporadically and are not typically updated. Thus, a reader should contact a magic dealer (see the list at the end of the Appendix) in order to learn what directories might be presently available.

RESEARCH COLLECTIONS

As attractive and refreshing as the postcard pretty Midwestern town in which it is located is the American Museum of Magic of Marshall, Michigan. Opened in 1978 by Robert Lund, the museum is a visual feast for all lovers of conjuring; for over four decades, he has been collecting every variety of magic memorabilia. Over 250,000 items (original posters, magazines, books—the library has over 8,000 volumes—letters, photographs—including over 40,000 by the "Ansel Adams" of the magic world, Irving Desfor—tapes, records, advertisements, and 8,000 biographical files on magicians of every station throughout the world) are lovingly displayed and preserved. The collection, which spans the period from the sixteenth century to the present, is marked by its great heterogeneity; all under one roof are a magic prop used by Doug Henning on Broadway, the milk can from which Houdini escaped, and magic sets, both vintage and contemporary. Recognized as the largest collection of its kind in private hands, the holdings are housed in a nineteenth-century, Victorian-style, two-story building that was renovated by Lund himself and for which he received the "Historic Restoration Award" by the city of Marshall. A prize-winning journalist, Lund has contributed numerous writings to magic magazines and books; in 1971, his article in *The Linking Ring* earned him the International Brotherhood of Magicians' Trophy. Like magic itself, which proves emphatically how deceptive appearances can be, Lund is a plain-looking man, but behind this mundane shell is the excited, enthralled child who has never lost his sense of wonder. Best of all, his museum stands as a catalyst that can rekindle one's own sense of enchantment.

The Egyptian Hall Museum of Magical History (in Brentwood, Tennessee) is among the world's largest museums devoted to the memorabilia of magic and magicians. The museum is open to magicians and others by appointment.

The Houdini Magical Hall of Fame (at Niagara Falls, Ontario, Canada) sits squarely amidst the commercial squalor of wax museums, fast-food restaurants, and tastelessly stocked souvenir shops. In fact, the Hall makes its own contribution to the overall garishness of the street. One can hardly visit this enterprise without experiencing ambivalent feelings. Houdini went to his grave regretting the fact that all of his success and fortune had not won him an audience among the upper class. Imagine how he might react against the tawdry environment in which an institution dedicated to him is situated. In the lobby area, television sets show an excerpt from the 1953 film ''Houdini'' in which Tony Curtis played the role of the master escape artist. The movie, true to its Hollywood origin, took some liberties with the life of Houdini; more to the point, the film took considerable liberty with his death. In the spirit of dramatic license, Tony Curtis dies while performing an underwater escape. In reality, Houdini died in a hospital, with his wife, Bess, holding him in her arms. Thus, anyone familiar with Houdini's career will be disturbed by the fact that history is flaunted at the Hall of Fame, for the abovementioned film episode depicts Tony Curtis struggling to his death in an underwater stunt. Positively speaking, the museum contains a fascinating assortment of Houdini's posters, letters, playbills, and apparatus. His lock picks and the largest collection of his handcuffs are also on exhibit. Dioramas, populated by mannequins, portray favorite illusions of the day as presented by Houdini and such greats as Blackstone, Kellar, and Thurston.

The Library of Congress, Washington, D.C., like all public libraries, is limited in its holdings on magic; since much magic literature is suppressed and circulated only among practicing magicians. Researchers will, however, be pleased with the Library's McManus-Young and Houdini Collections, Rare Books Division. Complementing the Houdini materials at the Library of Congress is the Houdini Collection in the Hoblitzelle Theatre Arts Library of the University of Texas at Austin. Holdings include photographs, correspondence, unpublished writings, film scripts, posters, and research for a book exposing spiritualism.

Prominent among European institutions is the Musée Robert-Houdin in Blois, France. This museum is devoted to apparatus once owned by the father of modern magic. The Library of the London Ring of the International Brotherhood of Magicians affords members one of the finest collections of magic literature in the world. The Library of the Magic Circle, a prestigious organization of British magicians, is an outstanding collection and is also situated in London.

The Magic Castle is a lavishly appointed Victorian mansion that overlooks Hollywood, California. Here are collected posters, photographs, books, and the paraphernalia of famous magicians. Virtually all contemporary magic greats have performed in this elite establishment; membership is private and individuals can gain entrance only after having passed a proficiency test. Researchers wishing to use the superb library must apply for permission to the Academy of Magical Arts at the same address. Another California institution is The Society of American Magicians' Hall of Fame and Magic Museum, Inc., a nonprofit educational corporation that was conceived by leaders in the Society of American Magicians in 1963. Four years later, the first inductees were chosen, but the hall existed only on paper. In 1971, the hall opened; in 1979, it was incorporated. The original space of 2,500 square feet was divided into various rooms, including a little theater to accommodate 45 spectators. Dedicated to research and the advancement of the art, the hall preserves and exhibits magical artifacts and also honors distinguished magicians. Materials donated include magic apparatus (for instance, a set of linking rings with which Professor Cook entertained Abraham Lincoln), books (the Herbert Downs'

Memorial Library will be discussed below), magazines (dating as far back as the eighteenth century), costumes, posters, and other assorted memorabilia. In some exhibits, dioramas present scenes from the lives of magicians who have been inducted into the hall. One room, "The Ronald and Ruth Haines Gallery," boasts a superb collection of playing cards that is surpassed only by the holdings of the United States Playing Card Company of Cincinnati, Ohio. It contains cards of various sizes (from miniature to giant), shapes (round, oblong, football), and countries (including some French cards that were designed by the artist David under the commission of Napoleon). A unique collection of gimmicked cards is isolated in a separate room that is off limits to nonmagicians. The Herbert Downs' Memorial Library, a noncirculating and ever-expanding collection, is a valuable resource for scholars. It includes scrapbooks and S.A.M. publications as well as magazines and books. The address of the museum is the same as that of its corresponding secretary and librarian, Ronny H. Cortes: 1500 N. Vine Street, Hollywood, CA 90028. Richard A. "Pete" Petrashek (3409 South 89th St., Omaha, NE 68124) is the S.A.M. film librarian from whom local branches of the society may rent films or videotapes of magic performances by such past and present greats as Harry Blackstone, Howard Thurston, Hardeen (Houdini's brother), Slydini, Dai Vernon, and David Copperfield. Videotapes of recent international magic conventions in Hawaii, Switzerland, and Norway are also available. Admission to the hall is by invitation or appointment only. This institution is sustained by donations and by the proceeds of an annual public magic show.

The John Mulholland Collection, The Players, New York, contains not only rare books but antique pieces of magic apparatus, playbills, and art works devoted to magic by such magnificent artists as Hieronymus Bosch. While The Players is a private society, scholars may apply for permission to use the Mulholland Collection by contacting the curator. The Carl Waring Jones Collection, in the rare books division of the Princeton University Library, consists essentially of books, but scrapbooks are also included as are writings on related topics such as laws of chance.

Because most magic literature is distributed by small trade houses or private individuals rather than by large lay publishers, specialized collections like the above can be essential for the researcher. Unfortunately, such libraries are relatively few in number and may be inconveniently located; thus, the scholar may wish to consult the catalogs of magic dealers (see the list at the end of the Appendix) for listings or descriptions of most of the publications that are unavailable through public libraries.

DEALERS

Each of the following dealers can provide a catalog or price list for his or her apparatus and/or books.

Abbott's Magic Company, Colon, MI 49040. One of the largest manufacturers of magic apparatus in the country. Hundreds of books are described in their general catalog.

Academie de Magie, 47 Rue Notre Dame de Lorette, 75009, Paris. Dealer in basic apparatus.

Al's Magic Shop, 1012 Vermont Ave., N.W., Washington, D.C. 20005. A full-range magic store that is operated by one of the finest demonstrators in the United States, Al Cohen.

Ron Allesi, 11309 Urban Road, Dunkirk, NY 14048. Dealer who is well known for the high quality of the rare magic in which he specializes.

Mario Carrandi, 122 Monroe Ave., Belle Mead, NJ 08502. America's oldest and largest dealer in antiquarian apparatus, books, and memorabilia.

Chu's Magic Studio, P.0. Box 95221, T.S.T. Kowloon, Hong Kong. Dealer and manufacturer.

Collector's Workshop, 4335 Cathedral Ave., N.W., Washington, D.C. 20016. Dealer, manufacturer, and publisher. The proprietor, Rich Bloch, does custom manufacturing for professionals and caters to those seeking high quality in both new and antique equipment.

Davenports, 7 Charing Cross Underground Concourse, The Strand, London, WC24HZ, England. A leading British dealer, manufacturer, and publisher. Its booklists include magic texts, but also manuals on origami, shadowgraphy, ventriloquism, juggling, the tarot card, and Punch and Judy. Over 3,000 items are described in a recent catalog.

Paul Diamond Magic and Fun Shop, 903 Federal Highway, Searstown, Ft. Lauderdale, FL 33304. Dealer, manufacturer, publisher.

Flosso-Hornmann Magic, 45 W. 34th St., NY 10001. Oldest magic dealer in the United States.

Micky Hades International, P.O. Box 2242, Seattle, WA 98111–2242. Publisher and manufacturer. This is the world's largest supplier of books on magic and related arts. Thousands of books are identified by title and author under 24 categories. There are no descriptions; thus, this catalog is mainly of value to one who is already familiar with the contents of the books that are listed. It would be a great service, and an immense undertaking, to include even brief descriptions of the thousands of books that are for sale.

Haines House of Cards, P.O. Box 12527, Norwood, OH 45212. Dealer, manufacturer, and publisher. Emphasis is placed upon gimmicked playing cards of various types and sizes.

Lee Jacobs Productions, P.O. Box 362-L109, Pomeroy, OH 45769–0362. Dealer and publisher whose specialties include antique posters and reprints.

Klamm the Magic Man, 1412-L Appleton, Independence, MO 64052. Dealer who specializes in novel items (books on gospel magic) and utility props.

Hank Lee's Magic Factory, 125 Lincoln Street, P.O. Box 1359, Boston, MA 02205. Dealer and manufacturer with a full range of magic equipment.

Magic Hands, Oderstrasse 3, Postfach 1241, 7033 Herrenberg, W. Germany. Dealer and manufacturer noted for beautiful stage effects with silks, bottles, and other items.

Magic Inc., 5082 N. Lincoln Ave., Chicago, IL. Dealer, manufacturer, and publisher. Among the top few magic supply houses in the country, this operation features an exceptional selection of books; a multi-volume book catalog is available.

Magic Methods., P.0. Box 4105-L, Greenville, SC 29608. Dealer and publisher who emphasizes close-up magic.

Morrissey Magic, Ltd., 2882 Dufferin St., Toronto, Ont., M6B 3S6 Canada. Dealer who specializes in metal products.

Mystery Castle, 349 E. Cooke Rd., Columbus, OH 43214. Dealer who stocks such oddities as imitation shrunken heads and "voodoo blood needles."

Robert Nelson, 470 Forest Lake Circle, Kernsville, NC 27284. Dealer who specializes in used and antique magic apparatus.

O'Dowd Conjuring Books, 7313 Kohler Dr., Barnhart, MO 63012. Dealer who specializes in used books and magazines.

Osborne Illusion Systems, P.O. Box 36155, Dallas, TX 75235. Dealer, manufacturer, and publisher specializing in stage illusions.

Owen Magic Supreme, 934 N. McKeever Ave., Azuza, CA. Manufacturer of illusions.

Petrie Lewis Manufacturing Co., 5456 Peach Ave., Seffner, FL 33584. Considered the "Rolls Royce" of magic dealers, providing standard props of the highest quality of construction.

Show Business Services, 1735 E. 26 St., Brooklyn, NY 11229. Dealer in videotapes. Many magic shops now sell or rent videotapes that instruct one in the performance of magic. Some magicians abhor this burgeoning phenomenon, for it allows even "illiterates" to learn the secrets of magic. Defenders of tapes argue that only those seriously interested in learning magic are apt to obtain the tapes. In any case, videotape permits the student to observe important elements in the execution of an effect (such as timing) that books cannot capture.

Silk King Studios, 640 Evening Star Lane West, Cincinnati, OH 45220. Dealer, manufacturer, and publisher that specializes in silk magic.

Stevens Magic Emporiums, 3238 E. Douglas, Wichita, KA 67208. Dealer, manufacturer, and publisher.

Sun Magic, 5825 N. 7th St., Phoenix, AZ 85014. Dealer who specializes in used and antique magic apparatus.

Supreme Magic Co., 64 High St., Bideford, Devon, England. A leading British dealer, manufacturer, and distinguished publisher.

Sushi Magic, 17–2 Kabuto-cho, Nihonbashi, Chuo-ku, Tokyo 103, Japan. Dealer who specializes in silks and accessories.

Louis Tannen Inc., 6 W. 32nd St., NY 10001. Dealer, manufacturer, and publisher; best-known magic shop in the East.

Tayade's Magic, 64–65 Bhatia Bhuvan, Ash La, Dadar, Bombay, India. Dealer and manufacturer.

Readers should consult the yellow pages of their telephone books, under the heading "Magicians Supplies," for information on local magic shops.

AUTHOR INDEX

Abbott, David, P., 120
Abbott, Percy, 164
Ackerman, Alan, 66
Adair, Ian H., 38, 51, 92, 103, 105
Alan, Don, 83
Albenice, 110
Albright, Howard P., 55–56, 121
Aldini, Al, 54–55, 110
Alexander, C., 115
Allerton, Bert, 83
Allin, David, 110
Ammar, Michael, 19, 37, 153
Anderson, Gene, 100, 110
Anderson, George B., 36, 114, 163
Andrews, Max, 55
Andrews, Val, 97, 164–65, 168, 170
Andrus, Jerry, 22, 66, 79–80, 93–94
Annemann, Theodore, 16, 36, 56, 113, 115, 117
Armelagos, Adina, 151
Armstrong, George, 109
Arthur, R. E., 109
Auer, James, 115
Ayling, Will, 53, 101

Baker, Al, 52, 115
Bamberg, Theodore, 7–8, 99–100, 163, 169–70
Barnhart, Russell T., 63
Barnouw, Erik, 159
Baron, Harry, 39, 56, 81
Batchelor, Tom, 66
Beam, Steve, 98
Beaufort, Douglas, 164
Behnke, Leo, 66, 83
Bennett, Horace, 25, 83–84, 86, 88, 99, 104–5
Benzais, John, 84
Berg, Joe, 55
Berland, Samuel, 81
Bertram, Ross, 84
Bertram, Charles, 164
Bessent, Trent E., 12
Bey, Mohammed, 93, 99
Bigbee, North, 119
Binet, Alfred, 15–16
Blackstone, Harry, 4, 7–8, 19, 21–22, 39, 55, 164
Blackstone, Harry, Jr., 33–34, 170
Blake, George, 51
Blitz, Signor, 164
Boarde, C. L., 115
Bobo, J. B., 84, 97
Bohlen, Henry, 106
Bongo, Ali, 108
Bontjes, Gary, 124

Bonura, Aldo, 37
Booth, John N., 1–2, 100, 165
Braddon, Russell, 170
Branson, L. H., 169
Braue, Frederick, 54, 62, 70
Brent, Lu, 51–52, 56
Brooke, Ken, 49
Bruno, Joe, 23–24
Buckingham, Geoffrey, 44
Buckley, Arthur, 25, 66, 100, 114
Burgess, Clinton, 41
Burlingame, H. J., 5–6, 18, 164–65

Cameron, Charles W., 116, 122
Campbell, Loring, 39, 99
Cannell, J. C., 166
Cardini, Great, 147, 164
Carrington, Hereward, 167
Cecil, Harry E., 49
Chanin, Jack, 36, 88, 94, 102
Chapman, Frank, 117
Charles, Kirk, 95
Christopher, Milbourne, 3, 6–7, 19, 36, 39, 46, 48, 104, 118, 121, 163, 166
Claflin, Edward, 6
Clapham, Harry, 164
Clark, Keith, 102–4
Clarke, Harry, 39
Clarke, Sidney W., 4, 165
Clive, Paul, 55
Collins, Stanley, 53, 120
Cook, John B., 114
Corinda, Tony, 113–14
Craggs, Douglas, 48
Cramer, Stuart, 165
Crandall, "Senator" Clarke, 90, 94–95
Cremer, W. H., 7
Curry, Paul, 5, 39, 119

Dalal, Sam, 53, 118–19
Davies, Rev. C. M., 120
Davies, Robertson, 12, 16
Davis, Phil, 160
Dawes, Edwin A., 6, 38, 119, 124, 154, 165
De Baros, Jules, 99
Decourcy, Ken, 117, 123
De La Torre, Jose, 52–53, 92
Denhard, Howard, 104
Desfor, Irving, 8
Dessoir, Max, 18
Devant, David, 24–25, 48–49, 148, 155, 165, 170
Deveen, D., 102
Dexter, Will, 5, 40, 48, 117, 171
Dhotel, Jules, 81
Dircks, Henry, 158
Dodson, Goodlette, 101
Doerflinger, William, 34
Dorfay, 12
Dornfield, Werner C., 109
Downs, Thomas Nelson, 45, 97–98
Dunninger, Joseph, 40, 116, 120, 122, 164, 168
Duval, Ade, 103
Dyko, James, 26

Easley, Bert, 109
Edmonds, I. G., 3–4, 27, 158, 168
Elliott, Bruce, 40, 84
Enochs, Edward Loyd, 102
Epstein, Samuel, 167
Erdnase, S. W., 60, 63, 64
Ernst, Bernard, 167
Ervin, E. G., 52, 84
Evans, Henry Ridgely, 4, 5–7, 20, 107, 119, 163–64, 168

Falk, Lee, 160
Farelli, Victor, 60, 67, 98, 168
Feinman, Jeffrey, 34
Fetsch, Hen, 39, 117
Findlay, D. W., 7
Findlay, James B., 124, 164–65, 171
Fischer, Ottokar, 33, 60
Fisher, John, 160–61
Fitzkee, Dariel, 20, 24–26, 53, 89, 104–5, 118, 154
Fitzsimons, Raymund, 168
Fleischman, Sidney, 93
Florek, Bruce, 67
Foster, Neil, 102, 106, 152
Fox, Karrell, 67, 100
Francis, Douglas, 84
Frikell, Samri, 120
Fromer, Roy, 106

Frost, Thomas, 6
Fuller, Uriah, 121
Fulves, Karl, 56–57, 67, 77–78, 80–81, 84–85, 114
Furst, Arnold, 51, 164, 171
Futagawa, Shigeo, 98

Galloway, Andrew, 22, 61, 85
Ganson, Lewis, 21, 25, 45, 48, 50–51, 61, 66–68, 85–89, 91–92, 101–5, 110, 115, 118, 163
Garcia, Frank, 49, 57, 64, 68, 72, 89, 94, 102
Gardner, Martin, 33, 57, 92–93, 111, 120
Garrett, Teral, 117
Gaultier, Camille, 46
Gibson, Walter B., 40–41, 57, 61, 81–82, 111, 166
Gilbert, George, 5, 43
Gill, Brenden, 157
Gill, Robert, 4, 6, 21, 38, 40, 45, 50, 123, 165
Ginn, David, 82, 93, 105, 108
Gloye, Eugene E., 2, 26
Goldston, Will, 171
Good, Arthur, 7
Goodrum, John, 43
Goodsell, David R., 19–20, 147
Gordon, Gene, 49, 100, 165
Gordon, George M., 21–22
Gore, George, 105
Grant, Maxwell. *See* Gibson, Walter B.
Grant, Ulysses F., 57, 94
Gravatt, Glenn, 41, 57
Green, Cliff, 69
Gresham, William Lindsay, 167
Griffin, Al, 112
Griffin, Ken, 109
Griffin, Roberta, 109
Griffith, Tony, 52, 57, 86

Hades, Mickey, 106, 155
Hadley, Paul R., 118
Hall, Trevor H., 52, 55, 69, 123
Hamam, Ray, 22
Hanson, Herman, 165
Harbin, Robert, 5, 41, 107
Harris, Paul, 69–70, 86, 89
Hawkesworth, Eric, 158
Hay, Henry, 46, 109
Heinemann, Richard, 53
Henning, Doug, 147, 156–57, 160, 167
Heyl, Edgar, 123–24
Hilliard, John Northern, 33, 45, 61
Hiraiwa, Hakufu, 106
Hodson, A. S., 86
Hoffman, Professor, 38
Hofzinser, Johann N., 60
Holden, J. W., 168
Holden, Max, 164
Hollingsworth, Scott, 96
Holmes, Donald, 41
Hope, James, 19
Hopkins, Albert A., 4, 106–7, 111
Hopkins, Charles H., 22–23, 54, 61
Horn, Maurice, 160
Houdini, Harry, 3–4, 6, 8, 15–16, 20, 41, 111–12, 120, 154, 159, 161, 163–64, 166–68, 171
Howatt, Gordon, 37
Howie, John, 93
Hoy, David, 116
Hugard, Jean, 32–33, 41, 46, 54, 57, 61–62, 70, 82, 98, 103, 119
Hull, Burling (Volta), 20–21, 54, 102, 106, 113–14, 118
Hunt, Douglas, 5
Hunt, Kari, 5
Hurwitz, Abraham B., 38

Ireland, Laurie L., 8, 82, 91, 98, 105

Jacobs, Lee, 8, 158
Jacques, Pierre, 112
James, Bill, 48
James, Stewart, 58, 104
Janel, 122
Jarrett, Guy, 168–70
Jastrow, Joseph, 15
Jay, Ricky, 158–59
Jenness, George A., 169
Johnson, George, 48
Johnson, Roy, 49–50, 86–87
Johnsson, Rick, 87
Jones, G. Elmar, 108

Jones, Jan, 21, 109
Jonson, Wilfred, 46, 63
Jordon, Charles T., 70
Joseph, Eddie, 91, 93, 109, 112, 117
Judah, Stewart, 50

Kane, Peter, 70
Kaplan, George, 41
Kattner, Wilbur, 70
Kaufman, Richard, 37, 70–72, 82, 98, 101–2
Kaye, Marvin, 34–36, 41, 113–14
Kellar, Harry, 15, 150, 163, 168, 170
Kellock, Harold, 166
Kenyon, John, 36
Kerns, Ernie, 108
Kort, Milton, 71, 87
Kosky, Gerald, 51, 87, 119, 171
Kronzek, Alan Z., 25, 153
Kuethe, William F., Jr., 124
Kumar, S. K. V., 106

Lamb, Geoffrey Frederick, 4, 6–7, 33
Lamonte, Jack, 110
Langham, Jack, 41
Larsen, William W., 108, 115, 119
Laureau, Marcel, 7
Lawton, Don, 100
Leamon, Earl, 111
Lee, Wallace, 111
Leech, Al, 24, 63, 71
Lees, Walt, 101
LePaul, Paul, 71
Lewis, Eric C., 26, 108
Lewis, Shari, 38
Liebertz, Arnold, 41
Lorayne, Harry, 71–73, 87, 97, 124
Lorraine, Sid, 87

McCarron, B. W., 64
MacCarthy, E. Brian, 82
MacDonald, Gordon, 103
MacDougall, Michael, 64
McGill, Ormond, 115
McGuire, Eddie, 65
McMillan, S. A. S., 86
Majax, Gerard, 65
Majikans, 42
Maly, Charles, 123
Mardo, Señor, 42, 87, 91, 109, 160
Marlo, Edward, 58, 65, 73–74, 77–80, 95, 98–99, 101
Marshall, Frances Ireland, 8, 22, 48, 90, 107, 110, 124, 160, 169
Marshall, Jay, 8, 42, 44, 48, 160
Martineau, Francis B., 103, 109
Maskelyne, Jasper, 20, 169
Maskelyne, John Nevil, 6, 24, 49, 94, 119–20
Maskelyne, Nevil, 148–50, 155–56
Maurice, Edward, 21, 116
Mayoh, William, 101
Mendoza, John, 87–88
Mentzer, Jerry, 74, 79–80, 88
Merlin, Jack, 74
Merrill, R. D., 92
Meyer, Bernard C., 167–68
Meyer, Jacob, 4, 6, 112
Meyer, Orville, 53
Miesel, William P., 74
Miller, Charlie, 88, 110, 163
Miller, Gordon, 58
Miller, Hugh, 50, 103–4
Miller, Leonard H., 110
Minch, Stephen, 75, 121
Mishell, Ed, 89, 95, 110
Mole, H. C., 169
Morley, Henry, 158
Morris, Bud, 111
Moskowitz, Joel, A., M.D., 12, 26–27
Moss, Floyd, 65
Mulholland, John, 4, 6, 21, 43, 120, 124, 161
Musson, Clettis, 82, 111, 123

Nathanson, Leon, 25, 85
Neil, C. Lang, 43
Nelms, Henning, 18
Nelson, Earl, 88
Nelson, Robert A., 113–14, 116–19, 122
Nemoto, Takeshi, 88
Nightingale, F. B., 169
Norman, Anthony, 63
Novak, Robert, 105

Okito. *See* Bamberg, Theodore *or* Okito *in subject index*

Olsen, Fred, 108
Olsen, Robert E., 170–71
Osbourne, Tom, 91, 94, 99
Ostin, Bob, 88
Ovette, Joseph, 106

Page, Patrick, 43
Palmer, Tom, 103, 106
Parrish, Robert, 43, 88, 153, 163
Pecor, Charles J., 24–25, 82, 155, 157
Permin, Ib, 104
Podmore, Frank, 120
Poland, Ellison, 43
Pomeroy, John D., 119
Postgate, Bruce, 96, 103
Potter, Jack, 123
Price, David, 3

Racherbaumer, Jon, 89
Raffles, Mark, 112
Randal, Jason, 18
Randi, James, 46, 121–22, 161, 166
Rapp, Augustus, 170
Ravelle, 37
Rawson, Clayton, 95
Read, Bob, 82
Read, Ralph W., 94
Reneaux, James, 22
Reynolds, Charles, 8, 33, 157–58, 167
Reynolds, Regina, 8, 33, 157–58
Rhine, J. B., 122
Rice, Harold R., 103
Robert-Houdin, Jean Eugène, 4, 7, 20, 38, 148, 156, 168
Robertson, Robin, 63
Robinson, Benjamin, 2
Rogers, Mike, 89
Ross, Barry, 46–47
Ross, Richard, 105
Roterberg, A., 59
Roth, David, 98
Ruthchild, Myriam, 118
Rutledge, Ned, 75, 117
Rydell, Wendy, 5, 43

Sachs, Edwin, 46
Samp, Timothy E., 13
Sands, George, 104
Sankey, Jay, 154
Sardina, Maurice, 89, 168
Sartre, Jean-Paul, 149–50
Scarne, John, 44, 59, 95, 98, 170
Schatz, Edward R., 118
Schindler, George, 49, 57
Scot, Reginald, 38, 119, 155
Searles, Lynn, 63
Setterington, Arthur, 52, 122–23
Severn, Bill, 5, 37, 44, 82–83
Sharpe, Alton C., 53, 75
Sharpe, Samuel H., 101, 146–47, 153, 155, 168
Sheils, Tony, 123
Sheridan, Jeff, 6
Sherwood, Arthur, 25
Shine, Frances L., 170
Siegal, Paul, 116
Simon, Bill, 75–76, 89, 111
Sirridge, Mary, 151
Skomp, Stephen, 117
Sorcar, P. C., 1, 5, 44, 164
Spooner, William E., 99
Staar, Janii, 158
Staar, Will, 158
Stanley, Harry, 59
Stanyon, Ellis, 63
Starke, George, 89
Stebbins, Robert A., 153
Steele, W. F. Rufus, 59, 76, 163
Steinmeyer, Jim, 168
Steranko, John, 76, 87
Strong, David, 37
Sugar, Bert Randolph, 166
Swinford, Paul, 78

Tan, Choon Tee, 76
Tan, Hock Chuan, 55
Tanner, Don, 55, 102
Tarbell, Harlan, 4, 32, 36
Tarr, Bill, 46–47
Taylor, Gerald, 111
Taylor, Tony, 164
Tenkai, 51, 88, 98, 170–71
Tessler, Marc, 52
Thompson, James G., 48, 59, 63, 75, 89–90, 117, 163

Thurston, Howard, 8, 21, 159, 163–65, 168, 171
Tigner, Steven S., 3, 11, 161
Tong, Danny, 90
Torino, Señor, 76
Triplett, Norman, 13, 20
Trixer, Hans E., 93
Trost, Nick, 91, 95, 119
Tucker, W. M., 112
Tuff, J. Elsden, 44
Turner, Bill, 59
Tyler, Wilfred, 108

Vermes, Hal G., 44
Vernon, Dai, 18, 50–51, 68, 72, 86, 90–91, 98, 105, 163
Victor, Edward, 47, 98, 101–3
Volkmann, Kurt, 92

Walsh, Audley V., 65, 91, 95
Walton, Roy, 77
Warlock, Peter, 51–52, 90, 117–18
Wass, Verrall, 44
Weibel, Richard, 11–17, 21, 26, 167
Weigle, Oscar, 43
Wels, Byron G., 106
White, Joseph, 117
Wiersbe, Warren, 77, 103, 119
Williams, Beryl, 167
Willmarth, Philip, 77, 89–91, 93, 113–14
Wilson, Eric P., 109
Wilson, Mark, 32, 91–92
Wright, L. B., 158

Yates, Jack, 114, 117
Young, Morris N., 111, 124, 166

Zavis, William, 90
Zweers, John, 165

SUBJECT INDEX

Academy of Magic Arts, 2, 102
Acting, 150
Actor, magician as, xi
Aesthetic attitude theory, 148–49
Aesthetics of magic, 153–54
American Magic Museum, 158
American Museum of Magic, 8
Anderson, Harry, 110
Anderson, John Henry (Great Wizard of the North), 6–7, 154, 158, 161, 164
Andree, 37
Andruzzi, Tony, 122
Animal magnetism, 115
Animals, 2, 15
Aristotelian principles, 147–49
Art, magic as, 145–51, 153
Ascanio, 92
Assistants, 109
Astral projection, 115
Astrology, 121
Auteur theory, 149
Automatic writing, 115
Automaton: chess playing, xii-xiii, 6; cups and balls, 170

Balls, 45–48
"Bazarada," 154
"Bead-diffusion," 34
Beardsley, Monroe, 149
Bibliographies, 123–24
Biddle move (card technique), 61
Billet reading, 115
Billiard balls, 45–46, 102
Bizarre magic, 122
Black art, 35
Blackston, J. Stuart, 159
Blindfold, 45, 84, 115
Body loads, 109
"Book Tests," 39, 115
Bosch, Hieronymus, 154
Bosco, Bartolemeo, 7
Bottom dealing (card technique), 60
Bradbury, Ray, 34
"Brainwave," 114
Breaks (card technique), 79
Brown, Edward G., 69
Buckinger, Matthew, 154
Buckling (card technique), 73
Bullet catching, xiv, 164, 166, 171

Canadian magicians, 2
Card apparatus: card box, 55; daub, roughing fluid, and wax, 54–55; marked cards (stripper deck), 54, 64; prearranged deck, 57; trick deck, 55
Card cheating, 60, 64–66

Card magic, 34, 37–46, 53–81; card control, 66; card fans (stage magic), 101; card flourish, 47, 63; cardicians, 57, 79; card-scaling, 159; card switches, 80; card throwing, 159; mathematical principles, 57; psychology, 22; psychology of card expert, 63. *See also* Card tricks
Card tricks: "Card on Ceiling," 74; "Card and Mousetrap," 82; "Card to Pocket," 61, 68, 74, 76, 84; "Card Warp," 77; "Immaculate Connection, " 69; "Interlocked Hands," 69; "Invisible Card Change," 87; "Linking Cards," 73; "Oil and Water," 74; "Out of this World," 5, 40, 119; "Out of this Universe," 72; "The Persistent Card," 56; "Rising Card," 57; "Six Card Repeat," 76; "Three Cards Across," 63, 67. *See also* Card magic
Carroll, Lewis, 160–61
Carus, Dr. Paul, 5
Changes (card technique), 62
Chapeaugraphy, 44, 158
Chavez School of Magic, 83
Chemistry, 111
Children, 12, 16, 26, 35, 44, 49, 51, 105, 107–9; as magicians, 37–38
Ching Ling Soo, 6, 170–71
Chop cup, 92
Christ, Henry, 69
Chwast, Seymour, 158
Cigarettes, 45, 47, 102
Clairvoyance, 115
Clark, Hyla M., 163
Close-up magic, 41–42, 46, 49, 51, 88–99. *See also* Magic with everyday objects *and names of specific objects*
Clown magicians, 108
Code, 117
Coin magic, xiv, 42–46, 97–99. *See also names of specific tricks*
"Coins Through the Table," 84–85
Cold reading, 118
A Comedy of Errors (Shakespeare), 155
Conan Doyle, Arthur, 167
Confederate, 114
Copperfield, David, 26, 160
Costumes, 109
Craft, 145
Creativity, 25–26, 148, 154–55
Crimp (card technique), 64
Crystal gazing, 115
Cups and balls, xii, 34, 40, 47, 82, 84–85, 87–88, 90–92, 154

Dance, 145, 151
Dante, 164
Dart, Edward, 170
Debunkers, 121–22
"Decapitation Illusion," 155
Deck switches, 64
Deja vu, 122
De Kolta, Buatier, 7
Dice, 94–95; loaded, 64, 95; stacking, 94
Dickens, Charles, 3, 154, 158, 161
Dingle, Derek, 70–71
"Disappearing lollipops," 37
Doctor Faustus (Christopher Marlowe), 155
Dorny, 93
Double lift (card technique), 61, 68, 72
Dover Publications, 3
Doves, 103
Downs' palm, 99
Dowsing, 121
Drama, 8, 147–49, 155–57

East Indian mysteries, 115
Ectoplasm, 115, 123
"Egg Bag," 42, 49, 84, 110, 163
Egyptian Hall, London, 165, 169
Electronics, 111
Elmsley, Alex, 72
Elmsley count, 74
Escape artistry, xiv, 111. *See also* Harry Houdini *in author index*
E. S. P., 119, 121–22. *See also* Mentalism
Estimation, 80
Ethics of magic, 16–17, 22, 35, 65, 116, 169
Euripides, 155
Exposing secrets, 27–28, 36, 65

False count (card technique), 74
False cuts (card technique), 63, 73
False deals (card technique), 63, 65, 75
Faust (Goethe), 155
Feather flower bouquets, 109
Fechter, Eddie, 74
Finnell, Gene, 78
Fire-eaters, 107, 111
"Five Card Mental Force," 90
Flash string, 83
Floating ball, 105–6
Folding coin, 99
Forcing, 36, 60, 65
Fortune telling, 121
"Fraidy Cat Rabbit," 100
Frauds, xiii, 120–22
Friar Bacon, 158
Frikell, Adalbert, 169
Fu Manchu, 92
Full-evening magic show, xiv, 44, 156

"Gaze into My Crystal Ball," 83
Geller, Uri, 121–22
General studies, 32–44
Germain, Karl, 165
Ghost shows, 122–23
Ghosts (spirit conjuring), 4
Gibbons, Cathy, 147
Gimmick, xi
Glide (card technique), 22, 62
Glimpsing (card technique), 60–61, 170
Goethe, Johann Wolfgang von, 155
"Goldfish Eating," 90
Goldin, Horace, 170
Goldsmith, Oliver, 154
Goldstein, Phil, 72
Goshman, Al, 90
Le Grand David, 157
Graphology, 121
Great Cardini, 147, 164
Great Masoni, 21
The "Great" Virgil, 21
Gwynne, Jack, 4
"Gypsy Thread," 86

Hahne, Nelson, 71
Hamman, Bro. John, S. M., 71
"Hathaway change" (card technique), 75
Haunted Man (Dickens), 154, 158
Heller, Robert, 164
Herrmann, Adelaide, 166
Herrmann, Alexander, 6, 15, 18, 163, 165
Herrmann, Carl, 6, 18, 165
Himber wallet, 97
Hogarth, William, 154
Hold-out (card technique), 110
"Homing Stones," 25
Houdini, Beatrice, 100, 166
Hull, Ralph W., 55
Hume, David, 16

"Illogical Double Lift" (card technique), 72
Illusion show, 109
"Indian Rope Trick," xiii-xiv, 33, 160
International Brotherhood of Magicians, 1, 6
"Invisible Pass" (card technique), 85
Ireland Magic Company, 47

Jadoo-wallah, 2
Jaks, Dr., 76
Jardine Ellis ring, 93
Jogging, 79
Jugglers, 107; juggling, 3

Kaps, Fred, 92
Kardyro, Tony, 76, 88. *See also* Señor Torino *in author index*
Kilgore, Al, 34
Knife, color changing, 45
Koran, Al, 50
Krenzel, Ken, 72
Kreskin, 116

Lagerould, Terry, 67
Lapping, 25, 84
Laurel and Hardy, 165
Leipzig, Nate, 4, 50, 67, 163
Levitation, xiii, 28, 105–6, 115–21, 150–52, 155
Light bulbs, 42
Lincoln, Abraham, xiii
Linking cards, 73. *See also* specific card tricks

The Linking Ring, 1–2, 12, 17
Linking rings, 35, 43, 45–46, 104–5
"Living and Dead" tests, 117
Logic, 18
Lund, Robert, 8, 124, 158

MacMillan, Ron, 101–2
Magic: ancient, 6, 8; seventeenth century, 6; eighteenth century, xii, 6; nineteenth century, xii-xiii, 5–7, 13; twentieth century, xiv-xv, 6–7; used in WWII 20, 169
Magic as an art, 7, 17
Magic circle, 164–65
Magic defined, 148–50
Magic with everyday objects, 34, 42, 44, 46–47, 49–51, 81–83. *See also* Close-up magic *and names of specific objects*
Magic Factory, 164
Magic Inc., 47, 78, 99
The Magic Show, xv, 147, 157
Magic on stage, 147, 156–57; English, 154–55, 158
Mail order, 34–35
Make-up, 109
Malini, Max, 51, 163
"Mandrake the Magician," 160
Manfredi, Arthur, 85
Marco the Magi, 157
Marlowe, Christopher, 155
Martyn, Topper, 100
Maskelyne family, 4
"Masquerades and Operas" (William Hogarth), 154
Matches, 93
Mathematics, 111
"Matrix," 84
Mechanic's grip, 78
Mediums, 113, 118, 120, 123
Medley, Joshua, 170
Méliès, George, 156, 159
"Mental Epic," 117
Mentalists, 170
Mental magic, xv, 42–43, 49, 51, 87, 113–19
Merlin, xv, 18, 156–57
Mind-reading teams, 107
Mirror ring, 64
Mirrors, 35
Misdirection, 12, 18, 19, 22–25, 44, 46
"Miser's Dream," 47, 98
Motion pictures, xiv, xv, 4, 107, 150, 159; special effects, 159–60
Multiple shift, 75, 79
Murray, 168
Muscle reading, 17, 118
Music, 109, 145
Myth, 145, 155

Nail writing, 113, 117
Nash, Martin A., 75
Native American conjuring, xiii, 4
Night, Arthur, 159
Nikola, 58
Nominalism, 151–52
Numerology, 121

Okito, 7–8, 99–100, 163, 169–70
Okito coin box, 98–99
"One Hand Double Turnover" (card technique), 73
"One Hand Palm" (card technique), 74
One-way principle (card technique), 58
Ontology, 151–52
Opera, 158
Oriental magic, xiv, xvi, 2, 7, 170

Packet tricks (card technique), 81
Paddle (Knife), 92
Palmistry, 121
Palms (card technique), 22, 62
Pantomime, xi
Paper-cutting, 44
Pass (card technique), 22, 62, 63, 72, 152
Patter, 24, 41, 45, 63, 113, 149, 158
Pavel, 51
Peeking, John Henry, 154, 158
"Phantom Tube," 103
Philosophy of conjuring, 43, 49, 100
Pickpocketing, 112, 146, 166
Plato and Platonism, 152
Pocket tricks, 34
Poe, Edgar Allan, 6
Poster, 8, 157–58
Predictions, 116–17

"Professor's Nightmare" (rope trick), 53
Psychics, 116; detectives, 121; phenomena, 115; surgery, 121
Psychokinesis, 114, 121
Psychology of magic, 11–15, 18, 35, 92
Psychometry, 115

Ramsay, John, 85
Readings (sealed messages), 118–19
Reel, 110
Religion, 4, 8, 28, 35, 147
Religious magic, contemporary, 110
Restaurant/bar magic. *See* Close-up magic
"Revolve Vanish," 85
Rezvani, 89
Rhomer, Sax, 154
Robert, Etienne Gaspard (Robertson), 159
Robinson, Hector, 170
Robinson, William E., 170
Roots of magic, 3, 5, 6
Rope, 104; cut and restored, 47
Rosini, Paul, 76, 163
Ross, Faucett, 51
Rossini, Carl, 170
Routining, 45, 164
Roy, Marvin, 148
Ryan, Jim, 77, 89, 91

Sawing a woman in half, 34, 42, 106–7
Scenery, 109
Schoke, Chic, 93
Schulien, Matt, 90, 93
Science and magic, 6, 111
Scott, Walter I., 65
Seances, 121
Second deal (card technique), 63–65, 68, 75
Senior citizens, 12
Seth the Sensational, 157
"The Shadow," 41
Shadowgraphy, 42–43, 158
Shakespeare, William, 155–56
Shoplifting, 112
Short card, 64
Short change, 112
Showmanship, 20–22, 41
Shuffles, 77–80; false, 62; Faro, 70, 72; Klondike, 78; one hand, 63; riffle, 67
Side steal, 71, 80
Sightless vision, 117. *See also* Blindfold
Silks, 85, 103–4. *See also names of specific tricks*
"Six Card Repeat," 76
Slade, Henry, 120
Slates, 118
Sleeving (card technique), 36
Sleight of hand, 5, 17, 39, 44, 47, 59–60
Slip cut (card technique), 61
Slydini, Toni, 25, 84–86, 92, 98, 163
Smith, J. Stewart, 76
Society of American Magicians, xiv, 12, 48
Sociology of magic, 153
"Soft Soap," 103
"Southwick Fair" (William Hogarth), 154
Spirit apparitions on stage, 158–59
Spirit manifestations, 115
Spirit photography, 113
Spiritualism and mental magic, 39, 41, 113–123
"Splitting the Knots" (silks), 85
Sponges, 90–91
Statue of Liberty, xv
Stepping (card technique), 79
Street magic, xv, 6
"Sucker Tricks," 108
Suez Canal, 169
Swami Gimmick, 113
Swift, Jonathan, 154
Sword-swallowing, 3, 107, 111
Sympathetic magic, 73
"Sympathetic Silk Mystery," 50, 85

Table lifting, 123
Table tipping, 115
Tarot, 121
Telepathy, 115
Television magic on, xv, 160
Tenkai, 51, 88, 98, 170–71
Testot, Felix, 171
Theme parks, magic in, xv-xvi
Therapy, magic as, 26–27
Thimbles, 44–46, 85, 102–3

Three card monte, 47, 65–66, 68
Three shell game, 45, 47, 88, 90, 94
"Thumb Tie," 84
Thumb tip, 2, 36–37, 85
Tolstoy, Leo, 149
"Tomato Trick," 89
Top change (card technique), 62
"Topit," 37
Trade-show magic, 2
Trance phenomena, 115
Transposition methods, 72
Trick decks, 55
Trick photography, 107, 159

Universal appeal of magic, xi-xii

Vacca, Amadeo, 49
Vanishing cane, 35
Vanishing effects: birdcage, 7, 100; cage of doves, 103; elephant, xiv; lady, 39, 41; waterglass, 43
Ventriloquism, 107, 170
Video-tape lessons, 89

Walsh cane, 103–4
Welles, Orson, 40
White House, xiii-xiv
Wiersbe, Warren, 77, 103, 119
Witchcraft (occult), 119–20, 123
Women as magicians, 8, 12, 13

X-ray vision, 115

Zarrow, Herb, 72
"Zig-Zag," 107
"Zombie," 33

About the Author

EARLE J. COLEMAN is Associate Professor of Philosophy and Religion at Virginia Commonwealth University. He is the author of *Philosophy of Painting by Shih T'ao* and *Varieties of Aesthetic Experience*. He has contributed entries to the *Abingdon Dictionary of Living Religions*, and has published articles in *The Journal of Popular Culture*, *The Journal of Magic History*, *The New Tops*, *Virginia Commonwealth University Magazine*, *Philosophy East and West*, and *The Baum Bugle: a Journal of Oz*.